ANATOMY OF DECLINE

The Political Journalism of Peter Jenkins

BRIAN BRIVATI is Senior Lecturer in Modern British History at Kingston University.

RICHARD COCKETT is Lecturer in History at Royal Holloway and Bedford New College, University of London.

POLLY TOYNBEE, Peter Jenkins's widow, is Associate Editor and columnist of *The Independent*.

LORD OWEN was Chairman of the International Conference on the Former Yugoslavia between 1992 and 1995.

ANATOMY OF DECLINE

The Political Journalism of
PETER JENKINS

Edited by
BRIAN BRIVATI
RICHARD COCKETT
Introduction by
POLLY TOYNBEE
Foreword by
DAVID OWEN

INDIGO

First published in Great Britain 1995
by Cassell

This Indigo edition published 1996
Indigo is an imprint of the Cassell Group
Wellington House, 125 Strand, London WC2R 0BB

A catalogue record for this book is
available from the British Library.

ISBN 0 575 40051 X

Printed and bound in Great Britain by
Guernsey Press Co. Ltd,
Guernsey, Channel Isles

96 97 98 99   10 9 8 7 6 5 4 3 2 1

Contents

Foreword

by Lord Owen

Peter Jenkins was fun to be with. He bubbled with life. Yet behind the *bon viveur* image was a serious mind, a philosopher, playwright and art critic as well as a political commentator. My memories of him are vivid. He would switch from discussing who was going to win the first race at Newbury that afternoon to a passionate defence of social democracy, while pausing only to fill his glass and deplore the quality of my wine. He had his share of sorrow, losing his young first wife through a long debilitating illness, but he never lost his zest and occasional childish exuberance. Even a few hours before he died he was weighing the odds for a lung transplant.

We first met in 1960 in the Bistro near Sloane Square when he had just joined the *Guardian* and I was a clinical medical student. Peter described that extraordinary place where we spent many hours as 'a club, a hideaway, an emotional poste restante, a debating society, a womb to climb back into, an intellectuals' employment exchange, and a Salvation Army soup kitchen for down-and-out Etonians ... in short, a state of mind, not a catering establishment.' Of the woman who ran it, Elizabeth Furse, he wrote, 'In London SW1 she performs the useful function of a Mittel European poltergeist'. It was there that I began to live the politics of Europe, with Britain's first application to join the European Common Market starting to be a divisive as well as a dominant issue.

Soon the European issues in British politics became the leitmotif of Peter's journalism. Given that he was a quintessential continental European Social Democrat, it is appropriate that one of the pieces in this book should be about the former German Chancellor, Helmut Schmidt, who, along with the annual Anglo-German Konigswinter conference, did much to shape his attitudes. To Peter, Social Democracy was 'the most successful and bountiful mode of left-wing politics in the postwar Western world', a form that combined 'a liberal economic regime with the pursuit of collective social goals'.

In January 1970, before the General Election, but after watching the collapse of Barbara Castle's attempt to reform the trade unions, which as a result of his time as Labour Correspondent of the *Guardian* he understood perhaps better than anyone else, Peter wrote, 'The notion of Social Democracy still rests heavily on three assumptions – that trade union interests are closely aligned with the interests of the community as a whole; that the planning of production is the most important tool for shaping the quality of life; and that class solidarity works towards the eradication of poverty and need. As none of these assumptions is any longer valid the first task for the Left in the seventies is to break loose from them. We could still if we wish describe the result as Social Democracy and even go on talking about the Labour Movement.'

Angry about Britain's continued economic decline and the behaviour of the trade union movement in the Winter of Discontent, he was still searching in October 1979, after Labour's electoral defeat, for a way forward for Labour. He wrote, 'so it is no way true to say that Social Democracy is dead. In Europe it is very much alive. There it is Socialism which is dead or dying. Social Democracy has not come to Britain chiefly because the Labour Party has yet to bury Socialism.'

By 1980, with Tony Benn establishing an ever greater hold on Labour policy, Peter became convinced that Labour could no longer be reformed only from within and that it was impossible to expect a significant section of centre-left opinion to continue to be associated with a party that was heading inexorably to fighting the next election with a manifesto commitment to take Britain out of the European Community without even a referendum, with an economic policy that was deeply hostile to the market economy and a unilateralist nuclear defence policy that was the despair of his continental Social Democrat friends. He judged that only the shock treatment of facing a new political party, with new ideas and policies, would galvanise the good people within the Labour Party to fight back or perish.

In his heart I think Peter knew that it was folly for a seasoned political commentator with deep roots in the labour movement to declare for the SDP. But he began to feel that he had to put his money where his mouth was and risk his reputation on what he always assessed were very long odds against success. Peter was not alone in doing this. Many other people well advanced in successful careers suddenly took an exposed political position and even became SDP candidates for council and parliamentary elections. Peter characteristically took the plunge with self-mocking humour. 'It is not my practice to engage in local political activity on the grounds that I have quite enough of that sort of thing without doing it in the evenings or the weekends.' Then in a genuflexion to the *Guardian*'s women's page, he referred to his wife as Ms Polly Toynbee, who was standing for the SDP in the Lambeth Council elections, and informed his readers, some of whom he knew would be gnashing their teeth with anger, that he would canvass for her but then added, mischievously, the all-important qualification, 'if weather permits'.

On the Falklands, Peter savaged Margaret Thatcher for her jingoism. The two pieces included in this book, 'Taking leave of our senses' and 'The islands will become a besieged Antarctic Berlin, without importance or meaning, doomed to wither on the vine of distance and unconcern', are in the best tradition of radical dissenting journalism. We passionately disagreed and had to give up arguing.

It is not easy for a political commentator and a political leader to remain friends. Some people thought our friendship would not survive my reading over the breakfast table at an SDP Party conference in Portsmouth after the 1987 General Election the headline in which Peter described me as 'megalomaniac'. But it did. In truth we both knew what each had to do. Peter had to break with the SDP and re-establish his independent credentials, and I had to stick with the SDP until the best of its members could accept that it was doomed to die. Why? Perhaps because, unlike Peter, I had canvassed in the rain.

Even in February 1988 Peter realised that Neil Kinnock's Labour Party reforms were not going to be enough, and he wrote, 'what Gaitskell was after in 1959 and what the German SDP achieved in that year was a symbolic break'. It is a tragedy that Peter is not alive today to chronicle Tony Blair's progress. He would be looking with an astringent sympathy for clear signs of a real break with the past. He would be wanting to believe that Labour had become a continental

Social Democratic Party, and if he felt convinced that that had been achieved by the next election, I have no doubt that he would once again have voted Labour.

Introduction

by Polly Toynbee

For most of the time Peter thought journalism the best possible life. It combined for him the serious business of analysing and describing the world as he saw it, probing ideas and exploring most aspects of how we live and organise ourselves. As a columnist he had the freedom to range over everything in society he thought mattered. At the same time it was a lifestyle congenial to him, with his taste for intense talk and debate, long lunches, many friends, and manic fits of writing against the clock. He never missed a deadline, even when he was writing four columns a week, but as with any journalist there were days when he panicked and thought it couldn't be done.

The problem was juggling a large number of highly complex issues, so in the course of one day there might be the issue he knew he was going to write about, say defence, but also a long pre-arranged lunch on prison policy, and perhaps a meeting at Chatham House about the Gulf. The day's column had to be written while storing away the information on several other things at the same time.

The life of a political columnist can be tricky. Success depends on getting in close to political sources and interpreting what their words mean. There is always the danger of getting too close, of becoming beholden to your politician friends, or simply liking some of them too much. Treading a delicate line between access and impartiality, Peter was always aware of these dangers. Politicians like the company of commentators, partly because they often have few real friends among their colleagues in that seething competitive world at Westminster. They enjoy bouncing their ideas off those with whom they are not competing. On the other hand they can be easily affronted if they find themselves mocked or criticised in print. Peter thought the job could never be done by anyone who didn't basically like politicians, sympathise with them, and believe that most of them were essentially engaged on attempting to improve things. Those who write from a cynical standpoint – 'They're all just in it for themselves' – usually miss the point.

He saw and avoided the danger of being forced back time and again on the insularity of British Westminster politics. He strove to keep broad horizons, in Europe and America. It is all too easy for political commentators to fall into the petty but increasingly unimportant squabbles in and around the Commons. He was sometimes frustrated by the repetitive narrowness of the issues, which British politicians often approach as if they have never existed before, here or elsewhere in the Western world. We behave as if problems and ideas for their solutions were all our own, exclusively, scarcely lifting our myopic eyes beyond the Channel, rarely seeing the bigger picture.

Peter's working habits were a curious mixture of the highly organised and disciplined and the disordered. His little notebooks, squared and bright-covered, are crammed with tiny neat lines of writing, recording every conversation and everything he read. He would whip one out at odd moments and flatter those he was with that he was taking down their *bons mots*. In truth he was usually writing down his own thoughts or words.

He was oddly reticent and shy about the telephone. The best time to catch leading politicians is at home on a Sunday morning, but often he used to have to screw up his determination to call them.

It is hard to assess the importance of political commentators. They interact with the political process, sometimes at crucial junctures. How much of their writing feeds into political decision-making we can never know. Peter had no grandiose illusions about that, and regarded the job of the journalist as exclusively to explain matters for the benefit of his readers, and not as a pseudo politician. He felt passionately that once you start to delude yourself that what you write actually affects policy, it is the start of a slippery slope towards dishonesty with your readers.

However, journalism is the front line in the making of contemporary history, and Peter would have liked to have thought that he had contributed to the understanding and interpretation of the times in which he lived and wrote. This collection of his columns, written very much in the heat of battle, provides one well-informed eye on events as they happened. His ear was probably as close to the ground as anyone's, and his evidence will I hope add to the portrait of the politics of the last 25 years.

Profile of Peter Jenkins

by Brian Brivati and Richard Cockett

On one of the worst days of Michael Heseltine's political life, with his own party as well as the Opposition in uproar over his pit closure programme, the President of the Board of Trade put politics on hold and attended the memorial service for Peter Jenkins at St Margaret's, Westminster. He read an extract from John Donne's 'For whom the bell tolls'. The presence in church that day of so many senior politicians was a testament to the place that Peter Jenkins had come to occupy in British public life. When he died in May 1992 at the age of 58, he was one of perhaps half a dozen political journalists of the postwar period who had become an integral part of the British political scene.

He was born in Bury St Edmunds in 1934 and educated at the local public school, Culford. Although only a few miles from his home, he boarded there between the ages of eight and 18. His father owned a chemist's shop in Bury and had met his mother at London University – they were both the first members of their respective families to graduate from university. His father's social status was uncertain because as a chemist he hovered between the professions and trade – such social ambiguity afforded the young Jenkins a keen insight into the petty social snobbery of English bourgeois life. It was a provincial world which he, like so many of his generation, was desperate to escape. The one positive feature of Bury was the writer Angus Wilson, an early influence, and a source of protection and encouragement.

Jenkins escaped through National Service in the Navy, and then went up to Cambridge to read law. After Part I he switched, despite pressure from his father to return to Bury as a solicitor, from law to history, and went on to get a first.

He had always wanted to be a journalist and on leaving Cambridge he applied for a job at the *Financial Times*. He had worked his way through Cambridge because his father had refused to contribute towards his grant and it was his mother who scraped together the price of an interview suit. Unfortunately, Jenkins managed to lose the money on his first night in London in an illegal casino. To recoup the money he became a croupier in a travelling casino that moved from house to house in a pantechnicon full of little gold chairs. He earned enough money to buy the suit and got the job.

He joined the *Financial Times* under the editorship of Sir Gordon Newton and became one of the remarkable stable of young journalists – Nigel Lawson, William Rees-Mogg, Sam Brittan and Shirley Williams – that Newton recruited straight from university. Having escaped from the provinces and landed a job on a national without a period of apprenticeship on a local paper, Jenkins quickly made the most of his chance and had attracted sufficient attention by 1960 to move to the *Manchester Guardian*.

The paper he joined in the early 1960s still lumbered under the weight of its inheritance from the politics of Manchester liberalism, personified in the austere editor, Alistair Hetherington. They had an uneasy relationship – the editor seeing the young Jenkins as a bit cocky and extravagant, Jenkins seeing Hetherington as a puritan – but this did not prevent him from becoming Labour Correspondent in 1963 in succession to John Cole, inheriting Bernard Ingham as his number two. It is difficult to imagine a sharper contrast in personality and journalistic styles. Jenkins later recalled of Ingham: 'He was very nice to work with: extremely conscientious. He probably thought I was a bit flash and metropolitan.'

A mutual colleague remembers the relationship thus:

'Peter would be turning out the airy features while Bernard hammered our four news stories a day . . . complaining about Peter's absence but actually revelling in it because it gave him an opportunity to make a name for himself.'[1]

The 'airy features' actually paid off rather more for Jenkins than the

---

[1] Both quoted in Robert Harris, *Good and Faithful Servant: the unauthorised biography of Bernard Ingham*, Faber and Faber, 1990, p. 47.

plodding did for Ingham when the *Sunday Times*, then at the height of its stature under the editorship of Harold Evans, offered him the chance to write a column. Not to be outdone, Hetherington trumped the *Sunday Times* offer and gave Jenkins his own political column on the *Guardian*.

As is clear from the first article reproduced in this collection, Jenkins relished the intellectual challenge of being a columnist, of 'trying to make patterns out of torrents of words'. He was happiest writing twice a week, as he did on the *Independent*, rather than three times, as had been the case for a period on the *Guardian*, or once a week, as he was forced to do on the *Sunday Times*. As a political columnist he could range across both domestic and international politics, utilizing a correspondingly wide range of sources. He had a formidable range of personal contacts, especially in Germany and the United States. He was especially knowledgeable about Germany and was a key figure at the annual Anglo-German Konigswinter conferences. He also spent two years as the *Guardian*'s Washington correspondent and thereafter wrote with particular authority on American politics – although he felt rather like a small fish in the very big Washington pond.

As far as British politics is concerned, Jenkins formed close and lasting friendships with several politicians, mostly from the Gaitskellite wing of the Labour Party. He was a social democrat, and remained loyal to this tradition of British politics both when it was contained within the Labour Party and, after 1981, when it found expression in the Social Democratic Party (SDP). He was most drawn towards politicians of the centre of British politics. Foremost among these was Anthony Crosland, the great intellectual of the postwar Labour Party who died in office in 1976. The closest political friendship of the latter half of Jenkins's career was Crosland's successor at the Foreign Office, Dr David Owen, whom Jenkins had known since the early 1960s. For Jenkins, as for many others, Owen became the great hope of social democratic politics in the 1980s, and many of the articles in this collection chart the often stormy relationship between the two. They never quarrelled mortally, despite the often harsh tone of Jenkins's coverage of the merger debate after the disastrous SDP performance in the 1987 election ... Owen understood and forgave.

Jenkins also liked and admired Roy Jenkins, Jim Callaghan, Denis

Healey, and Harold Lever; and had, like so many social democrats, a very high regard for the political writings of John Macintosh. As he makes clear in *Mrs Thatcher's Revolution*,[2] and in the interview included here, he liked Neil Kinnock as a person but felt that he would never have reached the top of British politics without the procedural reforms that reduced the power of the Parliamentary Labour Party. On the other hand, as several articles in this collection demonstrate, he despaired of the political posturing of the likes of Tony Benn and Michael Foot.

As the Conservatives replaced the Labour Party as the 'natural' party of government in the 1980s, so Jenkins cultivated a new network of contacts among the new governing class. However, as with his Labour Party contacts, he was most at home with those Tories who gravitated towards the centre-ground of politics, such as Michael Heseltine, Ian Gilmour, Douglas Hurd, Chris Patten, and Kenneth Baker. He was both appalled and fascinated by Mrs Thatcher and the phenomenon of Thatcherism, something which he saw much more as a style of politics rather than as an ideology.[3] He charted the rise of Thatcherism and its apparent successes during the mid-1980s in *Mrs Thatcher's Revolution*, which made an immediate impact on publication, being a very fine example of contemporary British history, and which will remain a key text on the period. Reviewing the book, Professor Anthony King wrote, 'I think this is a brilliant book, and brilliant is not a word I use lightly (or often). It is one of the best books on British politics to have appeared since the war.' With this book and in his journalism, Jenkins was one of the first to chart courses through the politics of what he called the 'Post-Socialist era', which became the dominant theme of his later work.

He had made his reputation as a political columnist during the 1970s by virtue of his lucid and prescient analyses of Britain's relative economic and industrial decline; indeed, he won Granada TV's Journalist of the Year award in 1978 for his series on British decline reprinted in this collection. Given his pedigree as one of the founders of the school of Declinology, it was not surprising that he embraced certain aspects of the Thatcher revolution, such as trades union reform. That he felt that relative decline had been halted and was

[2] Peter Jenkins, *Mrs Thatcher's Revolution. The Ending of the Socialist Era*, first published by Jonathan Cape, 1987, paperback edition by Pan Books, 1988.

[3] See *Mrs Thatcher's Revolution*, pp. 321–2 and, particularly, pp. 369–79.

prepared to say so publicly led many to believe that he had moved further to the right than was in fact the case. It is arguable that it was the centre of British politics which had moved to the right and that Peter Jenkins was simply articulating this shift.

In analysing government, Jenkins was acutely aware that politicians might come and go, but civil servants stayed. A civil servant's career might span 15 or 20 years at or near the top of British politics, irrespective of changes of government, and he therefore developed friendships with civil servants whom he followed through their careers; some of them later even became politicians, like George Walden and Douglas Hurd. But most ended up as permanent or assistant secretaries in the most important departments of state such as the Foreign Office, Treasury, Defence and, to a lesser extent, the Home Office. These contacts were probably his greatest strength as a journalist, allowing him to get to grips with the real issues beneath the artifice of political debate at the Palace of Westminster. He would lunch and dine with civil servants, diplomats and foreign ambassadors at least as often as with politicians. He was a popular lunchtime companion, with a love of food and champagne and a great zest for life and conversation. It was said of him that even when he was depressed, he was depressed with gusto. He was always open to ideas and had the journalist's permanent state of awareness. David McKie, a fellow *Guardian* journalist, recalled, 'It was flattering over a lunch or a drink to find Peter pulling out one of his famous notebooks and noting down one's comments.'

This love of life and conversation reflected a wide range of intellectual and artistic interests away from the world of politics; what Denis Healey has characterised as a 'necessary hinterland'. His major love outside politics was the theatre. He was an enthusiastic theatre-goer, a critic for three years on *The Spectator* in the late 1970s and a playwright himself.

It is evident from the content of his notebooks that Jenkins felt the limitations of political journalism as a medium for expressing personal feelings and complicated ideas. He regretted the rare occasions when he allowed his personal feelings to surface in his column, as for example with his declaration of support for the SDP. His omnivorous and eclectic reading and his notes on it covered an enormous range of topics from the decline of the Venetian Empire to studies of the life of Christ. Only a small amount of the scribblings in his notebooks on the books he was reading and the people he was talking to found its way into his columns.

Jenkins also used play-writing as a way of channelling his deeper feelings on life and politics. In *Merrie England* he wrote about the Bury society of his youth, and although it did not quite work as a play and was never performed, it did contain acute observations about the sort of English provincial life that he so detested. He had more success with his play *Illuminations*, which ran for a month at the Lyric, Hammersmith in 1980. It concerned the dilemmas of a politician closely modelled on his friend Anthony Crosland. It is an apocalyptic piece built around a dialogue between the social democrats and the Bennite Left during a Labour Party conference. It was followed by a TV series, *Struggle*, satirizing the antics of a 'loony left-wing' council, led by a Ken Livingstone-type figure, not unsympathetic but beleaguered on all sides by the unions, the Trots, the Greens, and a huge deficit . . . not unlike life under his own Labour Lambeth Council. If these productions had enjoyed more commercial success than in fact they did, Jenkins might well have tried to become a full-time playwright. The fact that he was not obsessed by politics to the exclusion of everything else undoubtedly made him a more sophisticated and interesting political writer, but he wore his learning lightly and never let it suffocate the columns.

His other great interest was painting. He did not himself paint, but was a keen and respected student of modern art, writing often in his later years for Peter Fuller's anti-art establishment magazine *Modern Painters*. John Rosselli, an old colleague from the *Guardian*, recalled that 'to go through an exhibition with him was to share a clear vision, simply expressed; one saw new things.'

The job of political columnist was not as well developed a tradition in the UK as it was in the USA. In giving Jenkins his own column on the *Guardian*, Hetherington implied that he wanted 'a Walter Lippmann'-style input to the paper. This, as Jenkins realised, was not possible on a British paper, but in his years on the *Guardian*, perhaps because of the range of political opinions on the paper from Trotskyist to Manchester Liberal, his writing flourished. The atmosphere was such that he found himself increasingly the right-winger on a left-wing paper, a position that brought out the sharpest quality of his writing. The wit that he brought to many of these *Guardian* columns was less obvious in his later writing.

After his brief stay in America, between 1972 and 1974, Jenkins returned to a Britain in the grip of a three-day week. The contrast was stark and the tangible nature of decline in these years was an everyday reality through the chaos caused by power cuts and the ravages of inflation. Like other journalists of his generation and outlook, Jenkins felt decline personally and, as British politics increasingly polarised the office politics of the *Guardian*, became more embattled. The SDP period was particularly painful and the level of abuse hurled from the Labour Party at those who had left to form the SDP was acute. When the *Sunday Times* renewed their offer of his own column in 1985, offering a substantial salary, the *Guardian* had ceased being such a congenial home and there was a certain appeal in being a left-wing columnist on a right-wing paper. However, the *Sunday Times* of Andrew Neil in the 1980s proved to be a very different creature to what the *Sunday Times* of Harold Evans in the 1960s would have been. It was not a happy experiment. His pieces were the wrong length; he disliked the rest of the paper and felt more like a sort of freak on display than a part of the policy and soul of the paper. He particularly disliked Sunday journalism, where reporters have to scavenge around for something new to say about the week's events. When the *Independent* lured him away in 1987, it was a welcome return to bi-weekly journalism and a fresh challenge on Britain's newest quality newspaper. It was exciting to be part of the 'heroic phase' of the *Independent*'s history, and he was deeply involved with its future and was consulted on a whole range of journalistic matters outside his immediate brief. That his journalism in these years lacked something of the spark of his *Guardian* years could simply have been due to the fact that the real debate was in the house papers of the Conservative government, and that politics, aside from Thatcherism, was somehow less exciting – partial economic recovery makes for less gripping copy than a country on the verge of collapse. However, this brief hiatus ended with the revolutions of 1989 when international politics became a source of renewed inspiration, and in the final years Jenkins was writing some of his most authoritative pieces on the need for Britain to play a central role in the process of increasing European integration and for the West to contribute to the reconstruction of Eastern Europe after what he memorably called 'the long Communist nightmare'.

The articles included in this collection are only a sample of the political journalism of Peter Jenkins, which in turn was only a part of his output as a writer. We have tried to achieve a balance between a set of articles that read as a chronological account of politics between 1967 and 1992 and a breadth of coverage that does credit to the range of topics addressed in his journalism. It would be wrong if the reader took away from this collection the idea that Peter Jenkins was only interested in domestic politics. This collection is weighted more towards domestic politics because we felt that in this aspect of his development we could achieve a fairly complete picture. It marks the journey of a social democrat from the age of the collective to the age of the free market. As such it is representative of a political road travelled by many voters in the United Kingdom.

Inside Story

To introduce this collection of Peter Jenkins's political journalism we reprint here his own reflections on the art of the political columnist.

This is the last column I shall be writing on my present three-times-a-week basis. Since I began almost 10 years ago to the day I have tried doing it twice, four times, once and three times a week; there remains only five or total abstinence. Instead I am going back to a weekly Friday column although I shall hold myself manfully in reserve to deliver instant commentaries at moments of great national crisis of which no doubt there will be many.

When I began the idea was to imitate the American-style column. The then editor of the *Guardian* seemed to have Walter Lippmann in mind. There was nothing novel about columns, of course, although Fleet Street's idea of a column was, and largely still is, a star turn with the emphasis on turn: the columnist's job was to take an ego trip and to entertain his readers, preferably by annoying them, with strong opinions on each and every subject.

Political columns existed in three basic forms. There were regular or occasional comments or background features by political correspondents. There were, in the Sunday papers and weeklies, personalised and usually stylised Westminster journals of which Massingham's in the *Observer* had been the modern classic. There were political gossip columns, insiders' chit-chat, of which Crossbencher in the *Sunday Express* was the prototype and still is.

The American column was something quite different. Indeed, and as I soon discovered, it was not for import. To begin with the American columnists were syndicated which meant that they commanded readerships vastly greater than the readership of any one newspaper. This gave them the kind of power or influence which we attribute to the mass-circulation national dailies. A man addressing the readers of, say, 150 newspapers three times a week could see just about anybody he wanted to see in Washington, and have his telephone calls returned.

Moreover, the syndicated columnist would often be if not the sole the chief source of political information apart from the news agencies in most of the newspapers in which he appeared. So if what appeared in the centre spread of the *Washington Post* sometimes seemed a bit on the trite side to the home town audience it had to be remembered that the same column was playing to the millions from coast to coast.

None of this applied in Britain. The columnist could not command a readership larger than his newspaper's; indeed, his would be a good deal less than for the front page story or the sports results. Nor did he enjoy any kind of monopoly in high political information; indeed the reverse because some of the functions of the American-style column were amply and ably discharged by his own specialist colleagues, the Political Correspondent, the Diplomatic Correspondent, and so on.

However, there was something to learn from the manner of the American columns, their blend of reportage, analysis and editorialising. There was also a great deal to be said for their inter-disciplinary reach, especially as the coverage of government in Britain had become so highly compartmentalised. Trying to combine foreign and domestic affairs was, perhaps, easier in Washington where they were combined in the activities of the Presidency and therefore more central to the business of government than under the British system. However, it seemed to me that foreign affairs ought not to be left entirely to the specialists and ought to be treated as a part of politics. Opportunities for trips abroad were also a consideration.

It took a while to accustom Number 10 Downing Street to dealing with a creature calling himself a columnist who wasn't a Lobby Correspondent or the Foreign Office to speaking to somebody who wasn't an accredited Diplomatic Correspondent. The Treasury, and the lesser economic departments, I had been more accustomed to dealing with as a Labour Correspondent, but basically – and it is still true, although much less so – the Whitehall departments prefer to control the flow of information through groups of specialised correspondents who themselves have some interest in establishing a monopoly.

The problem with the politicians was to persuade them to be less than totally preoccupied with the next morning's newspapers. A columnist who might write a 'think piece' several days after the event was scarcely worth bothering with; opinion, they thought, was formed chiefly by the way the news was slanted, and so it was and, to a large extent, still is.

Moreover, the commentator's needs are consuming of the politician's time. He doesn't require merely to be briefed or given 'the story'. He needs to discuss things in a more wide-ranging and leisurely fashion. Most important of all, he needs to get to know the people he is writing about and the way their minds work.

Politicians have romantic notions about the way political journalists work in the same way that journalists are accused of entertaining wild fantasies about the inner workings of government. All information in the press is assumed to be the result of a 'leak'. More often it is the result of piecing together public information, asking supplementary questions of press officers and coming to the same sort of tentative or inadequate conclusions as the decision-makers themselves. High-level sources seldom spell things out, but they sometimes drop hints which enable mysteries to be solved. One of the arts of political journalism is to make a little information go a long way.

The political columnist, however, suffers not from too little information but from far too much of it. The difficulty is to know what it means. To be sure, governments are unnecessarily secretive, but the characteristic problem of a modern mass democracy is not scarcity of information but rather a surplus vastly in excess of what most ordinarily busy people can process. The writer of a political column spends a great deal of his time reading the papers on behalf of his readers, trying to make patterns out of torrents of words.

Guardian, 3 June 1977

CHAPTER ONE

The Radical Creed of Civilised Men

The Last Years of the Wilson Government, 1967–1970

In May 1967 Peter Jenkins wrote his first piece as a political columnist for the Guardian. He was writing a year after the Labour Party's landslide election victory of 1966, following their narrow defeat of the Conservatives in 1964. Harold Wilson was Prime Minister and still the dominant personality of the Government. The unpredictable George Brown was Foreign Secretary and James Callaghan was Chancellor of the Exchequer. The latter was already deeply embroiled in the ongoing balance of payments crisis that was eventually to lead to the devaluation of sterling and with it the end of many of the radical hopes invested in the Labour Government. It also spelt the end of Callaghan at the Treasury. On 30 November he was replaced by Roy Jenkins, then the rising star of the social democratic wing of the Labour Party and at this time one of Peter Jenkins's favourite politicians. Beside the recurring economic problems that had plagued the Government since it took office in 1964, the three issues that dominated politics in these years were immigration, Europe, and the problem of trade union power.

Jenkins's first article introduced a theme that was to recur throughout the rest his career and which gradually came to dominate British politics: the European Economic Community. The Treaty of Rome had been signed by the original Six in 1957, and the subsequent economic success of the EEC persuaded the Macmillan Conservative Government to apply for membership. However, Macmillan's bid for entry by the British was rejected by de Gaulle in January 1963. The Labour Government, particularly George Brown, had set about reopening the road to joining the Community with renewed determination. At this stage everything was in the balance and dependent on the General.

Anglo-Saxon virtues

A nice way to have begun this column would have been to reveal to the world what is truly in President de Gaulle's mind. For it is not to be expected that he will oblige us by doing so himself at his press conference this afternoon.

He may drop a few characteristically ambiguous hints – probably no more at this stage. First, we want to know whether the General has taken on board the remarkable extent to which Britain 'has come round to transforming itself enough to belong to the European Community without restriction and without reservation, and placing it ahead of anything else . . .'

These were his terms when he uttered his famous 'No' in 1963. He promised that when they had been met, France would place no obstacle in Britain's path.

Mr Wilson's tactical approach can be seen as a literal application of this Gaullist text. The first task is to make it clear at the Brussels negotiating table that there is no excuse for saying 'No' or 'Not yet' on account of British 'reservation' or 'restriction'. The second task is to convince him that we are placing the Community 'ahead of anything else' – that is to say, that Britain intends to follow a 'European policy' and there are therefore no grounds for a political veto.

The Prime Minister thus begins by playing the game strictly according to the book – and the book, of course, is the Treaty of Rome. It will be British policy to raise only matters covered by the Treaty or on which the Six are agreed. There are no matters on which the Six are less agreed than international monetary reform, political unity and defence.

Mr Heath was right in the Commons debate last week to remind Mr Wilson that before he finally leads us into Europe he is likely to have to show that he is thinking about these wider questions 'in terms of Europe'. But there is nothing to be gained at this stage from making

British proposals in these areas, if that was what Mr Heath was suggesting.

Everything that General de Gaulle has ever said indicates that if he wishes to fault our eligibility, he will seek to do so not on 'baggage train' items such as sugar or butter, but by the discovery of some persisting, deep Anglo-Saxon vice. It is easy to see ways in which the technical negotiations in Brussels can lead to global considerations which will fundamentally test our 'Europeanism'.

For example, it can be argued with fairness that Britain's too frequent overall deficits on balance of payments – a potential source of weakness to the Community – are within the power of Britain herself to avoid by substantial reductions in Government overseas expenditure. To make the point this way is to make it politically, for it amounts to saying 'you are not financially fit to belong to the EEC until you abandon your military commitments to the Commonwealth and the United States east of Suez.'

'Europeanism', in Gaullist eyes, requires freedom from overriding commitments outside of Europe, in particular from dependence on the United States. 'A European Europe,' he has said, 'means that it exists by itself for itself; in other words, in the midst of the world it has its own policy.' But what exactly is this policy?

Mr Wilson's probes in the capitals of the Six provided no evidence whatsoever that General de Gaulle intends to demand some 'European' price involving NATO defence arrangements or is interested in this stage in Mr Heath's Anglo-French *bombe des patries*.

French policy, no less than British, has been consistently concerned with avoiding German acquisition or control over nuclear weapons. It is always possible that France might at some stage be interested in some form of Europeans-only McNamara committee, or in the development of a European delivery system. But these possibilities – which would not involve any change in control of warheads – are not seen in London as immediate problems.

If, however, our military commitments beyond the Alliance are held to be an obstacle to membership, Mr Wilson will soon be ready to answer that we are removing the obstacle. The Cabinet has recognised the limit of our resources and by about the end of the transitional period (1975?) our military presence on the ground east of Suez will have been liquidated: our role as junior partner in the exercise of United States world power will have been exchanged for a European posture.

If the Nassau agreement – 'an allegiance foreign to a Europe that would be one' – remains an obstacle, Mr Wilson will be able to answer that he intends in any case not to perpetuate it by the purchase of Poseidon missiles to replace Polaris.

If sterling is seen as the fifth column for the dollar and the Europeans decide that they want a European reserve currency or payments union, they will find Mr Callaghan willing enough; the interests of the United States Treasury will not be allowed to stand in the way.

What more can we do for the General, short of abolishing the English language and banning cricket?

Guardian, 16 May 1967

In April 1968, at a party meeting in Birmingham, Enoch Powell made his famous speech attacking mass immigration in which he said, 'As I look ahead, I am filled with foreboding. Like the Roman, I seem to see the River Tiber foaming with much blood.' He was immediately sacked from the Shadow Cabinet by the Conservative Party leader, Edward Heath. But Powell continued to play the politics of race from the back benches in his bid to destroy liberal conservatism. In June 1969 he returned to his preferred theme in a speech to his constituency in Wolverhampton, and Peter Jenkins, recognising the importance of Powellism, offered an early and critical analysis of Powell's ideology.

The Joe McCarthy in our midst

Why immigration again? Why wait until now to take Mr Heath to task for the speech he made at Walsall on January 26? Why this week to make a new bid for the headlines?

Conservative MPs are searching for an explanation for Mr Enoch Powell's behaviour. He did not embarrass the Central Office by asking it to release the speech he made at Wolverhampton on Monday night; but he did, hopefully or provocatively, send an advance copy to every Conservative Member of Parliament. Nor was the speech a sudden outburst on the subject which has come to obsess Mr Powell; it was carefully planned weeks in advance.

One theory is that Mr Powell has amended his strategy for capturing the leadership of the Conservative Party. Until quite recently he was basing his hopes on the Conservative Party under Mr Heath's leadership losing the next election. Then there would be a great inquest and upheaval of the kind that afflicted the Labour Party after 1959. That would give him his chance; the party would turn to him as the true prophet, the man with the alternative policy and approach.

Now, according to his friends, his thinking has developed to take account of the probability that the Conservatives will win. In that case his hopes lie with Mr Heath's government failing to solve the problems of the country just as Mr Wilson's government failed. Mr Powell will be able to say: 'I told you so'; he will have chalked the sign of the plague on both houses; by then the system will have been held to have failed and he – perhaps the patience with destiny shown by General de Gaulle is somewhere in the back of his mind? – will be ready with the alternative to the bankrupt regime of postwar politics.

The great majority of Conservatives in Parliament believe that Mr Powell stands no chance of grabbing the leadership in either situation. Equally they are in no doubt that lust for the leadership of the party is the clue to his behaviour. The party managers estimate that if Mr Heath were to be run over by a grand piano Mr Powell would score no higher than the 15 votes he received when he 'left his card' in the 1965 leadership election.

At Westminster many may sympathise with him on some points, very few agree with him on most points. But in the country it is a different matter. The support for Powell on the immigration issue shows no sign of abating; there is a great deal of sympathy with his claim to be the only man prepared to speak the truth in the liberal consensus of politicians and opinion formers.

This is the danger of Mr Powell. He returns again and again to the immigration issue, I suspect, because it most dramatically makes the more general point he is trying to get over. This is that the politicians are conspiring against the people, that the country is led by men who have no idea about what interests or frightens the ordinary people in the backstreets of Wolverhampton, that government – the men at Westminster and the man from Whitehall – are entirely to blame for the country's difficulties.

More dangerous than the racial prejudices that his speeches encourage are the profoundly anti-political attitudes they invite. If things do continue to go badly Mr Powell will have played an important part in creating an atmosphere in which the governed might turn in unreason against government itself, making scapegoats of the values which hitherto have sustained a stable, moderate, and improving society.

His latest speech sounds some ominous notes. Britain is 'threatened from within'; 'the people of this country are being misled'; the situation 'is fraught with danger and disaster'; 'time is running against us'. This is the language of political paranoia. I suddenly remembered where I had heard it before.

'How can we account for our present situation unless we believe that men high in this government are concerting to deliver us to disaster? This must be the product of a great conspiracy, a conspiracy on a scale so immense as to dwarf any previous such venture in the history of man.'

'We live in an age of conspiracies. They are far more successful and well-managed conspiracies than the conspiracies of history . . . the age of the old-fashioned conspirator is no more. He no longer gathers with his fellows in tiny groups, admitted by password to huddle round a dark lantern in a dingy garret. Today the conspirators sit in the seats of the mighty, at the desks of Ministers and editors; they live in the blaze of continual publicity; their weapons are the organs of opinion themselves.'

The first quotation is Senator Joseph McCarthy in 1951; the second is Mr Enoch Powell in 1968.

On Monday night Mr Powell sneeringly attacked the people 'whose business or ambition it is to change their fellow men and improve human nature.' The people who took this line were what he called 'the best people'. McCarthy used to attack 'striped-pants diplomats'. He said in 1950: 'It is not the less fortunate or members of the minority groups who have been selling the nation out but rather those who have had all the benefits the wealthiest nation on earth has to offer – the finest homes, the finest college education, and the finest jobs in the government that we can give.'

For clues about the sort of politician Mr Powell is, I recommend an essay by Richard Hofstadter, *The Paranoid Style in American Politics* (Jonathan Cape, 1966). Paranoia is a feeling of persecution systemised into grandiose theories of conspiracy. The political paranoid, unlike the clinical paranoid, does not see the conspiracy directed against himself but 'against a nation, a culture, a way of life whose fate affects not himself alone but millions of others.'

Hofstadter analyses the literature of political paranoia of which there is a rich American tradition. The conspiracy is always 'gigantic' or 'vast'; the message is always apocalyptic; it is always a turning point; time is always running out. The enemy is firmly ensconced in high places; usually he controls the press. The paranoid is often a pedant. 'The enemy, for example, may be the cosmopolitan intellectual, but the paranoid will out-do him in the apparatus of scholarship, even of pedantry.'

Paranoid literature tends to begin with defensible assumptions but proceeds, through amassing facts or what appear to be facts, towards an overwhelming proof of the conspiracy and a total, or final, solution of the crisis brought about by the conspirators.

From Mr Powell's collected speeches I have composed this short anthology:

'Lift the curtain and the State reveals itself as a little group of fallible men in Whitehall . . .'

'The politicians and the pundits have contrived to cheat the nation, to bewilder its choices, and to destroy its good conscience by weaving around it a cat's cradle of falsehoods and fallacies.'

'The politics of the last few years have been little more than a series of conspiracies conducted by the politicians and the press against the common sense of the people.'

'The Higher Nonsense is a mightier instrument of mass repression than the machine gun, grapeshot and cavalry charges ever were.'

'Inflation, with all its attendant evils, comes about for one reason and one reason only: the Government causes it.'

Politicians are 'the real culprits' – 'Theirs is the dishonesty, theirs the thriftlessness, theirs the unwillingness to face the facts of life.'

There is a 'gulf between the overwhelming majority of people throughout the country on one side, and on the other side a tiny minority, with almost a monopoly hold upon the channels of communication, who seem determined not to know the facts and not to face the realities and who will resort to any device or extremity to blind themselves and others.'

One more quotation, this time from Mr Powell's beloved

Thucydides. Thucydides got the measure of the paranoids of his day, the anti-politicians and the enemies of politics in civilised society. He wrote: 'The meaning of words no longer had the same relation to things but was changed by them as they thought proper. Reckless daring was held to be courage, prudent delay was the excuse of a coward; moderation was the disguise of unmanly weakness; to know everything was to do nothing . . . He who succeeded in a plot was deemed knowing, but a still greater master in craft was he who detected one.'

Guardian, 13 June 1969

The Labour Government's response to the Powellite agenda was a mixture of immigration control and the passing of anti-discrimination acts. These measures, together with legislation abolishing the death penalty, legalising abortion, and decriminalising homosexuality, helped to create what became known as the 'permissive society'. The political architect of the permissive society was the unlikely figure of Roy Jenkins, who proved to be one of the very few radical Home Secretaries in British history. The legislation that he passed during his tenure at the Home Office, between 1965 and 1967, was one of the few lasting achievements of the Wilson Governments. On the strength of this success he became Chancellor in 1967 and, for many, the main challenger for Wilson's position in the Labour Party. As the inheritor of the Gaitskellite mantle he was the consummate craftsman of consensus politics.

The radical creed of a civilised man

Mr Roy Jenkins spoke up forcefully at the weekend in defence of the 'civilised society'. In a speech at Abingdon, Berkshire, the Chancellor sought to rally liberal opinion in the country. 'The forces of liberalism and human freedom,' he said, 'are now to some extent on the defensive. The permissive society – always a misleading description – has been allowed to become a dirty phrase.'

I talked with Mr Jenkins about his speech and asked him why he had thought it necessary at this time to make a restatement of his 'libertarian creed'. He replied:

'It certainly wasn't wholly, and I am not sure that it was chiefly that. There were a number of themes in the speech. It was intended to say that we had become almost too self-critical and too un-self-confident in this country. It was intended to put the balance of payments problem, which I had talked about a great deal in the last eighteen months, in a slightly wider context. But it was also intended, as you rightly say, to restate a "libertarian creed". Those are your words but I don't quarrel with them.

'I thought it an appropriate moment to do this because I haven't changed in any way from the views which I put forward in a Penguin book (*The Case for Labour*) ten years ago and which I tried to put into practice while I was Home Secretary.

'I think there is a certain danger at the present time – as I put it in the speech on Saturday – of liberal opinion being put on the defensive. There is a growing idea that liberal reforms have a bad effect on society. I don't believe this for one moment. And I think some rallying of the liberal lobby is desirable.'

Were the problems of personal freedom the problems which now urgently required the radical attentions of a Labour Government? Mr Jenkins thought not; otherwise he would have been very foolish to have ceased being Home Secretary and become Chancellor of the Exchequer. But he added that he regarded race relations 'as a continuing crucial test of the radicalism of any political party.'

I tried to explore further into a political philosophy in which the word 'radicalism' appears more frequently than the word 'socialism'. Why was he so attracted, I asked, by the paradox of radical achievement made by cautious, even rather conservative men? For example, he had written of Asquith's Budgets: 'He was highly successful in achieving the maximum radical result while arousing the minimum of conservative opposition.' Did this in fact represent his own approach to government?

'I am not sure that it does. And I am not sure that "attracted" is the right word. I think "intrigued by" is the phrase I would have chosen because I have certainly been struck when looking back over the one hundred years before 1964 how the three left-wing Prime Ministers under whom governments of the Left made radical achievements of various sorts – Gladstone, Asquith and Attlee – although very different types of individuals, were all of them men of very conventional habit of mind on a great number of other issues.

'It was that paradox which intrigued me. But I am not sure I would define my own approach as radicalism by stealth. I do think it is on the whole more important to achieve results than to announce you are going to do things, cause a great stir but not do them. I don't think that is a very sensible approach.'

I suggested to the Chancellor that not many people would dispute his achievements as a reforming Home Secretary. Indeed it might one day be written of him, as he had written of – again – Asquith: 'He was a successful Home Secretary in an unsuccessful government.' But what of his own record at the Treasury so far? What 'radical' achievements was he proud of?

'The context in which I had to try to operate, right from the very beginning, was quite different from the context in which I was working as Home Secretary. Although in the speech at Abingdon I tried to put the balance of payments problem in context, when I am trying to do my job at the Treasury I cannot pretend this is not the dominating problem. Indeed, I have made it the dominating problem because I believed that unless we could get this right it would frustrate a great many other things we wanted to do.

'Therefore I have had to concentrate on dealing with this single, not tremendously exciting, issue. And I think we are now making real progress in getting it right. Nearly everything else has had to take second place to this. But I have always had a balancing objective in mind. If you were to ask me to define my central policy objective as Chancellor I would have said to get the balance of payments right as quickly as possible and to combine with this the highest practicable rate of economic growth.'

I suggested that even at an unsatisfactory rate of economic growth there was still an important choice of priorities – for example, between public expenditure and private consumption. He said that the inhibitions on a Government doing what it wanted to do were very much greater if there was not a good rate of economic growth. Decisions about the balance between the public and the private sector were not only decisions for government – the community as a whole had to accept them. And the community could frustrate such decisions.

'I don't see a future of achieving our social objectives by constantly shifting resources over from the private to the public sector so that people have a less and less proportion of their incomes to spend as they choose. One, I don't think it is desirable; two, I don't think people will accept it.'

I reminded Mr Jenkins of a Fabian Essay he had written in 1952. In it he had said 'Where there is no egalitarianism there is no socialism.' Was that still his belief?

'Yes. I certainly think that the test of any left-wing party should be whether it is promoting a more equal spread not only of opportunity but also of living standards and freedom of choice throughout the whole community. To a greater extent now than in 1952 I believe that a generally rising standard of living, which of course is tied up very closely with economic growth, is an important equalising factor. It is incomparably easier to open up new windows to new groups of people on the basis of a rising standard of living than in a purely redistributive framework.'

In what sense did the Chancellor call himself a Socialist? It was not a word he used very often.

'It's not a word I use very often, probably consciously so. That's because in the fifties, and even in the early sixties, the word had become a political football within the Labour Party. People just kicked it around saying "I'm a better Socialist than you. You are not a Socialist at all." I became rather antipathetic to people who believed they could prove their socialism not by their actions but by how often they used the word in their speeches. Therefore I have been extremely sparing in the use of it in my speeches and writings.

'But I am a Socialist because I want not only full equality of opportunity – that is not nearly enough in itself – but full access to the means to a satisfactory life spread throughout the community.

'I don't regard the question of whether a particular industry should be under public ownership as the ultimate test of socialism. I regard the Race Relations Act as a more important piece of Socialist legislation than the nationalisation of a particular industry.'

How did he apply his philosophy in, for example, the field of education?

'We have made considerable progress in getting rid of selection at 11-plus. The traditional pattern of English education, with the rigid class division between the private sector and the public sector, is in the process of withering away. And I want to see it wither away. Oxford and Cambridge have lost their monopoly of excellence in university education. I think this was one of the things wrong with British university education.'

And in the social services?

'I don't want to see a system in which large numbers of people, and those the most articulate and the most influential, contract out of the Health Service. If that were to happen a deterioration in the standards of the public service would follow inevitably.

'I don't regard the question of charges on teeth and spectacles as being the crucial issue in the Health Service. The crucial issue is whether within the competing demands upon our economic resources we can provide a thoroughly good service for the community.'

Finally, I asked Mr Jenkins how he thought the 'Gaitskellite' or 'revisionist' approach had fared during Labour's period of office. He said:

'The essence of the old Gaitskellite approach – I don't find "revisionism" a particularly attractive word – was that it was essential for the Labour Party to have a very broad national appeal.'

Had the recent affair with the trade unions damaged Labour's appeal to all sections of the community? Nobody, the Chancellor said, should underestimate the toughness of the Government's approach in the first six months of this year.

'It involved great risks for the party. The risks were run and a very considerable achievement was made. I think this was a very good indication of the very strong desire in the Government to be a national party and not a sectarian party.'

I put it to Mr Jenkins that some commentators, mainly on the Left of the Labour Party, had been arguing that the disappointments of the Government were really the failure of Gaitskellism. 'I don't think for a moment,' he replied, 'that you can attribute any of the disappointments to the revisionist or Gaitskellite or – as one should perhaps now call it – the Wilsonite approach. If this approach had not been adopted in 1964 and 1966 we wouldn't be discussing the disappointments of the Government, for there wouldn't be a Labour Government. And I don't think there will be a Labour Government to discuss in the future unless the party keeps in touch with the leftward half of the country generally and not just a very small minority within that leftward half.'

Guardian, 10 July 1969

One of the great challenges to consensus politics was the increasing militancy of the trade union movement. By the late 1960s even the Labour leadership had come to acknowledge that the power of the trade unions needed to be curbed. The Secretary of State for Employment, Barbara Castle, published 'In Place of Strife', her proposals for trade union reform, on 19 January 1969. However, after a bitter struggle between most of the Cabinet and the trade union paymasters of the Labour Party, the proposals were withdrawn. In this article, Jenkins looks beyond the party politics to assess the long-term implications of Barbara Castle's defeat.

The terrible trinity

Good orthodox Labour Party men are expected to believe in a Trinity. The trade unions were the Father, the Labour Party is the Son and the Co-op, I suppose, is the Holy Ghost. The three form a godhead known as the Labour Movement. Tritheism – the belief in three distinct gods – is still a heresy for which you can be burnt at Transport House.

In election year we shall be hearing a good deal about the Labour Movement. 'This great movement . . .' the speeches will begin. But can anybody really believe in it? The past few years ought to have dispelled any remaining illusion that the trade unions and the Labour Government are in pursuit of the same goals. Not much remains of working-class solidarity. The relative deprivations within the mass of the working community are more keenly felt than the injustice of extreme wealth or extreme poverty.

The idea of a Labour Movement is a harmless enough sentimentality if it helps to hold together an alliance of interest groups for the purpose of achieving progressive government. The party of the Left must always be a kind of alliance between those who need and those who care. But the foremost challenge for the Left in the seventies, as I see it, is to prevent an outdated sociology from setting government tasks it cannot or should not perform while obscuring the tasks it ought to be undertaking.

The problem of the trade unions is by no means the only problem here, and may not even be the chief one, but let us glance at it first, for it involves a fundamental choice between a regulatory or managerial conception of State power. The Labour Party continues to behave as if the industrial and political wings of the Labour Movement are engaged in the common task of building something called a Socialist society.

Mrs Castle last year decided that the unions were not pulling their weight in this enterprise. She set out not so much to regulate the conduct of industrial relations, in the way that the State, for example, regulates street trading, but to intervene in industrial relations, more in the way that the State, for example, intervenes to secure orders for the shipbuilding industry.

Before the end of that unhappy affair Mrs Castle's honesty was forcing her towards the conclusion that the interests of the unions are intensely sectional and inimical to the programme of a progressive party and that they are either incapable or uninterested in operating priorities in favour of the underpaid and hard done by. A Government basing its policy on such harshly unsentimental assumptions might do two things: legislate minimum standards, not only of pay but also holidays and many other fringe benefits; and bring collective bargaining within a regulatory framework acceptable to public opinion and for the rest leave the two sides of industry to get on with it.

Two principles underlie this approach. One is that the State would become more concerned with regulatory functions and less ready to become involved in interventions of a managerial character. The other is of a social conscience divorced from the false notion of class solidarity. These principles have applications in many fields other than industrial relations.

Labour's attitude towards industry, for example, has become too producer-orientated; the role of the State as a doer and provider has become overemphasised, its role as a preventer neglected. Progressive government in the seventies will have to be more concerned with preventing misuse of land and amenities, noise, poisoning, and despoliation. Government intervention for, say, increasing steel production is of much less importance now than it was in the fifties.

Labour in the sixties became dedicated to positive or 'purposive' interventionism and one result is a vast bureaucratic *Zaibatsu* in the form of the Ministry of Technology. The intervention consists very largely in giving public money or gratuitous advice to private enterprise while hogging the supply of scientists and technologists. For some reason this is seen as a kind of socialism and is generally applauded on the Left of the Labour Party.

In taking on the function of a super management consultancy – which it performs poorly – government has neglected its duty to protect the consumer and the worker. It has been more concerned with promoting mergers than with curbing the growth of corporate power. It has done little about a situation in which people in the City of London can get away with things which would mean prison in capitalist America. In motorised America the car manufacturers have been forced to suppress exhaust fumes, but not here. The restrictive practices of the professions have received little of the attention lavished upon the restrictive practices of the trade unions. There is no difficulty in compiling a long agenda for a left-wing government which would give higher priority to protection and regulation, and less to promotion and direct intervention.

In social policy the Labour Party remains inhibited by its persisting belief in class solidarity. Ways and means of financing the social services (and the need is for extensions of the Welfare State and increased public expenditure) could soon enough be devised if social conscience could be directed towards poverty and need instead of at the condition of the working class as a whole.

One way of approaching this might be to raise taxes for specific programmes, earmarking sixpence of the income tax or whatever for a programme of primary school building in the slums, another sixpence for hospital building, etc. Social taxes of this kind could be made more progressive and lower and higher incomes and more regressive in the middle spread than the standard income tax. At the moment few people have the slightest idea of the way in which the social services are financed or of the Government's priorities in public expenditure. But everybody can understand the economics of handing round the hat for a deserving case.

Spectacular task force programmes might be devised for dealing with particularly disgraceful social problems. Instead of the scratching away at the slums why not totally raze the slums of Glasgow for a start? One thing is certain: the 85 per cent of the community which lives in bearable circumstances will not consent under the present system to pay enough taxes both to eradicate poverty and at the same time to maintain, let alone improve, the dwindling standards of the universal Welfare State.

Social improvement must be given a more dramatic appeal and Government spending connected in people's minds with visible social results. That social conscience is not yet dead is shown by the success of campaigns with limited purposes, such as Shelter.

The notion of Social Democracy still rests heavily on three assumptions – that trade union interests are closely aligned with the interests of the community as a whole; that the planning of production is the most important tool for shaping the quality of life; and that class solidarity works towards the eradication of poverty and need. As none of these assumptions is any longer valid the first task for the Left in the seventies is to break loose from them. We could still if we wish describe the result as Social Democracy and even go on talking about a Labour Movement.

Guardian, 2 January 1970

1970 was likely to be election year, and for the Conservatives Iain Macleod was the outstanding political personality – eclipsing even Edward Heath. In January the Conservative Shadow Cabinet met at the Selsdon Park Hotel, Croydon, for a pre-election policy meeting. Little of substance was actually decided at the meeting, but Harold Wilson seized on it to attack the Conservatives for swinging to the Right. He dubbed the new 'ruthless and uncaring' Conservative 'Selsdon Man'. Peter Jenkins, like many other journalists, used Wilson's line and the Conservatives thus found themselves being discussed in these terms throughout 1970 – not necessarily to their disadvantage. Macleod's answers to Jenkins, in the following interview, illustrate the extent to which Wilson's creation was an exaggeration – there was, though, a growing minority in the Party who were all too ready to breathe life into Selsdon Man.

One nation, which Macleod?

'A Tory radical', 'nothing if not a traditional Tory', 'a moderate', 'a mixed-up Conservative' – where does one place Iain Macleod who uses all these phrases about himself?

Twenty years ago he and Enoch Powell collaborated in the first intellectual Conservative critique of the Universal Welfare State. As Minister of Labour at the time of the 1958 London bus strike, Macleod had the reputation of being a toughie. Later as Colonial Secretary he came to be seen by important sections of his party as a softie, if not a leftie. Today Iain Macleod expects to be the next Chancellor of the Exchequer and has been preparing his plans. Which Macleod would it be at the Treasury?

I asked him to try to put a name to the sort of Britain he would like to bring about. I suggested 'capitalism', and he said: 'Oh, no, no. That's a very old-fashioned word with nineteenth-century overtones. I am not a capitalist. I prefer to look at the sort of society I want to see as an exciting society, but it's very important that an exciting society doesn't become a ruthless society. It is this aspect of the cartoonist's image of the capitalist society which I detest.'

How exciting would the 'exciting society' be, I wondered? Wouldn't we finish up with no more than a modest adjustment of the balance between the State and the individual? Macleod said he was not in the least bit interested in taking the same cake and cutting it up again. But he didn't believe that his exciting society was going to come about through a few changes in the level of surtax or whatever. He was talking about a society of opportunity, and to bring that about the Government could do no more than set the climate; the people, particularly the next generation, would have to grasp the opportunity.

I was still not clear about how radical Macleod's proposals are, but he went on:

'I believe that there is untapped in this country an enormous will to save. People used to save a great deal in this country. Now, partly because of the levels of direct taxation, it is almost impossible to save out of taxed income. So if I had to boil down my tax proposals into one single sentence it is just this: I want it to be possible for people, particularly young people, to save out of taxed income. What they do with the money they have saved I regard as their business.'

What he hoped some of them might do with the money was to make greater private provision for their children's education, their family's health, for their retirement and for their heirs and dependents. But he wasn't talking about private medicine replacing the National Health Service. He said that his father was a general practitioner and his grandfather a doctor too, and that he regarded the NHS as 'a tremendous piece of social engineering in which I am a profound believer.'

But that didn't mean that people shouldn't provide for themselves over and above the standards provided by the State. The same went in education, and in pensions it could go further for, ideally, he would like to see everyone in an occupational scheme. He believed in choice; in his children's generation he detected 'a deep desire to save' in order to exercise choice.

What about the State's role in industry? Where would he draw the line between intervention and letting the market decide? He admitted himself an interventionist still, but in a way which he carefully defined. This was where he described himself as a 'traditionalist Tory' for he agreed with me (and Lord Butler) that Tories were by tradition unafraid to exercise State power. But he disapproved of indiscriminate intervention in industry and thought that where help was given it should be the result of a particular decision of government.

For example, he believed that the Macmillan Cabinet, of which he was a member, had been right to send the new sheet strip mill to Ravenscraig in Scotland although that had been the third out of four possible sites listed according to purely economic considerations. He believed this sort of governmental intervention must continue, might even become an increasing factor as the world became more complicated and industry more sophisticated. But you couldn't go on handing out £900 millions a year in indiscriminate aid to industry, not if you wanted to reduce taxation.

Perhaps 'selectivity' is the connecting thread of Macleod's political thinking. I took him back to the 'One Nation' days of 1950 and he said:

'The conventional wisdom now of the parties, particularly of the Tory Party but to a great extent of the Labour Party as well, argues for some form of selectivity, and the fairly simple proposition – which is so simple that it is almost a truism – that if you want to help those in true need you cannot equally help everybody irrespective of need. Now this doctrine, which today sounds so absurdly obvious, was put for the first time by Enoch Powell and myself in 1951 when he and I together wrote a pamphlet called "Needs and Means" which was the first considered intellectual attack on the basis of Beveridge.'

I said I still found it difficult to place him in the spectrum of Tory politics and he said he found it difficult to distinguish between Left and Right in the Conservative Party, much more difficult than in the Labour Party. 'Take Enoch,' he suggested. 'Until a year or so ago whether one was Left or Right was judged almost entirely on one's attitudes to the forms of personal legislation which were going through Parliament at the time.

'Now if one accepts that standard – abolition of capital punishment, hostility to corporate punishment, approval of the changes in homosexual laws, of easier divorce and abortion and so on – on every single one of these issues Enoch was on the progressive or radical side. And so was I; I always have been; I probably always will be.

'On the other hand, Enoch is much more ardent as a devotee of a pure market system than I am, although I'm quite a long way down that particular road. Now I do not see how this fits in. I do not see how you argue whether these attitudes are Left or Right. On that analysis, which is Enoch Powell? Which is Iain Macleod?'

Iain Macleod thought again for a moment and added:

'I think in one sense I am more than most people the child of my parents. My father was always a radical Liberal and my mother was always a staunch Conservative. Through the years, so my mother told me, they would cast their opposite votes for the opposite candidates, thereby fulfilling their civic duty and cancelling each other out. Now I don't think it requires much imagination to see both these strains in me. I do feel very conscious of both these inheritances.

'It's quite true that in my Colonial Office period I did reach a level of political fulfilment that I never did before and, frankly, which I think I shall never attain again. This was an office in which not only my head but also my heart was completely involved, and still is, in the cause of freedom not just for colonial peoples but all oppressed people, people who are minorities in any sense of the word. Whether that makes me Left or Right or just mixed-up Conservative, I don't know.'

Was there any particular book or great political event which more than any other had formed his political views? Iain Macleod gave a curious but perhaps prophetic answer. He said:

'I think the thing I remember most is Butler's first Budget in 1952. It had a very coherent philosophy in it and one which is very much part of my thinking today. You see what he did was to remove the food subsidies and this was greeted with fury by the Labour Party who made precisely the same sort of noises as Mr Wilson was making last weekend about the increase in the cost of living. The *Daily Herald* ran a headline, "The shilling egg?" But you see it hasn't happened.

'And the reason is that in fact we moved into an era of much steadier prices because Butler used the money saved from the food subsidies partly to reduce taxation and partly to recompense through the social services those whom reductions in taxation would not benefit. Now, although it's on a much bigger scale, the exercise which we are planning at the moment is precisely in the philosophy of Butler's Budget of 1952.'

Guardian, 27 February 1970

When the election finally came the economic situation had improved to such an extent that it appeared as though Labour would win. This was Jenkins's first General Election campaign as a political columnist and he filed daily campaign reports. In 'Rail tale' he gives a glimpse into the life of a hack on the road with Harold Wilson and captures the glories of British Rail catering, circa 1970.

Rail tale

For the last leg of his campaign the Prime Minister took the 4 p.m. train from Euston to Manchester. As usual he sat with his wife in one reserved compartment, his two Special Branch men were next door in another, and a third compartment was reserved for his staff. The rest of the coach was available to the public although in fact commandeered by the press.

Mr Wilson had a nap (with the blinds of his compartment down), a cup of tea, and then chatted with the journalists, squeezing in four to a seat in their compartment.

Beyond the reservation of the compartments, the two policemen, the courteous presence of the station master on the platform, and a handful of photographers there were no special arrangements, no fuss. In few other countries of the world today could a Prime Minister travel so unpretentiously, so undisturbed, and with such scant regard for his safety. Mr Alan Watkins of the *New Statesman* was so moved by the spectacle as to announce at the bar that his faith in democracy was much fortified.

Mr Heath's campaign has been just as English although he has travelled by plane – a nasty American habit – and not by train, and has mingled less with the crowds. The attention and protection he has received as Leader of the Opposition has been far less than a junior senator would be afforded in the United States. And the campaign as a whole has not been marred by a single instance of serious violence or real threat to the safety of its participants. It has proved conclusively that law and order is not a serious issue in this country.

But to return to British Rail, for it plays an important part in ensuring that nobody in our democracy, not even a Prime Minister, is afforded special condescension. The only instance of favoured treatment is the case of the man who wiped the window of the Prime Minister's compartment with a dirty cloth, but it is not known whether he was acting upon instructions or from some political motivation. Otherwise I can report that British Rail maintained strict impartiality and was not moved by the presence of the Prime Minister or accompanying reporters to abandon its belief that people don't eat or drink at weekends, that ice is an unnecessary luxury in hot weather, that supply is the iron determinant of demand, and that in its hotels the eating of dinner must not interfere with the laying of breakfast.

The railway approach to catering, as inflexible as the rails themselves, is well indicated at the foot of the bills where you are requested to report to the authorities anything in the way of what is ambiguously called 'unusual service'. There was very little of that on the election journeys.

You might think for example that when a Prime Minister, his staff, and a horde of newspapermen are booked on a train the catering authorities would anticipate an unusual demand for food and drink, certainly for drink. They might even, you might think, perceive the opportunity of obtaining some favourable free publicity. Not a bit of it. For example, on a late afternoon train from London to Nottingham a single buffet car attendant was so overwhelmed by the demand that Mr Alfred Richman, the Prime Minister's indispensable and resourceful gentleman's gentleman, himself cut Mrs Wilson's sandwiches in the kitchen car and made out the bill for them. I intend to report him for providing 'unusual service'.

British Rail must also be given credit for the best but unreported egg-throwing incident of the campaign. This occurred when a fried egg was thrown into the coffee of my colleague Ian Aitken. But to be fair, a few stars must be awarded – for a start to the buffet car attendant who asked me for my autograph, although I fear I owe this unusual service to the presence of Mr Ludovic Kennedy, Mr Kenneth Harris, Mr George Galt, and Lady Hartwell. Also a favourable mention to the Royal Station Hotel, Newcastle upon Tyne, for civility to its guests, to the Midland Hotel, Manchester, for its excellent restaurant, and to the bar on the sleeper to Glasgow which appeared to have been specially designed as a sort of El Vino on wheels.

However, my special campaign prize for unusual service goes to the restaurant staff at the North British Hotel, an astronomically expensive establishment (if my editor will forgive the expression) which boasts 24-hour service, 24-hour quality, and 24-hour satisfaction, or some misleading words to that effect. It was there that the following immortal exchange took place:

Nicholas Tomalin of the *Sunday Times*: 'Waiter, we've been waiting thirty minutes for the wine list.'

Waiter: 'Sir, I have been waiting for thirty years.'

Guardian, 18 June 1970

CHAPTER TWO

'At the Head of the Queue for Collapse'

The Political and Economic Crisis of the Mid-1970s

Wilson was defeated in 1970. The Conservative Government initially enjoyed considerable success. However, its attempts to introduce industrial relations legislation and impose a statutory incomes policy resulted in confrontation with the unions, particularly the NUM and the power workers. Jenkins was in the United States for much of this period, reporting on the Watergate scandal as the Guardian's *Washington correspondent. In a remarkable article at the time of the 1972 Presidential election he bitterly attacked Richard Nixon.*

Stink of success

Only a stroke of divine providence or a devilish curse upon all opinion polls now can save the United States and the world from four more years of President Nixon. Mr Nixon succeeds by bringing out the worst in people and the margin of his re-election on Tuesday will be the measure of his success. Now that the moment of choice is so close, it is time to stop carping at the inadequacies and errors of Senator George McGovern and do him honour for his endeavour to bring a basic decency to the conduct of public affairs, to revive a withering sense of justice and compassion in a society deformed by callousness, brutality and greed, and to gain recognition for the simple moral fact that killing people – even Asians – is wrong. But Senator McGovern has been whistling into an ill wind. Americans can favourably compare the state of their nation now with its state in 1968. It is true that the cities are no longer in flames and the campuses in turmoil. The nightmare of Vietnam has receded. An insecure nation frightened by war and crime and hallucinatory abandon feels more secure under the firm hand of a mean man. The psychologist Erich Fromm observed the Germans electing Hitler and called the phenomenon the 'flight from freedom'. I am not going so far as to compare Mr Nixon with Hitler. However, I do seriously contend that his re-election should be viewed with repugnance and deep foreboding.

His record over four years ought to be sufficient warning of the evil he could accomplish in four more years. The world sees him as the man who went to Peking and Moscow, and he has dazzled the eyes of his own people with these external diversions. The rapprochement with China and the signing of an agreement to limit arms and promote trade with the Soviet Union were achievements of historic importance. What the world does not so clearly see is what Mr Nixon is doing to the United States. At least as great as the dangers of Super-Power conflict is the danger involved in Mr Nixon's callously insensitive handling of the fragilities of a modern industrialised society. His manipulation of fear and greed, no less brilliant in execution than his diplomacy with China and Russia, has eroded basic freedoms and dignities which if not preserved in the US may not for long survive in lesser corners of the world. There is something almost ominous in the fact that the ghettos are not in flames and the campuses not in turmoil. It is as if an iron hand is holding down the lid of a giant pressure cooker. For the injustices and inequalities, the squalor, corruption, and primitive barbarisms which exist within this great rich land seem sure to convulse it again before long.

It is not easy to comprehend why the American people are queuing up to re-elect President Nixon. One theory I have heard put forward – by former Senator Eugene McCarthy, who has a keen sense of sin – is that people feel the need for a President who can without compunction shoulder the nation's burden of collective guilt. The evangelicalism of George McGovern scratches tender souls too hard. A *New Yorker* cartoonist made the same point another way with one hard hat saying to another in a bar, 'Nixon's no dope. If the public really wanted moral leadership, he'd give them moral leadership.' The more likely explanation is that a people nurtured to high self-regard, their confidence shattered by the lack of success and bloody cost of their latest foreign adventure, judge Nixon solely by the fact that he brought the boys home from Vietnam and left the Asians to do the dying. The news of imminent ceasefire in Vietnam has come as an anti-climax to the already accepted and welcome fact that America's physical, man-to-man involvement in Indo-China has already been all but terminated. The after-spasms of the Vietnam war have yet to be experienced, and nobody could be less equipped than President Nixon to nurse his country through a period in which qualities of humanity, gentleness and understanding will be at a premium. His rhetoric has all to do with enemies and war. He calls the police 'crime fighters'; he is at 'war' against drug addiction. And these are not just metaphors of determination but have to do with his crude, simple, and miserable belief that the only language anybody understands – be it the Russians, Chinese, and the North Vietnamese, or the poor, the unemployed, and the black – is a language of force and threat.

He has begun to do many bad things, and if given a mandate will do still worse. He has undermined the authority of the rule of law, mistaking it for a rule of tough cops and harsh judges. He has gone four-fifths of the way towards stacking the Supreme Court with reactionaries and if re-elected will finish the job. He has not only subverted the Supreme Court but has insulted it with his nomination of men supremely unqualified. Law and order, however, does not begin in the White House, which under Mr Nixon has been associated with crooks and thugs charged with the subversion of the processes of democracy in a so-called free society. The President deals in mendacious over-simplifications which encourage people to believe that the only practical politics are those based on a morbid view. With luck, the US will survive another four years under Mr Nixon's malevolent sway and then find a President who can bring some inspiration of humanity, decency and understanding to his difficult task.

Guardian, 3 November 1972

Jenkins reflected on these years in two articles published in 1974. He probably wrote 'Unhealed scar at No. 10' by candlelight, at the height of the industrial conflict between Heath and the mineworkers. It was a time in which the very foundation of postwar affluence had been undermined by the oil crisis and the basis of democratic government was being questioned on both sides of the Atlantic – Nixon facing impeachment and Heath about to ask the electorate 'Who governs Britain?'

Unhealed scar at No. 10

A diagnosis of the present bout of electionitis involves going back if not to the once upon a time of Selsdon Man at least to the events of two years ago when Ministers in confrontation with miners were forced to unconditional surrender. Perhaps a little blood-letting would do no harm suggested an official at the time, trying to look on the bright side. 'A little blood-letting!' said Lord Carrington. 'That's true blue Tory blood all over the carpet.'

What happened in 1972 has been in everybody's minds during the present crisis. 'We have learned from that experience,' said the Prime Minister during last week's emergency debate. Its experience with the seven-week coal strike two years ago prompted the Government this time to take no chances with electricity supply and to issue the drastic order putting industry on a three-day week.

Last time it had failed to plan the conservation of essential energy supplies, underestimated the coal miners. In the end abject terms of surrender were forced upon the Cabinet not only by the miners but also by the officials in Whitehall whose duty it was, as they now relate, to warn Ministers that within days whole cities the size of Manchester would be blacked out and utterly dislocated, sewage flowing in their streets.

But it was that true blue Tory blood on the carpet which left the deeper stain on memories. The Prime Minister sat in the Cabinet Room that night while upstairs the National Coal Board gave the miners' leaders everything they asked for. 'If they had thought of asking for an allowance for their racing pigeons they could have had it,' recalls an NCB official. The Wilberforce Report had already smashed the Government's wages 'de-escalation' strategy but the miners were able to extract more than even Wilberforce had said. The Prime Minister, according to another witness, had to sit there 'while they came round and removed his underpants.'

The consequence – a crucial factor in the calculations and miscalculations of the past few weeks – was that even had the Prime Minister been willing to surrender a second time he would have faced a grave situation within his own divided party, both in Parliament and in the country. 'This Prime Minister simply could not do it,' said one of his aides. 'It would have to be someone else.'

This consideration – call it constitutional or psychological, a matter of politics or pride – has carried more weight in the last few days than the inflationary consequences of making a special case of the miners outside Stage Three of the counter-inflationary pay code. Indeed, as the surrounding economic crisis intensified, and as the TUC made its intervention, both Ministers and officials became increasingly ready to admit in private that the economic consequences of giving way had become the lesser consideration.

Other constraints – the appalling underlying state of the economy – were reducing the likelihood that other groups of workers could breach Stage Three this year; the fact that Mr Jack Jones and Mr Hugh Scanlon had come to the brink of acquiescence in the pay code was a sign that they too knew what the score was. And in any case, as the Treasury peered dimly into the candlelit future, fighting for Stage Three looked more and more like fighting the last war – while Stage Four looked more and more like Stage One.

No, this was no longer the chief consideration; it was the authority of the elected Government. 'Ministers are mostly constitutionalists, not economists,' said one Cabinet Minister, adding: 'If pay is to be settled simply by force the army will end up with the highest wages.'

However, this did not mean that the Prime Minister wanted a snap election, still less to fight it in an atmosphere of confrontation. Again we must go back to the events of 1972 for not only did they inflict humiliation upon the Prime Minister, they also inflicted a profound change of his mind. Mr Heath's ideological conversion to incomes policy (the spectacular nature of which Mr Enoch Powell never ceases, and without mercy, to recall to him) and his long and patient search for a pact with organised labour were also the direct results of the last confrontation with the miners.

Believing passionately as he does in the power of reason and having learned through the Downing Street and Chequers talks – and also over the intimate late-night whiskies with such imagined ogres as Mr Jones and Mr Scanlon – that they and other leaders of the Trades Union Congress were reasonable enough men according to their lights, not wreckers or revolutionaries, part of the 'one nation', the Prime Minister can have had no conceivable motive, and certainly no wish, to engage in confrontation. Indeed, according to one witness: 'Ted rates his talent for talking to the union leaders second only to his talent for talking to Pompidou.'

But in the past couple of weeks his options (shades of Harold Wilson) have been closing fast. The cock-up theory of history rather than the conspiracy version offers the better explanation of why the Prime Minister is where he is now. Just before Christmas, notably at the meeting of the National Economic Development Council on December 21 at which he took the chair, the Prime Minister could have drawn back with honour.

The previous meeting of the Neddy council had produced a rare spirit of national unity around the table. At the December 21 meeting Mr David Basnett of the General and Municipal Workers Union went so far as to suggest that the council meet again on Christmas Day. The shock of the three-day week had been profound and salutary. The international energy crisis had created the sense that the world had changed for ever. But the December 21 meeting was an unhappy affair; the Prime Minister was exhausted, tetchy, unconciliatory. But it would have been easier then, before positions hardened all round, to have reached the compromise which the Prime Minister discussed with the TUC, at its initiative at the eleventh hour this week.

For in the meanwhile other powerful forces were pushing the Prime Minister into an election he did not want. When he told the *New York Times* on January 7 that rather than give way to the miners he was prepared to keep Britain on short time at least until the spring he was either bluffing or deluded. For officials were under no illusions by then, if ever they were, that from early February the industrial and economic consequences of the three-day week would become unacceptable.

Last night Lord Carrington was announcing a gusher of Saudi oil over his new carpet at the Department of Energy and simultaneously discovering that maybe the energy situation might not be so tight after all – perhaps enabling a return to a four-day or even a five-day week. This confirmed the general view which had formed in Whitehall, which was that something had to give before mid-February – an election, an accommodation with the miners or (and nobody canvassed this one) a dramatic change in the Government's version of the facts.

Economic prospects for the medium term all pointed to one conclusion – an early election if not an early February election. The forecasters were in the dark, all previous projections rendered worthless by the surge in oil prices and the three-day week. 'Nobody dares to think ahead,' complained one Minister. But the most optimistic assumption at the Treasury is for nil growth this year (that due to oil prices alone) with the gloom mongers talking of a 5 per cent recession. Treasury officials are predicting a 15–20 per cent rate of inflation and a balance of payments deficit in the region of £4,000 millions this year. On what terms can we hope to borrow abroad in such circumstances? Without the miners and without the three-day week the temptation for an early election is still strong.

Can an election help in such a crisis? The answer depends on the nature of the crisis which is believed to exist and the kind of election the Government chooses to fight. The real crisis is an economic one brought about in small part by the Government's imprudence but for the most part by developments outside its control – by the soaring price of oil and the surge in world commodity and food prices. Nowhere, except in a section of the executive council of the National Union of Mineworkers, is there evidence of class war.

In other industries militancy appears to be on the wane; the union response to the counter-inflationary policy has been moderate through stages one, two and three; trade union leaders are not looking for confrontation with Government, indeed through the TUC they have taken steps to avoid it. The only confrontation is between the Government and the miners and only the predictable statements of a handful of Communist leaders have given to this a constitutional twist. The miners simply want more pay and Parliament has passed no law which compels them to work overtime; they live in a world of their own and it is not the first time that they have been a law unto themselves. A 'who rules the country?' election would be as irrelevant as it would be destructive.

The case for an election now is to give a new government the authority it will need to negotiate a settlement with the miners, to put the country back to work and the economy eventually back on a course of growth. Can the Prime Minister perform yet another somersault without going first to the country? The next government, Conservative or Labour, needs a mandate to govern by consent – not by confrontation. A great measure of consent will be needed to see the country through the coming months. It is no time to be crying over spilt blood, however true blue and Tory.

Guardian, 18 January 1974

Guilt-edged

President Nixon has changed his plea to guilty and asked in effect for the mercy of the court. What for months has been apparent beyond reasonable doubt, that he possessed extensive knowledge of the Watergate crime and was a prime mover in the cover-up, specifically conspiring to obstruct justice, he has now at last admitted. He has thereby admitted – it is important to grasp – an impeachable offence and can no longer avail himself of a plausible defence under the Constitution. His only remaining defence is that the magnitude of his offence does not warrant the extreme political penalty prescribed by the Constitution.

The ambivalence which has characterised his long and desperate struggle thus persists to the very end. Mr Nixon, with oscillating emphasis, has insisted on the one hand on his innocence while on the other hand contending that whatever he may have done was justifiable or excusable, was no worse than others had done or would have done, and would be so regarded by the American people. This latter theme is prominent in the versions of the tapes he published on April 29 of conversations with his aides concerning the strategy for his defence: one of his underlying judgments was, in essence, that even if the American people were to find out the whole truth they wouldn't much care.

Had he resolutely backed that cynical judgment from early on, he very likely would have got away with his misdoings. If he had come clean immediately after the Watergate burglary in June 1972, and declared that some of his associates had acted over-zealously in their partnership for his re-election, in all probability he would have been re-elected none the less – given the hostile passions aroused by Senator George McGovern in that year.

Later, in the spring of 1973, when the cover-up was falling apart, he could have admitted his errors, pleading in mitigation his concern to protect loyal colleagues, and probably still then have escaped impeachment. But Richard Nixon, characteristically, pursued the tricky course, relying upon his old allies, innuendo and deceit.

Now the sheer aggregation of his lies, the contempt shown for the law and the democratic institutions of the United States, his insults to the intelligence of the public, and the utterly unprincipled, prevaricating, obfuscating and ultimately incompetent conduct of his defence have destroyed the credibility of his final plea which is that, after all, his virtues exceed his vices and the advantages of keeping him in office outweigh the inconveniences of dismissing him.

Whether he now resigns under pain of impeachment, thereby preserving his entitlement to pension, or stands trial to be convicted by the Senate is unimportant compared to the fact of his removal from office. Now that he has confessed publicly to his part in a conspiracy to obstruct justice, a criminal and not merely a political offence, the Senate can fail to convict and remove him only by setting a precedent that the President of the United States is above the law.

A mere censure – as Mr Nixon seems to be inviting by his latest tactic – would have the same condoning effect. It would be tantamount to accepting that criminality in the nation's highest officer is secondary to other considerations of national interest. This has been the key issue throughout the affair and has tested the capacity and the will of the American system to government to deal constitutionally with a grave and systematic abuse of presidential power. The removal of the President, whether he goes quietly or has to be dismissed, will be the vindication of the institutions charged with upholding constitutional liberty.

This was the fact Mr Nixon never could grasp. It seems it was beyond his moral reach. Not only in his public statements but in many of the recorded conversations which were intended to remain private he seemed to be unaware of the subversive implications for American democracy if its representative institutions, its courts, and its public opinion were to condone crimes, or at very least high misdemeanours, committed within the office of the presidency.

Mr Nixon continued to contend, and perhaps genuinely believes, that his diplomacy for peace, the interests of what he claimed to be 'national security' and the material interests of his so-called 'New American Majority', were ends overriding consideration of the means which he had employed.

Moreover, he purported to be concerned for the authority of his office while seemingly unable to grasp that it could have no authority within a democratic society if unanswerable even for common crimes. Whether he was by rational conviction a tyrant or merely morally deficient and, by the end, cut off from reality are questions which will be disputed for many years. That he was and is unfit to be President of the United States is now surely beyond dispute.

There can be no assessing of his presidency without reference to its central characteristic, the criminality of the President. It is not merely by the lists of crimes, both literal and political (many of which are not without precedent in American public life), that he will be remembered but for his character as revealed through the exposure of his crimes. The Nixon who went to Peking and the Nixon who signed the Arms Limitations Agreements in Moscow was the same Nixon whose mind we see at work in the transcripts of his tapes and whose corrupt wielding of power is now laid bare. Nor is it possible in honesty to see him as a good President who went wrong; for the Nixon now cornered is the old Nixon, previously convicted in the Californian courts for election fraud and with a long sordid record of smear and untruth going back to the beginnings of his political career.

The view of society, and of human nature, which underlay his policies at home was the same view which led him into crime. This does not say much for his capacity to have grappled with the problems of a turbulent and disfigured industrial and urban society. However, he came to office at the end of President Johnson's unsettling and hugely costly 'Great Society' experiment and the country was in the mood for Nixon's brand of Californian Republicanism. In any case he was never much interested in social or economic policy.

In foreign policy lavish claims are made for him and in that field he had the assistance of the only outstanding member of his otherwise second-rate administrations. The rapprochement with Peking was pending and overdue but it was Nixon who made it – on television in his re-election year. His detente with Moscow, an extension of previous policy, looks less glorious now than it did two years ago.

The Arms Limitation Agreements of May 1972 symbolise the new tacit condominium between the United States and the Soviet Union and – as it turned out this year – the ground rules for the next phase of the arms race. Nixon and Brezhnev did not make an attractive partnership. The war in Vietnam was ended but only after it had become 'Nixon's war', extended secretly and illegally into Cambodia. We now know more about the mind behind the terror bombing of North Vietnam in December 1972.

His fall – for it cannot be much longer postponed – is devoid of nobility. I hope to read no nonsense about Greek tragedies. There is nothing whatsoever tragic about Richard Nixon, nothing of nobility. His removal from office, the vindication of constitutional liberty in the United States, will be a cause for great rejoicing. The only tragedy was that circumstances and the temporary unwisdom of the American people ever should have made such a man the President. Prison will serve no purpose, Miami will do as well. The fitting end would be for him to slink away and disappear beneath contempt.

Mr Gerry Ford may not strike us as a potential world statesman but it would be hard to conceive of a more fitting symbol for the celebration of the bi-centenary of American independence in 1976 than the replacement of a villain by a well-meaning nonentity.

Guardian, 7 August 1974

The electorate's only answer to Heath's question in the February 1974 election was to vote in more Liberal MPs. This produced a minority Labour Government which was not expected to last long. Amid fevered speculation about coalitions and national governments, some feared the collapse of Westminster-style parliamentary democracy. Had Britain become ungovernable? Peter Jenkins never aligned himself with the pessimists on this question, but he did speculate about the possibilities for new alliances in British politics. In the following article, he advocated a centre-left coalition.

Labour's love loss

To discuss coalition within the Labour Party is as perilous as to lecture on genetics at the London School of Economics. The taboo makes it difficult to be realistic about the possibilities of our politics which at the moment, with first holidays and then the election to come, have the appearance of being stuck. The biggest log in the jam is the wooden inability of the Labour Party to develop the potential which exists for a winning alliance on the Left of the centre of British politics.

By an alliance I do not mean necessarily a coalition. In theory it makes no difference whether a coalition of interests and views calls itself a party or whether two or more parties form what is called a coalition; the simple test is whether the assembled forces can obtain a majority for a programme on which they are in sufficient agreement to carry out. A coalition between parties seems to me to be a second best to a functioning party government but the coalition which calls itself the Labour Party is not functioning very well at the moment and, regrettably, a good deal of life consists in settling for the second best.

The Labour coalition is failing, I argued here last week, not because of any general lack of competence in Mr Wilson's interim Government but because it has made so little attempt by word or deed to broaden the appeal which in February won it 38 per cent of the popular vote, its worst performance in 30 years.

Political commentators may award high marks to the ministerial team, or some of them, but 47 per cent of the respondents to the ORC poll (taken at the end of June) were of the opinion that Labour was running the country badly.

But whatever the reason, Labour has failed signally to expand its constituency. During its brief honeymoon its popular support (averaging out the polls) barely exceeded the 43 per cent which lost it the 1970 election. Since the latter part of June, when the Government perhaps would have won a snap election, Labour's support has fallen below the 38 per cent of February; ORC put it at 37 per cent, level-pegging with the Tories, and now a Business Decisions poll puts it at 35 per cent, with the Tories in a 6 per cent lead.

Last weekend Mr Roy Jenkins loudly drew attention to this deficiency and offered some explanations. Greatly as I agreed with most of what he said it seemed to me an ill-timed intervention which was bound to damage further his party's electoral prospects. Presumably his intention was to rally the 'moderates' but for me the speech was a powerful reminder of the good reasons for not voting Labour again in the autumn. Predictably it provoked denunciations from the Left; a sure way to scare off middle opinion is to provide television opportunities for Mr Ian Mikardo, a hideous embarrassment to a party endeavouring to win over non-Socialist opinion.

The technique of the low profile periodically giving way to the loud public outburst is the one which Mr Enoch Powell perfected. I had not heard that Mr Roy Jenkins had been especially active lately in pressing for alternative policies within the Government. In February I know that he believed that the mood in the country made it receptive to measures of dramatic austerity. Perhaps he was right. But when urged by some of his friends to press his case, and his claims to the Chancellorship, he pondered and drew back. Mr Anthony Crosland in a recent letter to his constituents stressed the 'responsible moderation' of the Government and gave reassurance that its central figures, including himself, were more than a match for the doctrinaire leftists. Mr Jenkins, by doing what the press was bound to call speaking out, contributed to the contrary impression.

In the speech Mr Jenkins drew attention to the disadvantages of coalitions and cogently restated the case for party government. He prophesied that the stalemate in British politics would not be broken until 'one or other of the major parties' commanded substantial support among what he called the 'great body of moderate, rather uncommitted opinion.' Essentially I believe he is correct, although how 'moderate' are the 'rather uncommitted' is not a simple question. But if Mr Jenkins is correct about the failure of the Labour Party to gain the allegiance of this uncommitted body of opinion, which is becoming a maverick third force in British politics, he is in effect prophesying that the stalemate will not be broken by the autumn and that we shall have another minority parliament. What then?

There are four possibilities worth considering although the first of them – National Government – is barely worth considering. The others are a continuation of Labour minority government, a Tory–Liberal coalition and a Labour–Liberal coalition.

A government of National Unity would be preferable to a military junta but that is about the best that can be said for it. It could only be formed in such a way as to deprive the electorate from passing judgment on what it would do. If all three parties in England were to receive an exactly equal number of votes that would be no more a mandate for National Government than was Julius Caesar's policy for Gaul a recipe for Gallic unity. A government of all the talents? What talents, you may well ask? The advocates of National Government are mostly those who wish to restore the *ancien regime* (statutory incomes policies, etc.) but that is now an illusion.

A prescription for continuing minority Labour government has been put forward by Mr William Rodgers, an extremely shrewd judge of politics who deserves more attention than he receives because of his reputation as an arch right-winger and Jenkinsite apparatchik. Mr Rodgers believes that a minority government seeking to rule with moderation and consent could for the most part avoid, or, if necessary, ignore defeats in the House of Commons. To do so, he contends, would be more feasible over, say, three years than, as now, over six months with an election in the offing. Probably he is right, that is to say it could if it would. But if the proof of the pudding is to be in the eating why not go the whole hog and share the pudding with the Liberals? A minority government prepared to govern without coalition might as well govern in coalition.

Indeed, a Lab–Lib coalition could be more progressive than a minority Labour Government surviving on the sufferance of the Tories.

A Lib–Tory coalition is generally regarded as the most likely actual outcome of a second minority parliament. This is because a substantial body of Labour opinion, inside and outside the Cabinet, believes that should Mr Wilson fail to win an overall majority he should go at once to the Palace and hand over to Mr Edward Heath and Mr Jeremy Thorpe to do the best they can. Their partnership would break down, such is the incurable optimism to be found in the Labour Party, and result in a Labour majority in plenty of time for North Sea oil in 1977.

A Lab–Lib coalition is the least discussed of the four possibilities because it has been ruled out, declared 'not on' by the Labour Party with scant regard for either the national interest or the possible wishes of the electorate. MPs who might like to discuss it know that the 20 or so dedicated activists who dominate their constituency parties would scream Ramsay MacDonald at the very mention. Yet according to the

Business Decisions poll – and it is an extremely interesting finding – no fewer than 46 per cent of intending Labour voters disapproved of Mr Wilson's pre-emptive veto of coalition.

Britain needs to be governed at this time from somewhere on the Left of centre. No government which excluded the unions and the non-doctrinaire Left would stand much chance of governing by consent in present conditions. Yet there is evidently insufficient support for what the Labour Party officially calls socialism. That should be clear when BBC newscasters start referring to 'militant consultants'. Substantial sections of the salariat have grown disabused of both major parties and are joining the still swelling Liberal ranks; a new kind of owner-occupier, working class by attitudes while middle class by interest, is becoming a factor in electoral politics.

Here is a potential ruling alliance – consisting of what in the Labour Party constitution are called 'workers by hand and brain'. If the Labour Party alone can command a winning coalition of voters then that is the end of the matter with no need to discuss further the merits of alternative coalitions between parties. But if it cannot, is the country to be denied what could be a working consensus of second preferences? The great majority of Liberal MPs and Liberal candidates would rather make coalition on the Left than be forced into harness with the Tories. Yet the Labour Party would rather no power than sharing it.

Coalition is not some form of conspiracy against Labour. Coalition, as the polls show, is not the people's first choice but the second choice of a majority if denied their first. If no party can win a governing majority it should be the duty of the party with the largest number of seats to form coalition with the forces in the middle. If in these circumstances the Labour Party were to veto power-sharing on the Left, arrogantly declining to serve the country save on its own terms, the suspicions of many would be confirmed that it has ceased to be a national party and is unable to arrest its secular decline.

Guardian, 2 August 1974

Wilson, however, preferred to avoid the compromises of coalition and instead called a snap election on 10 October 1974. The result was almost as inconclusive but Labour had a small overall majority. In his post-

election commentary, Jenkins not only considered the implications of this slender electoral advantage for the Labour Party but also turned his attention to the prospect of a leadership battle in the Conservative Party after Heath's second defeat within a year.

From pragmatism to magnetism?

Mr Harold Wilson finds himself in a unique situation. It as if the fates had contrived the supreme test of his rare political abilities. The skills and wiles which enabled him to transfer the wafer majority of 1964 into a wedge in 1966 and the minority of 1974 into a majority have now been recruited in the service of the nation in its crisis. Today, as he begins his fourth administration, Mr Wilson has nowhere to go but down in the pages of the history books as the man who saw the country through the worst crisis of decades or the man who failed to.

If this sounds a bit over-dramatic, too heroic for the Harold Wilson we have learnt to love or kick around, consider the extraordinariness of the situation. Short of a severe parliamentary crisis there can be no more elections for a year or two at least; the Labour Chief Whip, Mr Robert Mellish, said yesterday that another election was unthinkable 'for three or four years.'

This year, for the first year since 1910, two elections each have failed to produce a decisive result; Labour's overall majority of three rests upon the lowest share of the popular vote achieved by a winning party since the twenties, on less support than Labour received when losing in 1970. The economic crisis which engulfs the country is far more severe than when Mr Wilson first came to power in 1964 with a majority of only four. The political alternatives to Labour are for the time being bankrupt, the Tories in disarray under a three-times losing leader and the Liberals' pretensions exposed under their pretentious leader.

In short Mr Wilson's famous options are closed all round. He has no option left but to rise to the occasion. He is no longer in the electioneering business, he is in the national leadership business. The mandate he has received, such as it is, cannot this time be treated as the draft of his next election manifesto. He is left with no choice other than to lead the country by mastering the factions within his party; the

Churchillian cliché applies: he will have to put country before party. He has won the election but he must know that he has not yet won the country's consent to be governed. That he must now do and says he will.

Can he? The question is best left unanswered at this time. The task he faces entitles him to start with a cleaned slate, a replenished tank full of credibility, a second honeymoon, and a generosity of good will. He has the right to be his own new man in a new situation.

In his remarkable interview with Mr Michael Charlton of the BBC in the middle of election night he seemed aware that a moment bigger than any other had come for him. He seemed both chastened and excited. He seemed almost to welcome the prospect of his pitifully small majority, as if the election had released him from the prison of his reputation as the most politicking of politicians, the party manager supreme, famed for his short view of posterity. When he said 'but it's going to be a hell of a job' he sounded like he meant it, not as another Wilsonian exhortation but as an inner resolve.

On Monday when he speaks to the country on television he will have the chance to strike a truly new note. Policies take time, but a sense of new departure if it can be created buys time, the most precious of commodities for a politician who must build. A more open style, too, could help to inspire new confidence; it would help to emerge from his cocoon of morbid suspicion and open the doors of his kitchen cabinet to new talent.

A majority of only three (two, if the Government party must supply a deputy speaker) need not prevent him from mapping out his programme of reconstruction over a two- or three-year period. The parliamentary situation is quite different from 1964–66. Then, although his tactic was to prove that a Labour Government could govern, his strategy was to win an election not long distant; in the present situation the planning of a future election victory would have little acceptance as a valid national objective. Moreover, in 1964–66 he faced a united opposition; today he faces a multi-party opposition with conflicting objectives, united only for the time being in its equal desire to avoid an early return to the polls.

The first reaction of the few MPs and party officials who could be consulted yesterday was that the new parliament would allow a far greater degree of informal co-operation than did the last electioneering parliament. Providing only the Government proceeds in a conciliatory spirit there is no reason why Mr Wilson's new Government should lack authority.

The tensions within the Labour Party will not suddenly vanish, of course; but the discipline imposed by the slenderness of the Government's right to govern applies to all factions of the Party. The Left will resent the shift in balance brought about by the narrowness of the result; for it was the so-called 'moderates', and the pro-Marketeers, who were rejoicing yesterday in a situation which is bound to strengthen their hand both within the Cabinet and within the Parliamentary Party at large. With the luxury of revolt at a prohibitive price the Marketeers, who are in no position for the same reason to attempt to veto the promised referendum, will be much better placed to insist that its terms and conduct are conducive to a popular acceptance of the renegotiated terms of Community membership. Mr Roy Jenkins has immensely strengthened his position through his announcement, during the campaign, of his reconciliation to the goal of renegotiation and his endorsement of the ballot box pledge.

Of Mr Edward Heath there is little now to say. In spite of some loyal public statements to the contrary virtually nobody could be found yesterday who believed that Mr Heath (played four, lost three) will lead his party into the next contest. The question is not if he will go but when and how. The narrowness of the result may extend his time (some said for perhaps a year) but already there were moves afoot to hasten his end, by violence if necessary.

Among the first to declare in so many words that they would 'back Ted up to the hilt' – such as the honey-mouthed Mr Edward du Cann, chairman of the 1922 Committee – will be found the first to 'back him on to the hilt' when the moment is appropriate. Where it was conceded that Mr Heath's campaign had brought the Conservative Party far closer to victory than anyone had expected it was usually also claimed that the election could have been won if it hadn't been for the Ted problem on the doorstep. A typical tale was of the party worker who asked a voter at a walkabout 'Would you like to meet Mr Whitelaw?' to receive the reply 'Yes, but not until you get rid of that . . . Heath.'

Who will replace him? Mr Whitelaw is the near-universal prediction although by no means universally regarded as the ideal Leader. There is nobody else. Sir Keith Joseph? 'A brilliant fellow,' you will hear people saying in the way that only Tories have of wrapping a blackball in a compliment. Mrs Margaret Thatcher? Over the Tory Party's chauvinist dead male. Has she ever set foot in the Carlton Club?

Split between Josephite monetarists and middle-of-the-road Williests, some MPs yesterday were already drawing up an American-style dream ticket for the Tory Party – Mr Whitelaw as Leader with Sir Keith as Shadow Chancellor for running mate. That may in time be the answer. Meanwhile, for news of Mr Heath's demise watch three men: Mr du Cann, Mr Whitelaw, and Mr Heath's friend and confidant, Lord Carrington.

If Mr Heath is sentenced to pay the hard price of failure so, too, could Mr Thorpe come in for criticism, although there is no sign of moves to replace him. Perhaps it was inevitable that in the changed situation since February Liberal voters would backslide, as they did disproportionately to the Tories, helping to falsify the opinion polls and narrow the race. But the Liberal campaign was hardly a success, lacking clear direction and hopelessly confused on the subject of coalition since the subject was first raised by Mr David Steel in June. The injunction to 'smash the two-party system' came over as less than a battle cry from Mr Thorpe in his funny hats. 'He's just a big leg pull, isn't he?' asked one voter who had seen the show pass by. When urged last summer to set out upon a Midlothian campaign like Mr Gladstone's, Mr Thorpe replied, 'Yes, I'm planning a hovercraft tour.'

Guardian, 12 October 1974

The Conservative Party leadership election produced a surprising result. The standard-bearer of the right wing of the Party, Sir Keith Joseph, ruled himself out of the leadership contest after making a particularly controversial speech. Willie Whitelaw, the natural choice of the centre of the Party, was beaten on the second ballot by the virtually unknown Margaret Thatcher. It was not immediately apparent how far this would change the nature of Conservative Party politics: she was elected simply for not being Edward Heath.

Enter the unknown leader

Readers and viewers must be feeling saturated with Mrs Thatcher. There ought to be a word for it, Thatcherated. There is no doubt that she is an accomplished actress, an important political talent which Mr Heath lacked totally. More significant than the fact that she is the first woman to lead a political party in Britain is the possibility that she may turn out to be the first authentic media natural. She is the first to reach the top of the television generation of politicians and no politician in this country has yet exploited the full potential of that medium.

Within the Conservative Party in Parliament she won the leadership by an organisational coup d'état but in the country at large she is the overnight creation of the media. She has become a 'TV personality'. In barely two weeks viewers and voters have learnt more than they need to know about her family life, her domestic habits, her wardrobe and hairstyling than they have learnt something of her style as a politician; they have learnt next to nothing of the substance behind the image and the reason for that is that there is as yet very little substance there. Mrs Thatcher is the Unknown Leader of the Opposition; that is the most remarkable aspect of her astonishingly rapid rise to power and fame, the most important political fact about her, and it ought not to be obscured by the instant familiarity of her image.

So who is Margaret, what is she, that all our swains commend her? Quickie biographers busy knocking on publishers' doors will have to invent her past, for her political career contains remarkably few clues. The indices of Hansard for the years between 1959, when she entered Parliament, and 1970, when she became the 'statutory woman' in Mr Heath's Cabinet, reveal no theme to her career. Dip into those pages and you will find her competently handling briefs on a wide range of miscellaneous and mostly technical matters. Her maiden speech was of no note and curiously took the form of introducing a Bill – the Public Bodies (Admission of the Press to Meetings) Bill.

When she became Secretary of State for Education in 1970 she was instantly typecast as Selsdon Woman, the suburban hat-wearing exponent of the abrasive Heathism of those days. The similarity of her background and Edward Heath's, grammar school and scholarship girl, the daughter of a grocer, made her another symbol of the new-style Conservatism represented by the elusive, prickly public personality of the self-made Prime Minister. However, she made little impact beyond educational circles until she became involved in the great school milk controversy and it was only then that the gallery correspondents at the House of Commons can remember noticing her as a performer of above-average forcefulness at the Dispatch Box.

Officials who knew her at Education say that she showed few signs of real interest in her subject beyond a commitment to her own grammar school upbringing. What they liked best about her was that she was a tiger with a brief. This is what officials invariably look for first in a Minister, someone who will fight for the departmental view in Cabinet and against the Treasury. Her 1972 White Paper represented a spectacular victory over the Treasury; the school milk row was the result of a battle lost. She had fought hard over this one as well but not, according to her then officials, so much because she felt strongly about free milk for children as because she accepted the Department's line that milk ought not to be a charge on the educational budget.

There was nothing especially creative about her educational policy. She put the brake on comprehension, but it was a rearguard defensive action she was fighting; her criteria for approving or rejecting reorganisation schemes never became explicit and 'freedom of choice' remained a slogan more than a policy and was not zealously pursued. If she learnt one important lesson during that time it was, perhaps, that she had less power than she thought she had.

In so far as her aggressive right-wing reputation derives from her period at Education it does not owe to her achievements there – in fact she became increasingly pragmatic and was generally guided by her officials – but to her combative style and personal unpopularity in the educational world. She was cordially disliked by many and there seem to be few who were close to her who remember her with genuine affection. Even Mr Norman St John Stevas didn't like her as much as he now says.

Mrs Thatcher held only this one Cabinet job. She never became a member of the inner circle of the Heath Government. She was Heath's protégé but he came to dislike her. Several senior members of the Cabinet simply couldn't abide her. It is said that she was one who doubted the wisdom of the confrontation with the miners a year ago but she did not play a prominent role in the affair. Nobody can remember hearing her open her mouth on foreign affairs, Ireland and many other subjects.

So the record is one largely of grey obscurity and the adulatory build-up she is now receiving has little foundation in the experience of her career or in previous estimations of her. Apart from a few firm attitudes – for example, her devotion to thrift – which, according to prejudice, may be categorised as 'right-wing' – and they are mostly attitudes rather than systematic beliefs – Mrs Thatcher lacks a clear ideological profile as well as a great deal of experience. The best that her erstwhile opponents could find to say of her on the morning after was that she has a lot of growth potential, is 'low on the learning curve.'

For these reasons it is extremely difficult to guess about her future or the future of the Conservative Party under her leadership. The fear that the Party may have suffered a Goldwater-like lurch to the Right and will pay the same inevitable price as the Republicans paid in 1964 stems chiefly from some of the unsavoury elements who contributed to her seizure of power. A better analogy than with Goldwater is with McGovern who brought off an organisational coup within the Democratic Party in 1972 by being the first to understand and take advantage of its new rules. McGovern captured the nomination of his party but lacked a broad enough base in the country to have any chance of winning the Presidency. That may be Mrs Thatcher's problem when the euphoria of victory dies away.

There is some similarity also between her position and Mr Harold Wilson's on becoming leader of his party. In the Labour Party the Left liked to believe, and still sometimes do, that Mr Wilson was their man, one of them at heart, who owed his power to them. Mr Wilson plays on this sentimentality and this aspect of his past when it suits him, but it has not for the most part prevented him from pursuing a centrist policy and endeavouring to establish the Labour Party as a moderate party of government. We may well see Mrs Thatcher trying to use her right-wing credentials to the same end, holding her party together while steering a more moderate course than her ardent backers would wish.

She owes her victory primarily to two sets of forces. First she owes it to Mr Heath who by refusing to make way in good time for Mr Whitelaw and by fighting to the finish purportedly to save the Party from the Right delivered it into the hands of his enemies. Secondly, she owes it to a triple alliance consisting of herself, Mr Edward du Cann and Sir Keith Joseph. When Sir Keith threw down the baton in wild abandon, she picked it up; the deal then was that for as long as she looked a winner Mr du Cann would give her a clear run. Deals of this kind have a habit of coming unstuck but Mr du Cann did not rat on her.

The first interesting question now is how long the triple alliance survives ideologically. Mr du Cann, with City and family interests, seems in no hurry to claim his reward but Sir Keith has been telling friends that he expects his due as Shadow Chancellor. The first sign of Mrs Thatcher trimming will be if he doesn't get it as it seems he will not. More important, however, than her Shadow Cabinet – which may at first resemble a ceasefire in place – will be the appointments to her entourage. Her campaign manager, Mr Airey Neave, has already been named to head her 'private office', appointed – as one MP put it – to be 'her Marcia or her Haldeman.' How many of the zealots will surround her throne? If she dare not risk Sir Keith as Shadow Chancellor would Party unity survive his appointment to the key policy-making role in place of Mr Ian Gilmour, the ideologist-in-chief of the moderate wing at the Conservative Research Office?

There are also important questions about the tactics of opposition. Mrs Thatcher's hard-core supporters, the 90 or so who were committed firmly to her and not merely against Mr Heath on the first ballot, will be expecting a more aggressive style of opposition and that will be her instinct too. So what, for example, will now be the tactics over the referendum? Mr Heath's view, and Mr Whitelaw's too, was that the result of the referendum was the chief concern. The plan was to oppose the Bill at Second Reading but thereafter allow it an easy passage. The temptation now may be to use the referendum Bill as a means of wrecking the Government's business, notably Mr Benn's hated Industry Bill.

Is the Tory Party under Mrs Thatcher going to put itself on the Right of Mr Denis Healey on the question of the central management of the economy? The opinion of the Heath men, and of Mr Whitelaw, was that the Chancellor has struck just about the right balance between fighting inflation and preventing a too-deep recession. That will be another litmus test of how far the Party under Mrs Thatcher will shift in a Josephite direction. And what happens if there is an economic catastrophe and the Government needs Conservative support to carry emergency measures against a revolt on its own Left? The answer is less certain under the new leadership.

The posture of the new Conservative Party will gradually become clear through Mrs Thatcher's appointments and the tactics of opposition over the coming months. We may expect to see some change in the geography of British politics. Both parties are operating from a narrow base and each will be trying to extend its constituency at the expense of third forces. None of the parties is going to be quite the same again after the referendum which will bring about a temporary realignment. The key to Mr Powell's future in British politics depends less on whether Mrs Thatcher wants him eventually in her Shadow Cabinet than on the relationship which develops between the Conservative Party and the Ulster Unionists.

If the new Conservative Party shifts somewhat to the Right some in the Labour Party will argue that this will permit a more left-wing posture. Then the danger would be a further rejection of both parties, in the centre and on the fringes. Others in the Labour Party would see the opportunity to recapture the centre and condemn the Tories to permanent opposition. It is with such great issues to be resolved that the Conservative Party now ventures into the unknowable led by the unknown.

Guardian, 14 February 1975

Amid all the crisis and confrontation of the Heath Government one policy had been successfully carried out: Britain was from January 1973 a member of the European Economic Community. The Labour Party on the other hand was deeply divided on the issue, and once in power again a substantial section of the Party demanded British withdrawal from Europe. Wilson's typically brilliant tactical device to keep the Party together was to open the issue up to the British people with a referendum on the subject. In the end, 67 per cent voted to stay in the Community. During the referendum campaign many of the issues that would come to dominate British politics during the late 1980s were first publicly debated.

Community and independence

The word 'sovereignty' finds little favour with modern political theorists. This is because its meaning is unclear. Jean Bodin's classical definition – 'supreme power over citizens and subjects, unrestrained by law' – clearly will not do these days, although it is sovereignty in this sense which is attributed to the institutions of the European Community by their critics.

When the Government retorts that the ultimate sovereignty of Parliament is intact because Parliament can at any time, by repeal of the European Communities Act 1972, recover whatever powers it may have delegated, it is also following Bodin who argued that sovereign power, because absolute, must be perpetual. Hence, he observed: 'If power be held only for a certain time (it does not matter how long a time) it is not sovereign power, and he who holds it for that time is not a sovereign prince, but only a trustee or custodian of that power so long as it pleases the real prince (or the people) not to revoke it . . .'

More modern theorists have been concerned chiefly with distinguishing between kinds of power. For example, Dicey with the British Constitution in mind distinguished between 'legal sovereignty' and 'political sovereignty'. Hence it might be said today that while Parliament has the undisputed sovereign power to make laws, the trade unions, for example, have the power (sovereignty?) to obey or disobey those laws.

If we consider the problem of power in a pluralistic sense we can speak meaningfully of the 'power of Parliament' or the 'power of the European Commission', but not of the 'sovereign people' who are all sorts of people wanting all sorts of things at different times and therefore without exercisable power. Sovereignty, if it means ultimate power to achieve definable ends, similarly has little meaning in the international context and the sovereignty of states is held by some theorists to be in philosophical contradiction with the concept of international law. Either one law, national or international, is higher than the other, or neither may be said to be 'sovereign'.

For these reasons the word 'sovereignty' is a poor tool for uncovering the sources of power in a modern society or in a world of interdependent nation states. The 'sovereignty' issue in the referendum, except in so far as it is emotive of traditionalism or pure nationalism, is about who shall exercise what powers and for what purposes.

There is no denying that a consequence of Britain's accession to the European Community is the loss of some national power. The Government has lost some power. Parliament has lost some power, including some power over the British Government. The loss of parliamentary power means some loss of power to groups and individuals who might otherwise persuade the Government or Parliament to act in their interests.

In constitutional terms there has been a radical departure. For under the European Communities Act 1972 not only did Parliament accept the existing rules and regulations of the Community but also agreed to be bound by its future rules and regulations. Some of these require the unanimous consent of the Council of Ministers, and thus the specific consent of the British Government, but others do not and fall within the delegated law-making powers of the Commission.

The Labour Government's 1967 White Paper (Legal and Constitutional Implications of the United Kingdom Membership of the European Communities; Cmnd 3301) did not attempt to disguise the difference between entering into a treaty obligation, which might involve the application of its provisions as law in the signatory states (there is nothing novel about that), and joining a law-making community of states. The White Paper explained:

'The novel features of the European Treaties lie first in the powers conferred on the Community institutions to issue subordinate instruments which themselves may impose obligations on the Member States, or may take effect directly as law within them; and secondly, in the powers of these institutions to administer and enforce (subject to the control of the European Court) much of the law deriving from the Treaties and the instruments made under them.'

A more recent report by the directorate-general of the European Parliament (Preliminary Report on the Loss of Power by the Parliaments of the Member States as a Result of the Treaty Establishing the European Economic Community) reached a similar conclusion:

'The automatic application in the United Kingdom of future Community Regulations will involve a loss of power to the British Parliament as in many cases the context of such Regulations would formerly have required legislation in the form of Bills or Statutory

Instruments. Furthermore, in so far as Bills or amendment to Bills which may be passed by Parliament in future are found to be contrary to Community obligations, the courts are enjoined by the Act to rule that such provisions will have no effect.'

Power lost in this way cannot be said simply to have been transferred or delegated or, as some like to argue, pooled; for power-sharing is not like sharing out a basket of apples. The power of veto within the Council of Ministers, for example, is a negative power which can be used to prevent decisions against our national interest, but there is no equivalent power for obtaining decisions in favour of our national interest within areas which are the subject of Community decisions and hence no longer within the power of national decision.

However, these textbook formulations of the position grossly overstate the actual loss of power which has occurred. Although the Community is intended to be perpetual (and therefore, in Bodin's sense, sovereign within its areas of competence) the fact is that an omni-competent parliament such as the British Parliament can in theory and practice do anything that it likes including bring down the Government over a Brussels pig meat regulation, or legislate the repeal of the European Communities Act.

Moreover, the Commission like the Vatican has no divisions and when a government pursues its national interest in breach of the Community laws, as did the Italians last year, there is not much that it can do other than reprove the offender and assist him in his difficulties. The Community, as it has learnt with the French, can only work if its members choose to make it work.

The main areas in which the Government and Parliament have lost power concern the operation of a customs union and a common agricultural policy. It is not very helpful to debate these matters in terms of 'sovereignty'; people must make up their minds whether the advantages of belonging to a customs union outweigh the disadvantages, or whether it is wise to forgo the freedom to buy food at its cheapest price on world markets.

Any customs union requires rules and regulations, and somebody to administer them; the same is true of a free trade area. The powers which the Commission exercises in these areas, which are essentially the powers of a regulatory body, are similar to the powers which Parliament has on many other occasions delegated to statutory bodies, for example marketing boards.

It is true that Parliament has experienced difficulty in scrutinising the 4,000 or so statutory instruments issued each year by the Community institutions; but Parliament has had similar difficulties in scrutinising the 2,000 or so statutory instruments which are made each year under powers delegated in Britain.

A particularly emotive aspect of the powers surrendered to the customs union concerns Parliament's right of taxation. Customs duties can no longer be fixed by Parliament in the Finance Bill. Moreover, the Community's 'own resources' budget, which will automatically be funded by the proceeds of duties, levies and 1 per cent of the VAT is beyond the control of national parliaments. But once more the textbook approach is misleading. Parliament long ago lost effective control over the budgetary process. As the European Parliament's report points out: 'There is a great difference between the right to impose taxes and the decision-making powers in respect of the revenue and expenditure of a comprehensive budget of a modern state.'

In Britain, the allocation of resources for public expenditure takes place annually in the secret Public Expenditure Survey Committee without prior parliamentary debate. Parliament subsequently discusses, but does not vote upon, the resulting White Paper. Britain's contributions to the Community budget are a relatively minor item in a huge volume of public expenditure over which Parliament has already inadequate control. The Community has no powers to raise further taxes, and should the Council of Ministers unanimously agree on such powers Parliament's approval would have to be obtained.

As a result of the renegotiation the Government says it is satisfied that it will continue to possess adequate powers in the areas of regional aids, and aids to industry. This is the third main area in which the Community institutions wield powers consequent upon the establishment of a customs union. Any free trading area has to have rules of competition. The Government, having decided that the rules are flexible enough to allow it to do most of the things it might want to do, has no complaint about regulations designed to prevent an auction in State aids to regions or industries.

Providing State interventions are non-discriminatory there is nothing in the Treaties to prevent nationalisation and nothing to prevent the proposed National Enterprise Board from acquiring State holdings in firms and industries. The guiding principle of the

Community is 'fair competition' and the alternative to that is 'unfair competition'.

If discrimination is advocated, whether in the name of socialism or something else, then membership of the Community does involve an important loss of power. Those on the left wing of the Labour Party who contend that the Community is inimical to their brand of socialism have a strong point. However, their brand of socialism would find itself in conflict not only with the European Economic Community but also with the international trading order of the non-Communist world. A trading country such as Britain has to decide whether to compete within the rules or seek to thrive outside them. The practices which are prohibited within the Community are prohibited equally within the European Free Trade Area.

The debate about sovereignty is a debate about means and purposes. Membership of the European Economic Community does involve a loss of independent national power. In return, it brings the opportunity to influence the decisions of others who have also surrendered some of their independence. The power which is lost and the power which is gained cannot easily be quantified or weighed in a pair of scales. Sovereignty, or power in the abstract, is a mere slogan; those who argue the case for or against membership in terms of power must say exactly what it is they would do with it, and exactly what it is they cannot do without it.

Guardian, 7 May 1975

In the spring of 1976 Harold Wilson suddenly resigned. In contrast to the surprise result of the Conservative Party leadership contest the year before, Callaghan's succession to Wilson was a comparative formality.

Number one for No. 10

Mr James Callaghan was on stand-by for a call to the Palace last night. His acceptance speech was in type. Arrangements had been made for a ceremonial departure from Transport House. A case of counting chickens or of a deal which came unstuck? There is no doubt that Mr

Callaghan's friends were hopeful, on the strength of voting figures which turned out much as expected, that Mr Foot would concede and settle for the deputy Prime Ministership which is to be his.

Mr Foot's friends denounced the rumours as 'black propaganda' from the Callaghan camp. But it is hard to see the need for a conspiracy at this late stage, for the voting figures make it more certain than ever that Mr Callaghan is the victor. The race is all over bar the shouting. He is only 17 votes short of the final overall majority with 38 Healey votes plus five abstentions to play for in the final round.

Mr Denis Healey will now himself vote for Mr Callaghan and his campaign manager estimated that the overwhelming majority of the Healey vote will now switch to Mr Callaghan. So unless there is a miracle – or a thunderbolt, whichever way you look at it – Mr Callaghan has a few more days to ruminate on what sort of Prime Minister he will be and how he will lead his party.

Depend upon it, when a man knows he is to be Prime Minister in a fortnight, it concentrates his mind wonderfully. Five more days will help to concentrate it still more wonderfully. His intention is – and it is not surprising – to become a real Prime Minister, to be his own man. Beneath the benignly calm exterior Mr Callaghan is a prickly man and we may guess that he will be out to belie the comments to the effect that he will be a poor man's Wilson, a mere caretaker or the chairman of a board of feudal barons.

At the same time he knows that his days at the top are numbered, that he has little time for trial and error or for learning on the job, sitting next to Nellie. If he is to put the Callaghan mark on what can only be a brief age he must first of all put himself at least at half-arm's length from the old regime. That means not only clearing room in his Cabinet for fresh talent but also abandoning the Wilsonian method of Cabinet construction.

The present Cabinet is for the most part vintage 1966. It contains some half dozen whose abilities are less apparent than their services to old causes or vendettas. Mr Callaghan, graduating at age 64, will look as young and as vigorous as his Cabinet. By opening it to all the talents, without regard to the ancient civil wars of the Gaitskellites and Bevanites, he has the chance to invigorate the Government and end the morbid personnel management of the Wilson era.

The complexion of his Cabinet will be a clue also to how he intends to lead the Party. He will be obliged to take account of its yearning for a tilt towards the Left as revealed in the strength of support for Mr Foot. The broadly based alliance which formed behind the candidature of Mr Foot is not to be mistaken as the measure of support in the Parliamentary Labour Party for left-wing socialism but neither is it to be ignored as a demonstration in favour of principled, imaginative, and radical leadership.

Himself no ideologue, as resistant to Socialist as to any other kind of dogma, Mr Callaghan may seek to channel the radical energies of the Party rather than to manipulate or sublimate them as was Mr Wilson's way.

He will begin, it is expected, by institutionalising Mr Foot and thereby, he would hope, the 'broad Left' of the PLP. For he is entitled to regard the support for his chief opponent not as a demonstration against the policies of the Government but as an endorsement of Mr Foot's own betrayal of the politics of pure principle. The Left will not find it easy, for a while at least, to cry treason at a Government of which its own champion is the deputy chief.

So although Mr Callaghan is a man undoubtedly conservative in spirit, by a paradox – not uncommon in politics – the new Government may take on a more left-wing, or at least more radical, air than Mr Wilson's. By accommodating the 'broad Left', and also the reforming thrusts from the Jenkinsite wing of the Party, Mr Callaghan will be in the better position to put his policeman's foot down on the 'hard Left', in Parliament if necessary but particularly in the extra-parliamentary apparatus.

Mr Callaghan's stock in trade as a politician is to claim intimate communion with what he would describe as the decent, honest, patriotic folk of this country. It is said that he believes that those same folk are ready today for a greater measure of interventionism and reform. So he may not turn out to be as stodgily conservative as his critics anticipate.

Nonetheless Mr Callaghan is probably to old a Jim to learn many new tricks. He has put neither a foot wrong nor forward in standing, not running, for the leadership. 'You know me . . .' he is inclined to say in preface to some piece of worldly wisdom and it is true, we do know him; he brings no mystery to the highest office. The Labour Party's system of exhaustive balloting will in the end have legitimised the succession of, as I wrote at the beginning, the Buggins apparent and presumptive. By a process of elimination the mantle has fallen upon the Keeper of the Cloth Cap.

Guardian, 31 March 1976

The new Prime Minister and the Chancellor, Denis Healey, were almost immediately plunged into a financial crisis. At a Cabinet meeting in July the Government decided to ask for help from the International Monetary Fund. The resulting loss of financial credibility and the terms of the IMF package represented the nadir of Britain's postwar fortunes. The final IMF package was only agreed after a long series of Cabinet meetings which went on through to the winter. The complexity of the situation is captured in Jenkins's piece from December of that year.

Healey must grow

Massive deflation has been rejected by the Cabinet, but the decision it has reached will nevertheless tip the economy perilously close to a new recession. The economic recovery had already suffered severe setbacks this year.

First, there was the depreciation of the pound. A falling exchange rate pushes up the price of imports more quickly than it helps exports. This is the more so the more it is the case that physical constrictions are more important than price in determining export performance. Thus the falling rate of exchange (which the Treasury at times seemed to be encouraging) had the effect of imposing a sharper reduction of living standards on the mass of the people than had been envisaged in the terms of the Social Contract.

Partly because of the authorities' parity tactics, the Chancellor, Mr Healey, was pushed or inveigled into overtly deflationary actions. His July package was deflationary to the tune of nearly £2 billions, half of which he sprung upon the Cabinet at the last minute in the form of what was in effect a payroll tax – hardly a policy consistent with his undertakings to the TUC about reducing unemployment. If the July measures were justified at the time they are no longer, in economic terms, justified now when still for the most part in the pipeline.

The credit squeeze which the Chancellor has applied since then is probably no less deflationary than the fiscal measures. The minimum bank lending rate was hiked from 12 to 15 per cent (it is since fractionally down again) and 'corsets' of Victorian tightness have been applied to commercial bank lending, which is a roundabout way of restoring tight control over the money supply. One could only guess at the demand effects of all this but there is no doubt that a great deal of deflation is in the pipeline.

The erratic course of the Treasury's growth forecasts (and, to be fair, of the independent forecasts as well) is chiefly attributable to the uncertain and changing prospects for world trade. Nevertheless, the Chancellor in his Budget was talking about 4 per cent annual growth and at the time of the July package he projected an annual 4.5 per cent over an eighteen-month period from the first half of 1976. His public expenditure plans, as set out in the February White Paper, were based on an annual 3.5 per cent expansion of GDP over the five-year period 1974–79 while by August the Treasury was encouraging the NEDC to believe in 4.5 per cent growth next year on 'past trends' and, on more favourable assumptions, a preposterous 14.5 per cent.

In the Commons on Tuesday the Chancellor confessed that he had been obliged to halve the growth forecast for next year which he had made in July. But his latest forecast, 2.25 per cent growth, is based on present policy assumptions and will have to be downwardly revised again to take account of the deflationary measures contained in the coming pre-Christmas package. Moreover, the forecasts available to Mr Healey cannot have taken account of the Bank of England's 'corsets'. Some independent forecasters were already doubting whether there will be any significant growth at all next year and we are entitled to remember that Mr Healey, throughout his Chancellorship, has been consistently over-optimistic about world trade prospects.

The Chancellor, the Treasury and the Bank between them had effectively brought the economy to a near-halt before pen was put to paper in drafting the Letter of Intent to the IMF. Evidently the Chancellor hopes to do an income tax–pay policy trade-off in his spring Budget and this would be the best way of pumping demand back into the economy. But he isn't going to have a lot of room for manoeuvre. Thus the Government may have escaped a fate worse than death at the hands of the deflationists but mere death remains in clear prospect if it intends to serve out its term presiding over a stagnant economy.

The vanquished proponents of savage deflation keep complaining that 'deflation' is a dirty word unfairly used against them, that this is not what they mean at all when they demand substantial *real* cuts in the PSBR. The effect of their policies would not be 'deflationary' they contend because falling interest rates and rising business confidence would cancel out the demand effect of expenditure cuts. No doubt they sincerely believe this might be so but they have no way of proving it. There would have to be a time lag in which business activity would decline and unemployment increase. How long? They do not and cannot know. The social and political consequences of this indeterminate interregnum are among the factors which would affect business confidence. Interest rates are important certainly in determining investment decisions, and also in their contribution to the business atmosphere, but more important still are market prospects. Who wants to invest in a nil growth economy?

The prime need, as Mr Healey never ceases to insist, is for the three major surplus countries – the United States, Germany and Japan – to give a stronger need to the world recovery. But whatever the rest of the world does the problems of the British economy, and especially its structural problems, are not going to be solved by a nil-growth strategy. Nor will the British people for long put up with it. If virtual stagnation is the best the Government can achieve by its devaluations, its Social Contracts and its Industrial Strategies, the real winners of the argument in the end will be the New Cambridge economists with their protectionist remedy.

Guardian, 3 December 1976

Aside from the economic jeopardy in which the country was placed, the events of 1976 were a profound ideological challenge to social democracy. The IMF decision seemed to question many of the foundations on which the Labour Party had exercised power since 1964. It is also from this time that the position of the social democrats in the hierarchy of the Labour Party was increasingly undermined. The Left, although never dormant, had been kept at bay by the discipline of power. From the summer of 1976 onwards it became increasingly difficult to hold together the broad coalition that had traditionally been the Labour Party.

The first priority

Socialists of the revisionist school have called the tune in the Labour Party these past 20 years and the failures of Labour in government have been in large part their failures. There have been successes too, notably in redistribution through increased social expenditure. On each side of the coin, the failure of the economy to produce sufficiently and the propensity of the State to overspend, there are implications for democracy and freedom which until recently were largely unconsidered by Socialists.

The pursuit of equality was number one priority for the revisionists. It was central to their case that inequality was to be found, and could be reduced or eradicated, largely regardless of the ownership pattern of the economy. It followed, or at least it was assumed, that progress towards egalitarianism would not impede the efficiency of a mixed economy. Moreover, it was assumed that attacks on inequality would in general result in an extension of freedom also. In these ways, and in some others, problems of economic management and problems of social advance were uncoupled; at first economic growth was simply assumed, later it was merely observed that the slower the growth the more difficult the pursuit of equality.

Nowadays there is no shortage of voices, on Left as well as Right, who warn that the problems afflicting the developed democracies may defy solution within democratic institutions or under conditions of freedom. There are many varieties of this analysis but the essential point in each case is that the capacity of the State is exceeded by the aggregate demands which are made of it and that its authority is insufficient to arbitrate the conflicting and often irreconcilable claims upon it.

If Britain is seen at the head of the queue for collapse this is chiefly because the weakness of our economy is seen to render us more vulnerable to the forces which threaten what I will call The Social Democratic Order as a shorthand for the mixed-economy-Welfare-State-democracy aiming at a full employment objective while permitting free collective bargaining. That levels of Government spending or the overall burden of taxation are no higher in Britain than in most other countries does not affect the argument which rests not on the diagnosis of an 'English sickness' but on the proposition that there is a more general 'crisis', neither distinctively 'socialist' nor 'capitalist', but a crisis of the industrial State approaching the limits of its capacity to finance social expenditures.

Of course, the whole thesis may be dismissed out of hand as fashionable intellectual doom-mongering and it is true that many of the thoughts which have found an echo in Britain originated in the depressed mood of the United States in the aftermath of Vietnam, Watergate and the seeming failure of the Johnsonian 'Great Society'. However, our own recent experience – because the strains of modernity show up the more starkly against a background of economic failure – suggest the need to revise revisionism at least to take account of the economic consequences of egalitarianism.

The first question to ask is the extent to which egalitarian policies may impede an increase in general prosperity. That has to be the first question because if democracy does crack in Britain it is most likely to do so under the strain of persistent economic failure and national decline. Economic recovery becomes the first priority for ensuring the continuance of freedom and equalities which impede progress must be counted as costs. That is not to say that in many cases the costs will not be met but that egalitarianism can be regarded no longer as an overriding priority.

Egalitarianism does seem to have become an obstacle to growth in a number of ways. First it is inflationary to the extent that the State is unable to increase taxes to cover its expenditures. Inflation, generated in the name of equality, not only constricts the growth of the economy but also inflicts new inequalities through penalising the poor more than the rich. Second, the pursuit of equality has imposed a resource burden on the economy larger than its productive base can support. In the process a vast and cumbersome tax and welfare bureaucracy has been created to channel the flood of transfer payments. Third, it has spawned a politics of conflicting interest groups which increase the difficulties of the Government in making efficient allocations.

Examples of this last are myriad. The Chancellor's recent package of measures contained several instances in which egalitarian considerations prevail over considerations of productive efficiency (benefits to remain indexed, construction projects to be cancelled) while the trade-offs which are made in the name of the Social Contract, an instrument of egality, impose penalties on efficiency such as, for example, refusing to pay the rate for top-class managements of the nationalised industries.

Redistribution of income is generally unpopular and not least among the bulk of working people who now pay income tax. Relative adjustments in income, wealth and status cause the least friction when absolute standards are rising. The Labour Party revisionists, who knew that soaking the rich or nationalising everything were no answers, hoped that rapid economic growth would make their egalitarian task easier. But economic failure has made it virtually impossible while the continuing pursuit of equality assists in compounding our economic difficulties. Meanwhile, new and obnoxious inequalities based on rackets and wangles feed on the restrictive complexity of the bureaucracy and the tax system. It is more than time, therefore, for social democracy to place a higher-than-ever priority on the achievement of general prosperity and to weigh the claims for equality more critically and cautiously against the imperatives of freedom.

Guardian, 23 December 1976

CHAPTER THREE

The English Sickness

The continuing financial crisis provoked a wider debate about Britain's postwar decline. The symptoms of widespread industrial unrest, low productivity and high inflation were diagnosed as the British Disease. In 1975 Jenkins visited the German Chancellor to hear his views on Britain's deepening problems; in 1978 he wrote three articles on the theme of British decline which were typical of the period.

Diagnosing the English sickness

Class struggle, resulting in large part from the inferior status of the worker, is what is wrong with Britain in the steely eyes of Helmut Schmidt, Chancellor of the Federal Republic of Germany. He chose his words on this subject carefully and during a long discussion in his office at the Chancellery in Bonn last week was reluctant to be drawn into what might be construed as unfriendly criticisms of, as he put it, 'a partner and an ally'. But it was barely possible to explore our theme – the nature of the crisis in the Western industrial democracies and Schmidt's brand of social democracy as a response to that crisis – without exploring the question of why Britain's performance, economic and social, had been so markedly inferior to West Germany's.

It was no secret to me when I sat down with the Chancellor that he has a low opinion of the way we have been conducting our affairs in recent years. He finds it hard to choose as the greater culprit between the sleepy nine-to-five management of British industry (Schmidt believes in 14 hours work a day) and the narrow-minded insularity of the trade unions. Indeed, he has been heard to suggest that the TUC and the top management of industry should be tied together and dropped into the North Sea.

But he was clearly at pains to show tact (not his most celebrated quality) in the presence of my tape recorder and I promised to print the following passage: 'I do not want to give the impression that Britain has fallen incurably behind other countries. I personally am a very anglophile person – by upbringing, by tradition of my own city [Hamburg], and by everything I have experienced in life, including the war. Basically I believe that the British people if need be can be more stubborn than anybody else in Europe. There is an enormous potential in Britain for getting at a problem which the people have defined. [Here he mentioned Churchill and the blood, sweat and tears.] The British have an enormous potential for discipline and vigour if they understand what to do and what the need is. Therefore I am in no way despondent.'

He paused, thumped the table, and said: 'Please don't omit that. I really mean it. I want you to print it.'

We had got on to the subject of Britain when I asked him if he shared the view, common in Germany, that the name of our complaint was the 'English sickness' or whether perhaps we were in the forefront once more, experiencing difficulties endemic to advanced industrial societies and which before long could become just as acute in Germany.

Schmidt challenged my premise. 'I would not feel that Britain is advanced,' he said. 'By no means – not regarding her social set-up, not regarding her industrial set-up, and not even regarding her political set-up. I think that the English nation for too long a number of years has taken too many things for granted and this is not equivalent to progressiveness.'

He had distinguished earlier between two crises – the democratic and the international. Democracies lived in permanent crises, were accustomed to at least one a week. However, he didn't want to minimise what he called 'present critical developments' and these were by no means confined to parliamentary democracies. We were experiencing 'an inflation of incompatible desires, claims and expectations' at a time when the 'controlling disciplinary factors' in democratic societies had become too weak.

But there was also the international crisis and this took the form of the failure of the nation State to adapt to the requirements of interdependence. More and more problems were international problems but international co-operation had failed to develop since the immediate postwar period; indeed, had tended to decrease.

It was within this framework of analysis (and Schmidt since he succeeded to the Chancellorship last year and with an election to face next year has sought to place the blame for inflation and the resulting recession on factors external to Germany, notably OPEC) that he considered the question of whether Britain was a special case.

There were, he observed, structural problems to be found also in other countries, but outside Britain the repercussions of the worldwide economic crisis were by far the overwhelming reason for economic, social and political troubles. He went on:

'If one asks oneself what are the true reasons for the differentiated development of societies and economies between the British and most ones on the Continent I think it has something to do with the fact that British society, much more than the Scandinavian, German, Austrian, and Dutch societies, is characterised by a class struggle type of society. This is true for both sides of the class struggle society, for the upper classes as well as for the working classes.

'I think that the way in which organised labour on the one hand and industrial management on the other hand deal with their problems is outmoded. I think the organisation of British trade unions (How many do you have? It's in the hundreds isn't it?) is off course. By the very nature of being so divided and having so many small unions it has to be less effective than the organisation in this country, where we have only 16 unions.'

Was he suggesting that in general the German 'social market' formula was more successful than our more dirigiste approach to running the economy? 'I don't buy the term social market economy. I don't use it. The real difference is not the degree of dirigism. There is quite a lot – a great deal – of dirigism in Germany today and there always has been. No, the real difference is the fact of a very different organisation of labour and of the very different behaviour of labour organisations and of the industrial "partner" at the bargaining table.

'In Germany the trade unions have behaved extremely sensibly over the last twenty-five years. The number of strikes per one hundred thousand working days in Britain is on average ten, twelve or fifteen times higher than in Germany. Nevertheless, the British trade unions have not achieved in real terms for the workers what the German trade unions have got for theirs.'

He attributed this in large part to the system of co-determination, the legal framework for the conduct of industrial relations in Germany, and specifically the representation of workers on the boards and the system of freely elected factory councils. 'The strength of an elected labour council in a German factory causes acute horror in many British entrepreneurs but this is a very effective and very important part of Germany's economic performance.'

Was this a substitute for public ownership, I asked. No, he thought not, although in any case there was 'no pressure for public ownership in this country.' And what was the point of public ownership if the worker was treated in the same old way by the publicly owned management as he was treated by the formerly privately owned management? A mere change of ownership did not alter the manners with which unions and managements dealt with one another.

Schmidt, however, is under some pressure from the Left of his party to adopt what in this country we call 'Bennery', that is to say the planning of investment through State interventions. He is firmly set against it. He said: 'I don't believe in the direction of investment by the State. I don't believe in the growth of bureaucracy. I don't believe in the economic wisdom of the State as regards industrial management. And it's not going to be done.'

I put it to him that as a politician running for re-election he was behaving in a somewhat eccentric way. Instead of promising goodies he was promising expenditure cuts and tax increases. He replied that people placed trust in democratic leaders who told the truth and that most people in Germany knew it to be a truth that you can't spend more than you earn. He expected his programme of retrenchment to be a successful electoral strategy.

However, he pointed out that, even with the cuts, the aggregate budgetary deficit in Germany (including the state budgets with the federal budget) would this year be the equivalent of 6–7 per cent of GNP. This was by far the greatest exercise in deficit spending since the war.

Moreover, he stuck to the statement which he made when taking office last year – that he would prefer 5 per cent inflation to 5 per cent unemployment. At present the rate of inflation is 5.9 per cent (compared with our 26 per cent) and the rate of unemployment is 4.5 per cent which – at over a million – is roughly the same as ours. It would be easy, he said, to increase employment by allowing a much higher rate of inflation but in the long run Germany would finish up like other countries (no names mentioned) with high unemployment as well. But he stood by his statement. It was more necessary to decrease unemployment below 5 per cent than to decrease inflation below 5 per cent. 'I think that no democratic society in the long run will be able to sustain 5 per cent unemployment.' But it was clear from what he said that the speed of the German economic revival would depend on the speed of the revival of world trade.

During all this the Chancellor drank a cup of hot consommé. That, apparently, was his lunch. In keeping with his austere image, he was proposing to feed his Cabinet at its next meeting at his castle retreat on army-issue pea soup. He is plainly a hard man. However, he was not unsensitive to his reputation as a pragmatist or technocrat lacking in idealism, some allege not really a social democrat at all.

'What do they say about me in England?' he asked.

Of himself he said: 'I have no doubts at all about my identity. I am a social democrat. I have been a member of my trade union ever since I entered my role in life. But I have never seen it the political task of the SPD, closely related as it is to the trade unions, to be executing the orders of trade union leaders because they may have hundreds, thousands, or even millions of votes in their pockets. I regard myself as a middle-of-the-roader. I don't regard myself as a right-winger in the SPD.'

'You have to treat workers as equal members of society,' he said, and now he was talking again – with some passion – about the predicament of Britain. 'You have to give them the self-esteem which they can only have if they acquire responsibility. Then you will be able to ask the trade unions to behave and to abstain from those idiotic policies and embark on new ones. Then they will accept some guidance from outsiders – from the Government or the Party or whatever it is. But as long as you maintain this damned class-ridden society of yours you will never get out of your mess.

'And this, if you please, is a Socialist attitude not a right-wing attitude. British trade unionists are the right-wingers because they don't really want to have a say in the British economy and society. It's a lack of understanding of the social and psychological need of the worker. He wants to be proud of himself. I really do believe in co-determination.'

Guardian, 30 September 1975

Castles in the air 1: The industries that peaked a century too soon

It was only five years ago that Lord Rothschild, the head of the think tank, was rebuked publicly by the then Prime Minister, Mr Edward Heath, for warning that by 1985 Britain's domestic product might be only half that of West Germany and France, roughly the same as Italy's. Since then, and since the elections of 1974 when it was something of a novelty, the notion of Britain in decline has become a commonplace. A commonplace, that is, among a dispirited intelligentsia. The last five years, if we go back to the quadrupling of the price of oil in 1973 which sent the world into its worst recession since the thirties, have brought a keener awareness of the nature and extent of Britain's century-old relative decline as an industrial power.

More recently there has grown up among those who are in charge of the nation's affairs an awful awareness of how easily that relative decline could turn into a state of absolute decline. Instead of merely growing richer more slowly than others, Britain would grow steadily poorer. The political consequences of that are unpleasant to contemplate.

Decline, however, has remained a meaninglessly abstract concept for the public at large. It is not something people talk about in pubs. The league tables which consistently show Britain falling behind in economic performance make little impact on public opinion. Comparisons don't affect people's daily lives. To be sure, trade union negotiators make increasing use of Continental comparisons, but only a few people, mostly itinerant business executives, experience the humiliation of paying for a meal in a German restaurant or hiring a cab in Geneva.

A greater number of people encounter their German or Scandinavian opposites on holiday in Spain but console themselves, if they worry about it at all, with tales of the astronomical prices which these more prosperous Europeans pay for the necessities and luxuries of life. In this, by the way, they are correct in that the difference in living standards by any qualitative measure is a good deal less than the quantitative comparisons suggest.

Nor do foreigners visiting Britain in ever vaster numbers find it easy to reconcile the evidence of their own eyes with their received notion of a Britain sinking slowly into the sea. In the West End of London and in the southern counties where they mostly congregate, they see a people staggering cheerfully under the burden of prosperity. They would see much the same if they ventured north – a consumer boom reverberating down every high street – and they would be forgiven for suspecting that the idea of penurious Britain is the latest confidence trick by Perfidious Albion.

Ask people their opinion about Britain's decline and they will very likely reply: 'What decline?' 'How can we be in decline when everything is going up?' 'Most people think the country has passed safely through the eye of the storm.' 'People think we're not doing badly and that, even if we were, it wouldn't matter much.' 'People understand there's been a recession and they think we've come through it pretty well.' These are comments not from men in the street, but from people who keep an ear close to the ground. They are borne out by some unpublished opinion research. There is little doubt that the concept of decline does not relate to the experience of the great majority of the British people.

On a short view people are right. There are two ways of looking at the experience of the years since Labour returned to power, and which of them prevails is going to have an important bearing on next year's election. People with long memories may recall that in two years out of four living standards have fallen. Of course, they have fallen much more sharply for a few than for the majority and for some not at all, but on average real disposable income (which is what the pay packet will buy after all deductions) fell by about 1.5 per cent from mid-1975 to mid-1977. That compares with an average annual increase of 2.8 per cent during the last decade. It represents a hefty blow not to actual living standards but to previous expectations. It is not the sort of record on which you would expect to see a government re-elected.

If memories are shorter, however, the 6 to 7 per cent increase in real living standards which has occurred since the middle of last year compares very favourably with past form. It well exceeds expectations. Consumer spending is back nearly to its 1973 peak. New car registrations look as if they may break the record for that boom of boom years. Sales of consumer durable goods are 24 per cent up on last year. A good old-fashioned election boom is under way, financed from the North Sea and stocked by imports.

No wonder the idea of decline seems remote to most people as they go about their daily lives. They have become, perhaps, inured to gloom-mongering, to the pessimistic imaginings of a dispirited élite; the 'opinion-formers' are among those who have suffered substantial declines in their living standards. The politicians, for the most part, encourage the public in its reassuring air of complacency. 'If we keep our heads, the years of sacrifice are over,' said Mr Denis Healey in his Budget broadcast. But the sacrifice is a myth. Most people have been able to absorb without pain the marginal reduction in their real living standards – by putting off a change of car or new washing machine.

Moreover, people are being led to suppose that the recent difficulties have been due to international conditions and that Britain has done as well as most countries and better than some in riding out the crisis sparked by the Arab oil producers in 1973. This is not so. Britain's economic performance has been significantly worse than most other countries during the recession, just as it was during the postwar era of growth and prosperity. The worrying question of today is how much nearer Britain has approached to a state of absolute decline.

Britain's relative decline as an industrial power can be dated from some time after 1860. In large part, of course, it was inevitable that Britain's manufacturing primacy should give way to others as their industrial production grew. But at some time during the second half of the century Britain seems to have lost her technological lead. A convenient if symbolic date is 1862, the year of the Paris exhibition, from which visitors returned to write indignant letters to *The Times* about Britain falling behind in the new technologies – electrical and chemical. Great concern was expressed about the shortcomings of technical education which was deemed grossly inferior to that provided in Prussia and, later, in France.

Many reasons have been suggested as to why Britain suffered a failure in the application of science to industry during the 'second industrial revolution' which took place at that time. Note how they are echoed in our contemporary introspections. The Empire provided Britain with assured markets and left little incentive to innovation or restructuring; aristocratic values prevailed over commercial ones and country house life was the entrepreneur's ideal; the educational system was geared to administration not to business, indeed the public schools positively despised commercial values or technical skills; an

'Establishment', rich and secure in its ways, shut out would-be innovators and fresh entrepreneurial talent.

The huge momentum gained from the harnessing of steam to production was becoming spent by the end of the century. In 1900 it was noted that the productivity of American textile workers was four times higher than that of the British. Productivity missions trooped off to the United States before the first war and again after the second. They returned with the same story: more horsepower, more flexible work attitudes. Very little that is new has been said on the subject of productivity – which is at the heart of the British problem – for half a century or more. Here are two quotations which could have come from any recent Neddy report or government White Paper; in fact they came from the Lloyd George 'Yellow Book' (*Britain's Industrial Future*) of 1928:

'There was reason to doubt [before 1914] whether we weren't relying too much on casual, rule-of-thumb competitive enterprise, and too little upon scientific research and deliberate organisation.'

'The essential weakness is not national ... it is, rather, psychological. It lies in stubborn adherence to outworn methods, ideas, traditions, resulting in a general organisation of industry which fails to pass the test of twentieth-century traditions. Nor is it only business organisation in the narrow sense that is at fault. Our industrial efficiency is gravely impaired by unsatisfactory relations between employers and employed, bursting out every now and then in wasteful conflict.'

Since the war, Britain's growth rate has been good by historical standards, markedly inferior to the performance of others. By 1963 Britain's share of world trade in manufactured goods had fallen to 15.3 per cent; by last year it was down to 9 per cent. During the quarter-century since 1950 the economy of Japan expanded by 9 per cent a year, West Germany by 5.7 per cent, France by 5.1 per cent, the US by 3.5 per cent, and Britain by 2.8 per cent. Between 1955 and the coming of the recession output by head in British industry increased at an average annual rate of 3.2 per cent; in West Germany, France, Belgium and the Netherlands the annual increase averaged 5 per cent. From 1964 to 1974 unit costs of production rose faster in Britain – by more than 6 per cent a year – than in the other major economies, an average of 5 per cent a year.

Slower productivity growth and higher labour costs resulted, inevitably, in a slower growth of real earnings. Between 1961 and 1973 they grew by 2.2 per cent a year on average; with the others it ranged from 4.3 per cent in France to 8.1 per cent in Japan. Everybody else prospered at twice the rate that we did.

The litany is all too familiar. There doesn't seem much to be done about the British growth rate. From 1870 to 1913 it averaged 2.2 per cent. In the fifties it averaged 2.7 per cent, in the first half of the sixties 3.4 per cent, in the second half 2 per cent, in the first half of the seventies 2.4 per cent, since when the economy has virtually stagnated. The evidence of a hundred years would suggest that social, political and cultural deficiencies are the causes of Britain's relative decline.

Decline feeds upon itself. Its effects become the cause of further decline. By this process the relative can become absolute; relative decline is not a stable state. The most familiar theme of the exhortations which have been lavished upon the British people since the war is that only marginal improvement is required to ensure success. Unfortunately, by the same reckoning, it requires only a marginal deterioration to produce in the end a disastrous result.

Guardian, 26 September 1978

Castles in the air 2: The map for Britain's journey into the Third World

No country has yet made the journey from developed to underdeveloped. Britain could be the first to embark upon that route. That is what it would mean to move away from a century of relative economic decline into a state of absolute decline. Here is how it *could* happen.

Productivity continues to increase more slowly than in other countries. Wages grow at the same rate or faster. Unit labour costs and consumer prices thereby grow much faster. Britain's share of world markets continues to diminish. So does the number of persons employed in manufacture. Export trade ceases to be sufficient to keep factories open while imports strike more deeply into the domestic market. The moment comes at which it is no longer possible to finance a growth in real incomes. Relative decline will have brought about absolute decline.

It is vital to grasp that perpetual lagging behind is not an attractive option for Britain. It may not seem important that others grow richer provided we grow rich enough. Gentle decadence might prove an enjoyable state. Unfortunately it cannot go on; the loss of competitiveness leads gradually to industrial extinction.

Where is the motor cycle industry today? Dead and gone. Look at what is happening to British Leyland; it has been obliged to retreat from the volume car market in the United States. Since 1964 Britain's share of the world car market has fallen from 11 per cent to 5 per cent; of the shipbuilding market from 8 per cent to 4 per cent; of steel from 6.2 per cent to 3 per cent; of chemicals from 13.1 to 9.7 per cent; of non-electrical machinery from 16.2 to 10.2 per cent; of electrical machinery from 13.6 to 7.6 per cent; and of transport equipment from 16.3 to 6.1 per cent.

This is the process called de-industrialisation. It appears to have set in some time in the late fifties and to have marked a new stage in the course of Britain's relative decline. The most simple measure of it is the decline of employment in manufacturing. A decline in the manufacturing sector in relation to the growing service sector is a healthy feature of an advanced economy when it reflects the growing efficiency of the productive sector. In Britain it appears to have reflected the opposite, in striking contrast to what was happening in other countries.

Between 1955 and 1973 employment in the manufacturing sector of the economy in Britain declined by 13 per cent. Everywhere else it increased – by 13 per cent in France, 18 per cent in the United States, 31 per cent in West Germany, 57 per cent in Italy, and 155 per cent in Japan. Non-industrial employment also increased in these countries but not as quickly as in Britain where – as the Oxford economists, Bacon and Eltis, have chronicled – the exodus was from the factories into the offices of a burgeoning governmental bureaucracy. The result: a growing superstructural strain upon the productive sector of the economy.

The index of production gives some idea of what has been happening in key industries. Since 1970 manufacturing output overall has grown by 4 per cent – a deplorable performance in itself – but in key sectors it has declined; down 4.5 per cent in mechanical engineering, down 6.7 per cent in vehicles, and in engineering overall

– the heart of British industry – output barely kept up with the index.

The record of British industry during the recession does not inspire confidence in what will happen if world trade turns down once more. Between 1973 and 1976 output per head increased in West Germany by more than 10 per cent, in France by more than 9 per cent, and in Japan by more than 7 per cent; in Britain it increased by only 1.2 per cent.

Figures for industrial production are equally dispiriting. Since 1973, in spite of the recession, manufacturing output has grown by 7 per cent in Italy, 5 per cent in France, and 2.7 per cent in Germany; in Britain it was by last year still 6.1 per cent down. Overall growth in Britain over the same period was nil while with the others it ranged from 5.9 per cent in Germany to 12.8 per cent in Japan.

These figures show that Britain is emerging from the world recession in a further weakened state, less able to compete with the others than before. During the recession other countries managed to adapt to the higher price of energy and transfer a proportion of their national income to the oil producers. At the same time they were able to increase the living standards of their own people. This they did by increasing their productivity to make up the difference. Over the past 12 months real living standards have advanced sharply in Britain. North Sea oil helped to make this possible and so did last year's public expenditure cuts. Nevertheless, real living standards on the Continent will have improved twice to three times the British rate over the five years since 1973. The British pre-election boom is not justified by increasing productivity.

Low productivity and low wages are first the consequences of decline, then become its causes. It remains to be seen whether during this winter workers seek to obtain with their trade union muscle what they have failed to achieve in real living standards through their industrial productivity. The early confrontation at Ford is an ominous sign.

But the chief ingredient of a renewed inflation may be the cumulative effect of progressive taxation on take-home pay. The tax threshold as a proportion of median earnings is down to 50 per cent from 68.6 per cent in 1972–73, the standard rate of tax was up from 30 per cent to 33. That is the measure of the burden of public expenditure which had fallen upon the average working man.

Economic crises have taught the British to be unusually and

unhealthily preoccupied with the short term. The politicians from time to time deplore this but they do much themselves to encourage it. If it is believed that this strike or that price increase, this export contract or that Little Neddy report, this or that Budget, is of crucial importance then it is easy to suppose that Britain's economic difficulties are a series of contingencies rather than the chronic effects of a long-term deterioration. The late Iain Macleod used to say that he did not fear the precipice, only the long slide down.

That slide has been going on for a long while. It began in the 1860s; World War II destroyed a vast part of the overseas assets which had helped to subsidise the British standard of living; the liquidation of the Empire meant the loss of traditional markets; then from some time in the mid-fifties – in spite of an improved growth performance by historical standards – de-industrialisation began. Now the recession has made matters worse; the economy is less competitive than ever, more prone to import.

One more winter, one more phase of pay policy, one more Healey Budget is not going to be make or break. The transition from relative to absolute decline may be somewhat distant yet – beyond the next recession, or the one after that, or the one after that – who knows? North Sea oil will help to stave it off. And even if that absolute decline sets in it may at first be hardly discernible, scarcely painful for the majority.

For the great majority Britain should be a pleasant place to live for a good deal longer yet. There is time yet for the decline to be arrested and reversed. The prognosis is not an optimistic one but cure is not impossible. What can be said with certainty, however, is that the present pre-election boom, the glosses of the politicians in power and the panaceas to those who seek it, bear small relation to the truth of Britain's underlying economic state.

Guardian, 27 September 1978

Castles in the air 3: Britain's two nations locked together in decline

The underlying weakness of the British economy, made worse by the international recession, is in striking contrast to the buoyant mood in the country. Britain is a good place to live for most of its inhabitants. Life is good provided you are not one of the 10.4 million who are living at the supplementary benefit level (1976 figures) or no more than 20 per cent above it.

It is not easy to assess the sizes of today's Two Nations. Not all of the 20 per cent of the workforce who have no qualifications and do the unskilled labour or provide the more menial public services are locked in poverty or misery; but life can't be marvellous for many of them. By no means all of the 30 per cent of householders who are council tenants are among the disadvantaged, although an increasing proportion are – as many as 40 per cent; nor is life in an inner city high rise or on an overspill estate a form of gracious living.

Life leaves much to be desired for the 1.5 million who are unemployed and it isn't much fun being on the 600,000-long hospital waiting list, especially if you are one of the 40,000 urgent cases. Roughly speaking there are around 10 million people, or nearly 20 per cent of the population, who constitute the poor and the needy – the second of the Two Nations.

For the other nation, become the great majority since Disraeli's day, the general quality of life in Britain remains probably as high as anywhere in Europe.

What kind of house you live in is becoming the most visible sign of which nation you belong to. The proportion of owner-occupation has risen to 53 per cent and the proportion of council tenants who are welfare families has doubled in recent years.

Social changes seem to have played as large a part as economic factors in the gradual transformation of British class society. The reforms of the sixties which brought in the so-called permissive society extended the frontiers of personal liberty for the great mass of the people. The result is a much more equal society. Greater sexual equality is perhaps the outstanding change of the past decade; according to one shrewd observer of social trends women have ceased to be the more conservative of the sexes, at least in their exercise of consumer preferences, and if so this could have political consequences.

In spite of the complaints about the impoverishment of the middle class under Labour government you will find nearly everywhere better shops, more good places to eat and drink, improved amenities and cultural facilities. The impoverished middle class consists chiefly of people trying to pay school fees out of income.

But the past few years have left a severe dent in the self-confidence of the people who run the country, the decision-taking élite who we can call the ruling class. True, they are less at their wits' end than in the winter of 1973–74 when the country seemed ungovernable or than at the height of the 1976 financial crisis, but they know that they have no answer to the country's economic problems, no means of arresting its industrial decline. They are morally shaken, intellectually still in the hands of the receivers.

Loss of confidence applies not only to central government but also to local government and the administration of the Welfare State. There seems to be very little faith in the reformed two-tier system of local government among the people engaged in trying to make it work. The reorganisation of the National Health Service has been plainly an administrative disaster. In both of these cases increasing bureaucracy seems to have encouraged a paper-pushing nine-to-five mentality among the professionals, including the hospital doctors. Where there is no clear control no blame can attach – so pass the buck and home for golf.

Another aspect of what I have before called 'the politics of decline' is visible in the rapid growth of the 'parallel' or black economy. People who can circumvent the official economy are doing so in all manner of ways, creating their own market price system, escaping from the regulatory reach of the State, and evading the taxman.

This flight from the taxman – through which the small-time tax evader can grow richer than the highly salaried employee – is one reflection of a mounting unwillingness among the first nation to foot the bill for the second. Britain may have reached the limits of direct taxation during the recent recession.

Nevertheless, direct taxes began biting at well below average earnings and for the PAYE worker there is no escape. Some 2,500,000 more people are paying tax than in 1974 and the standard rate is up from 30 to 33 per cent. One of the consequences of a declining industrial base is that the disadvantaged, themselves likely to grow in number, preempt an increasing share of national resources. There is less disposable income for those who may consider they have earned it. Reluctance by the taxpayer to foot the welfare bill then becomes one of the motors of accelerating inflation, which in turn accelerates the decline.

Loss of position or influence in the world, which is another aspect of decline, does not seem to worry the public much. The rundown of Britain's defences has been accepted with equanimity. There is little sign of Rhodesia becoming a popular issue although it is the perfect case study in British weakness. Public resentment seems to be directed at the Common Market itself rather than at the ineptitude shown by Britain as a member. The oil sanctions affair was a cynical attempt to conceal Britain's true weakness.

Weakness abroad is matched by a weakness of the central government at home. It is still an exaggeration to describe the kingdom as breaking up but there is a drift towards a federalism which is not of design but rather by default of the centre. At the moment there is not much genuine desire within the English regions for assemblies of their own but if the Scottish and Welsh Assemblies prove effective instruments for obtaining favourable treatment from the centre, the English regions will not be far behind.

Finally, of course, there is the trade union problem. One of the most striking developments during the recession has been the growth in trade union membership especially among junior executive, technical, and professional workers. The growth of public sector employment has substantially increased the number of people with a vested interest in statism and the need, through affiliation to the TUC, of access to the Government.

At a time when competitiveness is the key to arresting the national decline the mood seems to be turning towards conservatism and resistance to change. There seems to be a feeling after a decade and a half of social engineering and efficiency-mongering that change has been tried and found wanting. And there is the mounting demand for shorter working hours which reflects renewed fears about technological unemployment. Understandable though it is the mentality bodes ill for the coming third industrial revolution, the application of micro-processing to factory and office.

I have no wonder cure to prescribe. Decline is not a moral question.

Its causes are social and political and in Britain they are deep-rooted. The recent record does not inspire great confidence in our national genius working in isolation. We would do better still to join wholeheartedly with the more successful, with open minds and readiness to change our ways.

Guardian, 28 September 1978

CHAPTER FOUR

The Backlash Against Decline?

The Impact of Thatcherism, 1979–81

Jenkins's analysis of decline seemed especially pertinent after the Winter of Discontent. In 1978 9,306,000 days were lost in strikes; the following year this figure had risen to a staggering 29,474,000 days. Despite, or perhaps because of, the Labour Government, trade union power had reached a zenith of what many people felt to be profound irresponsibility.

Hopes for the future have begun to die and with them patience. We may see the start of the backlash against decline

In the last few weeks we have seen the coming of the age of syndicalism. If the country threatens to become ungovernable it is not because of the power of the unions, it is rather because of their powerlessness to govern their own members. Their national leaders have lost control. I have never known them to be more alarmed. They fear that this is not just another wave of industrial unrest, rather something novel, something different.

What is happening bears more resemblance to the militant explosions of 1968–69 than the clumsy confrontation of 1974. A decade ago the Royal Commission which sat under Lord Donovan was already drawing attention to the duality of the British industrial relations system. There was the official trade union movement, national in character and formally structured, and there was the unofficial movement, local, sectional and informal. During the last decade it is the latter which has prospered.

As one national union leader said this week: 'We are seeing the factory union and the company union growing up under our eyes.' In part this is the legacy of the Jones era. Mr Jack Jones devolved power massively within his own gigantic trade union; he did so out of a quasi-mystical faith in the masses and without much regard for institutional functionalism; in the last two years of his reign the forces he had unleashed were catching up with him and today they have engulfed his successor, Moss Evans.

The causes of this peasant revolt in the trade union movement can only be guessed at. A decade and a half of intermittent incomes policy must be among them. The exponential growth of white collar and white coat, professional and executive, trade unionism owes in large part to the realisation that government was only too pleased to trample on the non-unionised while treating with the centralised trade union bureaucracies. These new trade unionists are of a different breed; their spirit of collectivism is not of the generous kind which imbued the old proletarian guard; their militancy is directed against the central government which is not only (in most of their cases) the employer of last resort but also, as a result of incomes policies, held responsible for the supply of money wages.

This new style of trade unionism derives also from the discovery of new weapons. Since 1972 when the miners first held the Heath Government to ransom, many other groups of workers have awakened to the power within their hands. We saw some demonstrations of it on Monday. People have discovered that a handful can stop a modern hospital in exactly the same way as a handful can stop a motor car factory.

It was some time in the early 1970s that groups such as doctors accepted the proletarian analogue and started to talk about 'industrial action'. Some power was thrust upon these flexing groups by the State itself, for example by its concentration of indispensable functions on single computer systems.

Changes in the law may have played some part in the siring of the new militancy. First the 1971 Industrial Relations Act drew attention to some forms of trade union power by seeking to restrict them. It was not until 1972 and Arthur Scargill that picketing became an offensive weapon. Michael Foot's repeals and reforms by implication sanctioned the activities which the previous Government had tried to curb, gave trade unions for the first time an almost total sense of their immunity at law, and thereby probably contributed to the unruliness of their members.

Economic failure is another factor. A decade or so ago collective bargaining was mostly concerned with the retail price index. Today it is mostly concerned with 'comparability', or envy; relative deprivation is its fuel and emulation its motor. It could be that we are also beginning to see envy of the more successful German or Japanese, born of a growing sense of national failure, vented against groups nearer at hand. The economic slowdown since 1974 may not so much have diminished expectations as foreshortened them. Hopes for the future have begun to die and with them patience. What we are today watching may be the beginnings of the backlash against decline.

Militancy should not be simply equated with left-wing tendencies. The present industrial unrests are probably as inimical to socialism as they are to capitalism. They may owe as much to the tax revolt as to any notion of proletarian solidarity. Combination may be the British response to a phenomenon which in California and elsewhere in the United States takes another populist form. It is important to bear in mind that the public's fervid dislike of trade unionism co-exists with a recruitment boom and the militant pursuit of higher wages by a broad section of the community.

There is a danger in this that the politicians will find themselves fighting the last class war over again. The Wilson and Heath governments tried to govern the country through the trade unions, by giving them more power at the centre; Mrs Thatcher is contemplating the alternative strategy of enfranchising the silent majority. The changes in trade union law she is talking about, the chief effect of which would be to enhance the rights of the individual against the trade union, may be desirable in equity but it does not mean that they will contribute significantly to an alteration in the balance of industrial power.

Mr Callaghan, for his part, is preparing to meet TUC demands for workers on boards, compulsory planning agreements and even – perhaps – measures to restrict imports in exchange for renewed endeavours by the national leadership to bring collective bargaining into line with national interests.

If I am at all right about what may be going on down below, these latest trade-offs offer small hope of success in reconciling the British system of collective bargaining with the pursuit of prosperity. Mrs Thatcher's legalistic tinkerings will not even address the problem. The difficulty is that the British system of collective bargaining is thoroughly inflationary and inimical to industrial success. Until it is replaced by something else Britain's decline will continue unarrested. If nothing else is clear from the experience of the last 15 years that should be.

The ultimate threat to the political system in Britain does not stem from the ambitions of trade unions to wield political power. The only threat to democracy comes from continuing economic failure. The coming crisis is of a systemic kind. Ever since strikers played football with the police in 1926 comfort has been taken in the non-revolutionary, often downright conservative character of the British trade union movement. Now another form of comfort is taken from blaming the unrests on Trotskyists or other troublemakers whose role is real but easily exaggerated.

In truth it is the brute instrumentality of British trade unionism, its disorderly, competitive but highly effective pursuit of money wages, which makes it so lethal – far more so than the Communist-directed trade union movements on the Continent.

Ruthless strikes and aggressive picketing are not the only symptoms of the chronic British condition. The present wave of industrial unrest is taking place against a background of falling production, eroding competitiveness and deteriorated productivity. To be sure the Government deserved credit for having brought down the rate of inflation into single figures but it had done this at a high price; faced with the institutionalised cost-push of the British collective bargaining system it had been obliged to pursue restrictive and deflationary policies, to appease the unions with measures inimical to the competitiveness of the economy, and to expropriate the North Sea revenues for the subsidisation of consumption.

Wages in Britain *are* low, living standards *are* becoming inadequate. When the Government last week raised its definition of low pay to a ceiling of £70 a week it turned out that a staggering seven million would qualify for the new minimum. We are living in an expensive and increasingly poor country. It is not much use lecturing people about paying themselves more than the country can afford. A better way of putting it is that increasingly the country cannot afford to pay people enough.

How is collective bargaining to be reformed? Successive governments have tried alternatively by pay policies and by legal reforms. They have failed. The union movement has tried to reform itself and it has failed hopelessly. Under a Conservative government the attempt may be made to allow market forces their play but we have Sir Keith Joseph's word for it that 'monetarism is not enough.' He and Mrs Thatcher believe that the balance of industrial power must be shifted. But how? The measures they are suggesting are trifling. For its part, a Labour government is likely to be drawn down the road of half-baked Bennery without finding at the end of it a solution to the industrial problem.

Standing in the way are the unions themselves; not malevolent men but conglomerations of vested interest which are not yet capable of exercising corporatist responsibility but which are no longer responsive institutions corresponding to a model of 'free' collective bargaining. The challenge to that kind of power now comes not from an exasperated State but from below – from people who are in the process of organising themselves into sectional combinations.

A way has to be found of relating this new syndicalism to the pursuit of national objectives. Reform of the existing 'formal' system whether by legal imposition or by corporatist embrace no longer seem promising strategies. The recent events ought to serve as a warning against the folly of empanelling the existing forces in the company boardrooms on the model proposed by the Bullock Committee.

A bold government might go for a wholesale legislative restructuring of the bargaining system around the enterprise itself, somewhat on the lines of the German works council system. If put to the people by referendum the chances are that such a reform would receive massive endorsement.

A psychological break is required from the dreary cycle of failure to come to terms with the union problem. The desire to escape from the prison of ancient structures is widespread and manifest. The tragedy is that a Conservative government which embarked upon any such ambitious undertaking would likely be destroyed by the powers-that-be while a Labour government can be guaranteed not to try.

Guardian, 26 January 1979

The natural party of government lost the May 1979 General Election. For the first time since 1970 a Conservative government was elected and for the first time since February 1974 the Government had a good working majority. This fact alone was a considerable asset to a newly elected Government with an untried leader. The fact that the Labour Party embarked on a period of unprecedented internecine warfare that ended in schism was also a considerable contribution to the beginnings of what Jenkins was to call 'the Thatcher revolution'.

Staggering towards a socialist future

Loser can't be choosers. That is the painful lesson which Mr Callaghan is going to learn in Brighton this week. Nor is he the only one: the biggest losers are the social democratic Right of the Party whose long reign as the dominant element in the Labour Party is coming to an end.

Mr Callaghan's weak position has three causes. He lost the election and not only that but he is open to the accusation that he bungled the timing of it. His power base in the trade union movement has been eroded; it let him down last winter in government and it looks like letting him down again in opposition. The third reason, however, is the most important. The right wing of the Labour Party has passed into the hands of the ideological receiver; intellectually it is bankrupt.

These are not matters worthy of individual blame but they are troublesome facts. In my opinion Labour would have lost the election whenever it was and Mr Callaghan's postponement made little difference. However, by postponing he presented the Labour movement with an alibi. Nor are the trade union leaders personally to blame, with perhaps two or three well-known exceptions, for they were not in control last winter and they are not in control now. As for the social democrats, it was the trade unions who bankrupted them; they gambled on the TUC and they lost.

The constitutional controversies which are making the headlines at the moment seem to me to be the first symptoms of a more serious and chronic condition. No doubt that Mr Tony Benn has scored a tactical victory over Mr Callaghan. For many months before the election he used his base at Transport House to lay the ground for a challenge to the failed parliamentary leadership of the Party.

Since the election he has adroitly rallied his forces around the word 'democracy' and constructed an alliance larger than any he could have built around the word 'socialism', or at least his meaning of it. Moreover, he has exposed the vacuum on the Right of the Party, advertised its ideological poverty and created the impression that its time is up; that is his most signal victory because, whatever exactly happens in Brighton this week, the way is now open for the Party to move in Mr Benn's direction.

The dispute about democracy within the Labour movement is really, of course, a dispute about power. If the Labour movement possessed a common philosophy broadly in tune with the opinion of the wider public which supports it at election time there would be no objection in principle or in practice to varying the balance of power between the Party in the Parliament and the Party in the country. But the way things are the choice is between the élite elected by the people as a whole and the activist élite of shop stewards and Party workers. The latter may only be said to be the more representative in a transcendental or *socialist* sense.

Which is the most democratic is a question to which there is no clear or simple answer. About which system of democracy is the most free the experience of modern history allows small doubt. If liberty is taken somewhat for granted in Britain one reason perhaps is that we have been far too cut off from the overwhelming experience of the twentieth century – the moral failure of socialism.

The Labour Party, proverbially owing more to Methodism than to Marx, seemed a million miles from Stalin; it was not Socialist enough to cause worries about liberty. But today it is moving in a Socialist direction at a time when the compatibility of socialism and freedom is more dubious than ever.

The argument here, we should be clear, is not that the policies now proposed by the Left, a muddled mix of statism and syndicalism, would of themselves tip the balance decisively or, perhaps, even significantly against freedom. Nor is the dispute about whether socialism and democracy are compatible in an abstract sense. There is only one threat to liberty in Britain. It is that persistent and worsening economic failure will eventually undermine our free institutions. The Labour Party ought to be asking itself whether, in the world in which we live, and in the face of the kind of economic decline which we are experiencing, there remains a future for socialism – or has it been one of the causes of the decline?

One of the distinctive features of the 'revisionist' position was, as Anthony Crosland many times wrote, that it was a doctrine equally about means. The essence of it was that societal goals, such as equality, could be achieved by making a go of the mixed economy and with only limited and pragmatic recourse to the direct instruments of state power which contained implications for liberty.

The difficulty facing the social democrats today is that they have patently failed to make a go of the mixed capitalist economy. That is why the whole centre of British politics has, for the time being at least, collapsed and opened the field to the laissez-faire Right and the interventionist Left.

Economic growth was the indispensable means to the social democrats' ends. Their commitment to greater equality was to be achieved chiefly by means of increased social expenditure. There would be continuing consent for this only if resources could be increased rapidly enough to provide for a steady increase in disposable incomes at the same time.

How was this growth to be achieved? There was never a very clear answer. The pursuit of social justice in itself would help to amend attitudes and break down some of the barriers to growth. A good deal of faith was placed in experts of one kind or another. Keynesian demand management policies favourable to growth would be pursued. By 1964 most of the 'revisionists' were convinced that an over-valued pound was one of the causes of the stop-go cycle which was so inimical to growth. But increasingly, and still more after faith in the once-and-for-all efficacy of a devaluation had been exploded, they came to depend upon the restraint of money wages through an incomes policy as the means to the economic growth which alone could justify, indeed permit, their social or 'socialist' ends.

It was on the 'trade union question' that the British version of social democracy became impaled and perished. This was not merely in the sense that the unions periodically broke free from pay restraint and, as happened last winter, inflicted not only defeat upon the Government but also a new bout of deflation upon the always declining economy. Just as important, it led Labour governments down the path of half-hearted statism. Trade unions were appeased and their negative powers enhanced; interventionism was more often than not directed towards the subsidy of inefficiency; enterprise was discouraged by taxation and other means; and all the while public expenditures increased faster than the nation's wealth. What had been put forward as a strategy for growth became a recipe for failure and decline. The elixir of British social democracy became its fatal flaw.

The structure, the history, and the habits of mind of the British Labour movement make it almost certain that a remedy for this failure, so central to the Party's claim to competence in government, will be sought some way further down the road to the Left. In the end compromises will probably be found not far along that road. The majority of the Party will convince itself that trade protection would be a good idea if introduced in the context of a (highly improbable) new international order.

Unfortunately it will lead the Labour Party still further down the road which leads away from the most successful and bountiful mode of left-wing politics in the postwar Western world. That is the form of social democracy which combines a liberal economic regime with the pursuit of collective social goals. In Germany, in Scandinavia, in Austria – wherever there has been a commitment both to wealth creation and to welfare there has been prosperity, far greater than in Britain and in conditions of assured freedom.

That prosperity has permitted higher standards of welfare, a higher quality of life, and (in most respects) a greater social equality than has been achieved by the British version of social democracy. There can be little doubt that had the Labour Party in 1959 adopted a programme along the lines of the German Social Democrats' the working people of this country would not have seen their living standards fall so far behind the Germans'.

So it is in no way true to say that social democracy is dead. In Europe it is very much alive. There it is socialism which is dead or dying. Social democracy has not come to Britain chiefly because the Labour Party has yet to bury socialism.

It is not certain whether Continental social democracy could be made to work in Britain. Things have gone too far for that. The negative power of the trade unions has grown too immense.

What is almost certain, and tragically so, is that the approach so successful wherever it has been tried will not be allowed to be tried here. The trade unions will see to that. The Labour Party is their political prisoner. Their commitment to competitive collective bargaining, their vested interests in declining industries and over-manned plant, and their inability to reform themselves or effectively lead their members are seemingly insuperable barriers to the adoption of a wealth-creating social democratic approach.

On the Continent social democracy has been conducive to growth and prosperity but its success has been in part also a consequence of growth. That growth slowed substantially in the last decade and will slow still further in the next. Many in the Labour Party will conclude happily that the 'crisis of capitalism' is at last upon the world and that soon everybody will be in slow step with Britain.

This is the kind of dismal ethnocentricity which has helped to bring the Labour movement to where it is today. The crisis is a British crisis and it is a crisis in part of the British Labour movement. The prosperous economies of Europe are continuing to expand at a rate faster than achieved in Britain during the peak postwar period in the fifties. For us the prospect is of near-nil growth.

This deepening crisis of the British economy makes it all too possible that the electoral pendulum will swing towards whatever is the next available alternative. It is no longer safe to assume that the Labour Party will lose an election if committed to more overtly Socialist policies. One of the strengths of Mr Benn's position is that he addresses the problem of decline and proposes policies for stopping it.

That is the full measure of the plight of the British social democrats. Their 'revisionist' middle way has failed. Their centreground has collapsed beneath them and they have nowhere to go. The road to Bad Godesberg is not open on the British Left. Increasingly, if true to their convictions, they are likely to find themselves more in disagreement with a substantial section of their own party than with most of their official political opponents. But most of them, I expect, will go staggering valiantly though dispiritedly down the road to the Socialist future, hoping – in the way of a wearied ruling class – to preside over whatever that future may hold.

Whether or not Mr Benn himself presides – and, I think, the odds are still against him – his approach is likely to triumph in large degree.

If in the preliminary rounds of the struggle at Brighton this week Mr Callaghan yet wins the game or forces a draw he will be beholden all the more to the unions. But Mr Benn will not so easily himself escape from what he likes to call *labourism* – that is from trade unionism posing as socialism. The unions will go most of the way with his 'alternative strategy' provided that protection is accorded to the inefficient as well as to the efficient, provided that control over investment can be used to defend jobs, and provided that industrial democracy makes no inroads into their monopoly of collective bargaining.

Like the social democrats before them the Bennites and their friends will be up against the huge negative strength of the trade union movement. Therein lies the future of British socialism.

Guardian, 10 October 1979

The early years of the first Thatcher Government continued to be conducted amid economic crisis, but added to this were the social consequences of increasing unemployment. In the last year of the Labour Government unemployment fell from a maximum of 1,608,000 in August 1978 to 1,464,000 in July 1979. By December 1980 it had peaked for the year at 2,244,000. Many in the Conservative Party lacked the faith of Howe and Thatcher that the Government could turn such a situation round. They also feared that the persistent application of 'monetarism' would result in what was already the most unpopular government of the postwar period being forced from office. Peter Jenkins's 'Commentary' from February 1980 captures the spirit of the times.

The Thatcher Revolution is nearing the end of its first flush of enthusiasm. The monetarist fad seems to be on the wane

Now that the Labour Party is past a joke, a great responsibility falls upon the Conservative Party for providing the entertainment without which politics would soon cease to be a popular spectator sport. The Conservatives are doing remarkably well; indeed, for the past two or three weeks they have been giving a passable imitation of the Labour Party in its prime.

There have been splits and leaks galore, slanders and back-stabbings, and even some examples of that most exquisite form of political misbehaviour, brought to a high pitch of perfection in the Labour Party: the personal attack.

Ostensibly the commotion has been about what to do about the trade unions in general and how to handle the steel dispute in particular; but the underlying instability of the Government has more to do with the half-hearted zeal with which a good few of its senior members are joining in the Thatcher Revolution. The split is between the Gironde and the Jacobin Clubs.

There was never much doubt, so far as I can discover, that Mr James Prior's approach to the reform of trade union law would prevail. Sir Geoffrey Howe consistently and sincerely holds to his belief (shared, incidentally, by Sidney Webb at the time of the 1912 Act) that it would be better to place union funds at risk than to expose individuals to the threat of legal process. The Chancellor expects that time will prove him correct, and Mr Prior wrong, but there was never much likelihood that he would win the argument this time round against the expert opinion of the responsible Minister.

Thus a misleading impression was given when Sir Geoffrey made his speech at Taunton on 8 February. It suggested that the issue was open in the Cabinet when to all intents and purposes it was closed. That speech, it is now known, was chiefly the work of the Prime Minister's own private policy adviser, Mr John Hoskyns, a former computer consultant with some sharp views of his own on the trade union question.

It was Mrs Thatcher herself who had another go last week, although this time on a different tack, when she tried to make the case for a one-clause Bill to outlaw secondary picketing. That was in the Economic Committee whose regular members are Whitelaw, Howe, Joseph, Prior, Nott, Hailsham. She failed.

The impression I have of these events is not so much of a running battle within the Cabinet, with one faction voting down the other, but rather of the weight or argument consistently and, in the end, almost entirely upholding the Prior position. So it was Mrs Thatcher and her Jacobins, who were the ones trying to reopen collective decisions. When she appeared on *Panorama* on Monday night she still seemed to be distancing herself from the Cabinet's decision.

Indeed, there was a nice Wilsonian echo to the homily about collective responsibility which Mrs Thatcher is said to have given to her Ministers at Cabinet last Thursday and which No. 10 leaked to the press at the weekend. Mr Prior throughout had been left to fight his own battles with Conservative backbenchers (which he did triumphantly at a meeting of the 1922 Committee) and in the grassroots whence there has been heavier fire.

It was somewhat odd, therefore, to see him being singled out in the Conservative press for reprimand on grounds of disloyalty to the collective decisions of his colleagues. It was still more odd to see him being ticked off like a naughty boy by 'mother' on television.

To be sure, Mr Prior's views about Sir Keith Joseph's handling of the steel dispute have been made as well known as Sir Geoffrey's and Mrs Thatcher's views about Mr Prior's policies for reforming the trade union law. It is not so easy to apply the doctrine of collective responsibility in the case of steel because the Cabinet has at no time played an important role in the matter. It is my understanding that Sir Keith merely reports to it from time to time, rather in the manner of General Haig reporting on the Flanders campaign.

The chief difference seems to have been that whereas Mr Prior has not received the unequivocal support of the Prime Minister, she has appeared guardian-angel-like at the elbow of Sir Keith at each attempt to jog it in the direction of compromise. That is what happened again last Friday night.

The significance of the steel strike, as I explained in my Commentary of 6 February, is that it has become a 'test case for "Josephism"' and by proxy, therefore, of Thatcherism. Since then the Government's intellectual foundations have received a further shaking, and this is really what the loss of nerve and all the rowing has been about.

The Government is not yet in a political crisis, but it is in something of an ideological crisis. And that is the backdrop to tomorrow's set-piece Commons debate when the Opposition will seek to censure the Government for its economic and industrial policies.

The loss of nerve has been most clearly visible among the Government's friendly commentators. The monetarist creed was majestically reaffirmed in yesterday's edition of *The Times*. In an earlier editorial it reminded us that monetary discipline is 'expected to affect inflationary expectations and govern in a general way the level of pay increases', but it went on to note, with some alarm, that a 19.6 per cent increase in earnings (December 1979–December 1980) is 'dangerously out of line with the index of production, with the underlying rate of productivity and [my italics] *with the growth of the stock of money.*'

Something clearly has gone wrong.

In the *Financial Times* Mr Sam Brittan seemed to be losing both his nerve and his temper. If people would not stop using 'monetarism' as a term of abuse Mr Brittan, so he threatened, was going to stop using the word altogether. Monetarism, he insisted, was 'not the same thing as the world outlook of Professor Friedman.'

Mr Ronald Butt, the *Sunday Times* columnist, seemed similarly eager to distance himself from Professor Friedman. 'Non-intervention,' he warned us – and presumably Sir Keith – 'cannot be applied mechanistically, as though politics and consent do not matter, and as though Friedmanism can be applied like a magic charm.'

Monetarism – and I'll buy Mr Brittan's definition with the addition of one word – is about the *useful* relationship between money and prices. Asked on television by Mr Robin Day when she expected inflation to come down, Mrs Thatcher replied: 'When the money supply really begins to take hold.' But she went on, as the monetarists always do, to speak not about a mechanical relationship between the control of money supply and the rate of inflation, but rather about people changing their attitudes. In other words, she departed the realm of economics for the realm of politics.

How does the supply of money determine the rate of inflation? Sir Geoffrey gave an answer to that one in a letter to the 1922 Committee. This document may become his Epistle to the Colossians who were, you may remember, heretics and unbelievers. 'Lower growth of money incomes will ultimately lead to lower inflation,' he told them. 'The speed at which this occurs depends crucially on expectations in both domestic and external markets, and in particular *on the effects on domestic negotiations*' (my italics again).

This missing link – between the supply of money and the hearts and minds of the people – is known in the trade as the 'transmission mechanism'. The phrase is attributed to Sir Charles Villiers of steel fame, who may have borrowed it from Lenin. Note the automotive metaphor applied to a process which would be better described as getting it into people's heads that the Government is not going to go on paying the wages. So *that's* the new science, the revolution in economic thinking!

As for Friedmanism, the master's weekly appearance on television cannot be doing much to steady the Conservative Party's nerve. So this is the guy Margaret and Geoffrey have been going on about, this potty-sounding professor wearing the confident smile of a flat-earther who seems to think we should shut up shop and 'buy Chinese'. My God, you can hear them saying, is this chap Keith's guru?

These and other tremors of disbelief lead me to suppose that the Thatcher Revolution is nearing the end of its first flush of enthusiasm. Even in the City the monetarist fad seems to be on the wane. The priesthood is in sectarian disarray. The religion is becoming increasingly ritualistic as ceremonies are performed which have no visible effect, and probably no effect at all on the real world at which they are directed.

When the Government's nerve eventually cracks, which it will, it will be because there is no visible connection between the levers the Government goes on pulling and the behaviour of the economy. Obviously, if demand is deflated sufficiently by monetarist or any other means, there will be in the end some change in the behaviour of organised labour.

But not only the social and political costs but also the industrial costs will before that have outweighed the kind of economic gains which the Government was hoping for. That will be primarily because the costs will be all too visible while the benefits will be concealed still in the darkness at the end of the tunnel. The tunnel down which Mrs Thatcher is travelling is simply too long.

It is precisely because it is a prisoner of false ideology that the Government is beginning to lose its inner confidence. There would be no reason for its nerve to show signs of cracking so early in the political cycle were it not for this sense, at Westminster and beyond, of policies being pursued without real regard to their prospects of success.

Where, ask the Jacobins, is the Gironde's alternative? The answer is easy: the alternative to being stupid is to be less stupid; the alternative to being unreasonable is to be more reasonable, etc.

Mrs Thatcher has three choices of U-turn.

She could turn to protectionism. I don't think she will because she would not like the degree of interventionism which that would in its turn imply.

She could turn back to incomes policy. She might have to do that, but I don't believe she will do a Ted Heath spectacular.

Her third U-turn, and I think the likely one, is to give up her money religion. She could, at least, become an Anglican monetarist.

Meanwhile, she's not sunk yet, but it ought to be beginning to occur to her that if you try to walk on water, your feet get wet.

Guardian, 27 February 1980

After a decade of political dealignment and persistent political crisis, British politics had polarised. The determination of the Thatcherites to stick to their developing new Right agenda was mirrored by the eclipse of the social democratic wing of the Labour Party by the Bennite Left. This was the political legacy of the 1970s, for social democrats like Peter Jenkins the polarisation of politics between Mrs Thatcher and Mr Foot the final fracturing of the postwar settlement.

The final collapse of consensus politics

Mrs Thatcher and Mr Foot make an odd couple but they have one thing in common, apart from a Methodist upbringing – neither is in full command of her or his party.

The Prime Minister cannot command a majority in her own Cabinet on a major issue. That is a most extraordinary state of affairs for a Conservative leader. The Leader of the Opposition could not command a majority in his Shadow Cabinet on the issues about which he feels most passionately – certainly not on unilateral nuclear disarmament and probably not on repeal of the European Communities Act.

Mr Foot and Mrs Thatcher are minority leaders who came to power in peculiar circumstances. Mr Foot is in some sense one of the consequences of Mrs Thatcher, and Mrs Thatcher is in part the product of the leftward shift which took place in the Labour Party in the early seventies. Ideological 'Thatcherites', however, remain a small minority of the Conservative Party at Westminster as well as being a minority within her Cabinet. The Left, from whence comes Mr Foot, remains a minority of the Parliamentary Labour Party and an even smaller minority within its elected Shadow Cabinet.

By virtue of being its leader, Mrs Thatcher receives the support of the vast majority of the Parliamentary Conservative Party. The Conservative Party is always loyal to its leaders until it throws them out. As a freshly elected leader, Mr Foot can expect the support of most of his colleagues, especially if he performs well at the Dispatch Box. The Labour Party is less loyal than the Conservative Party but it is also less brutal. So to say that Mrs Thatcher and Mr Foot are minority leaders is not to suggest that they lack the support of their followers or are at risk.

There is something unusual, nevertheless, about a pair of leaders in a two-party system of government who do not reflect the dominant tendencies within their parliamentary parties, who are potential or actual liabilities to their parties in the country, and who cannot be sure of the support of their senior colleagues on major issues of policy.

Mrs Thatcher and Mr Foot are the products of a decade of polarisation in British party politics. In that sense they deserve each other, although whether we deserve either of them is another question. In 1970 the Conservative Government, led by Mr Heath, moved quite sharply to the Right. There was little difference between his 'Selsdon period' and the Thatcherism which Mr Heath denounces today. The Conservative shift to the Right was one of the factors which contributed to the shift of the Labour Party to the Left from 1971.

That leftward shift, with its ratchet effects on the Labour Government which took office in 1974, helped to pave the way for Mrs Thatcher. Repudiating the Heathite middle way, which he had pursued from his 1972 U-turn until the debacle of February 1974, and repudiating by implication the whole of the Butler era of postwar Conservatism, the Conservative Party turned to a more passionately anti-Socialist leader.

A liberal tradition continued to run through British politics long after the demise of the Liberal Party. It was the basis for the consensual element in the two-party system. That liberal tradition was comfortably accommodated within Butlerian Conservatism and it was the success of that approach which helped to bring about the triumph of revisionism in the Labour Party in the late fifties. In 1964 the Labour Party led by Mr Harold Wilson captured the liberal-Left intelligentsia and the Labour Party remained the inheritor of the liberal tradition until Mrs Thatcher came along to break the image and smash the consensus.

In the 1979 election it was Mr Callaghan who offered the more conservative approach, steady and reassuring, while Mrs Thatcher preached her 'conviction politics', promising the country a radical alternative. Now, with Mr Foot in charge, we are to be offered the radical alternative to the radical alternative.

The process of polarisation is not quite complete, however, for Mr Benn – not Mr Foot – would be the opposite pole to Thatcherism; moreover, Mrs Thatcher is not wholly immune to the centripetal tugs of office, as the last few weeks have shown. Nevertheless, the election of Mr Foot to lead the Labour Party would seem to represent the final break in the old consensual mould of postwar British politics.

The old pattern has been broken in some other ways too. The generational gap between the two leaders is every bit as wide as the ideological chasm which lies between them. Mr Foot, like Mr Callaghan, is an old-fashioned figure; he is the political child of the thirties and formed his attitudes in the world of the slump and of the dictators. Mrs Thatcher is the political child of the forties and fifties; she is the first postwar British leader for whom the thirties had no direct significance. That marks her off. It leaves the Labour Party more associated with the past and closer to tradition than the Conservatives, a reversal of their usual roles.

Mr Foot is also an old-fashioned patriot. He wishes to see the European Communities Act repealed and full sovereignty restored to Parliament. That would be scarcely compatible with continuing membership of the EEC. When he was re-elected to the House of Commons 20 years ago he made his first speech on the subject of unilateral nuclear disarmament but his chief complaint was that British nuclear weapons could be used without the authority of Parliament. Now he has said that he would send the American cruise missiles home. Appeals to working-class patriotism or chauvinism used to be a Conservative stock in trade.

Mrs Thatcher's response to Mr Foot's accession was to make her clearest yet and most enthusiastic pro-European declaration. She said in Bonn that Britain was 'totally committed to Europe and the idea of the Common Market.' Having dealt with the problem of the budget for the time being she is now eager to play a leading political role within the Community; that is what her latest visits to Paris and Bonn have been about and that was what Lord Carrington was talking about in his important speech in Hamburg.

The Common Market continues to divide both of the parties. Mrs Thatcher was embarrassed on her return from Europe by a motion signed by 30 of her backbench anti-Marketeers. The European faction of the Labour Party remains strong enough to stop a Foot government taking Britain out of Europe.

There was a time when the country regarded the Conservatives as its natural leaders even if it didn't like them much. At least they knew how to run things. That cannot be said of Mrs Thatcher's Government. Sir Geoffrey Howe and Sir Keith Joseph, for example, do not look exactly as if born to lead; and nor does Mrs Thatcher have the air of a natural ruler although, like Mr Heath, she tries to make up for it with a bossy manner.

Ironically, Mr Foot is the one who was born to rule, coming as he does from a remarkable and distinguished family and having received the best of educations. Whether he would know how to rule, having until the age of 60 shown no interest in governmental responsibility, is altogether another matter. Putting the two parties side by side the conclusion might be that we have no masters now.

Neither of the two party leaders can have much confidence in the levers of power at their disposal. The Conservatives can no longer rely on the fear of God, the glory of empire or the love of country and have soon discovered that sterling M3 is no adequate substitute. Mrs Thatcher rode to power on a wave of excited expectations, promising to cut the taxes, bone up the defences and set the people free; now she faces the more traditional Conservative task of retaining the citizens' allegiance to the State while deflating their hopes, a task for which she no longer possesses the traditional tools.

Mr Foot is in a similar predicament. Socialism has been in intellectual decline for many years and no longer provides the moral cement of Labour's governmental authority. Through the sixties and seventies Labour rested its claim to competence largely upon the claim to a unique working relationship with the trade unions, whose co-operation or – at very least – acquiescence was seen to be essential to the ruling of the country. The fiasco of Mr Callaghan's last months exploded that claim. The co-operation of the unions, or rather of their members, is plainly in no way to be relied upon and, for the time being at least, any form of effective incomes policy appears to be out of the question.

Mrs Thatcher and Mr Foot both speak with the rhetoric of conviction. That will make them exciting opponents across the floor of the House of Commons and it will be fun to see who first gets the better of the other. But we should not be misled by this entertainment into thinking that 'conviction politics' are a substitute for a firm basis of governmental authority or that passion in advocacy is the same thing as strong or effective leadership.

A two-party system is supposed to produce a tendency towards consensus. In Britain's case that dynamic is reinforced by the first-past-the-post electoral system. Something has gone wrong with a two-party system which has thrown up Mrs Thatcher and Mr Foot at the same time. It shows that the parties themselves are too divided to uphold the consensus or have lost patience with it. The reason for that, presumably, is the accumulated frustration with economic failure.

Mrs Thatcher and Mr Foot present voters with a clearer choice between the parties but at the same time they narrow it – to Thatcherism or socialism. The politics of consensus are no longer on offer. There are still powerful forces within both of their parties seeking to restrain them and to pull them back towards the centre. But there is no guaranteeing that one more extreme government will not lead to another just as one more extreme leader has led to another.

An unwelcome choice encourages volatile and unpredictable behaviour – as we saw in America this year – but there is no need for a consensus in order to win an election. The question is whether the country can be effectively governed in its absence. The Thatcher–Foot era does not present an encouraging prospect.

Guardian, 26 November 1980

Even with the rhetoric of Thatcherism during the early 1980s Jenkins was one of the few journalists to note the change in the Government's policies from the summer of 1981 onwards when, in the face of mounting economic difficulties, 'punk monetarism', as it was sometimes referred to, was quietly abandoned. Whatever Thatcherism later became, the early flush of enthusiasm for strict monetary targets gradually faded and Jenkins rightly chose this moment to write the obituary of the first phase of the Thatcher Revolution.

A brief obituary of Thatcherism is now in order

Sir Geoffrey Howe's statement to the House yesterday was more interesting than it sounded. In his inimitably dull fashion he was announcing the major change which had occurred in the Government's economic policy.

The figures do not do justice to what has happened. Calculations can be done to show that the Government's fiscal posture remains resolutely deflationary, and the arithmetically gullible may even be persuaded that Sir Geoffrey's Medium Term Financial Strategy remains in force. The truth, however, is that political decisions have been made which will in time effectively rubbish the Government's declared policy.

Sir Geoffrey was in reality announcing the failure of the Treasury to obtain cuts on anything like the scale necessary to sustain his monetarist strategy. Attention, inevitably, will at first focus on his latest inflictions on the unemployed, on prescription charge-payers, and the purchasers of NHS teeth and specs. Small consolation to them that Sir Geoffrey is sending his monetary target for a burton and abandoning his prescribed borrowing limit. But for those who have hoped to see the monetarist heresy burn itself out, yesterday was a day for some rejoicing.

Arcane calculations can be made to show that the £5 billion increase in public expenditure for next year, when offset against a £3 billion revenue windfall, is compatible with the Chancellor's original and precious borrowing target. Nothing can make it compatible with what is happening to the M3 target, but be that as it may. Such economic arithmetic, however, fails to take account of the political reality. The Chancellor in his next Budget can scarcely avoid raising the income tax thresholds to cancel out a year's inflation. He failed to do it last year and this year will have to – or very nearly – on grounds of party politics, social justice and efficiency of revenue collection. That is goodbye to most of his revenue bonus. It is goodbye also to his borrowing target. In so far as he goes on to cut taxes – as he will be pressed to do with an election looming – the louder the goodbye to the PSBR target.

More important than the computations is what Ministers believe to have happened. Most of those who sat through the recent series of Cabinet and the committee meetings have little doubt that they have attended the funeral of the Government's original economic policy. The general opinion around Whitehall is that a considerable relaxation of fiscal and monetary policy will now flow from the political change of tune which has taken place.

Whether the Chancellor is fully aware of the change in his policy is not clear. By one description he is like a man strapped to the stake, blindfolded, the firing squad assembled and brought to attention, who realises that something is up but can't quite put his finger on what it is. The Prime Minister is said not to be afflicted by the same monetarist disorientation; with her economic convictions, no doubt, still intact, she has been showing distinct signs recently of political self-preservation. For example, the higher lunacy of the Treasury's proposed further onslaught against the local authorities received short shrift from her. She is also nagging daily about too-high interest rates.

The abandonment, in effect, of the Government's monetarist strategy leaves it heading towards an exchange rate policy as the next means of trying to control inflation. Accession to the European Monetary System can be expected in the New Year. Within the Treasury the argument rages between those who, including the Chancellor, see the EMS as a new instrument of discipline and those who see it as a cover for neo-Keynesian devaluations. The Chancellor's view, it is said, is that if you can't beat inflation with the British money supply you had better do it with the German money supply. But with an election due in less than two years, his view seems unlikely to prevail.

The revolt of the 'wets' – which stole the show at the Blackpool conference in October – may have contributed a little to the change in the Government's policy. The decisive factor, however, has been the repudiation of Treasury Ministers by influential non-wets, among them Mr John Nott and Mr John Biffen, and by Mrs Thatcher herself who has shown new impatience with the Treasury team's unpolitical view of the world.

The posture announced yesterday is ostensibly still deflationary and even when its political implications have worked through will by no means put the economy on an election-winning path. The prospects are for inflation remaining in double figures (yesterday's Treasury forecast of 10 per cent next year is a fraud) and for little, if any, reduction in unemployment. But at least the Government will be desisting from further worsening the recession which has devastated British manufacturing.

A brief obituary of Thatcherism is now in order. True monetarists may complain, and with some justice, that neither the Prime Minister nor the Chancellor were truly of their religion but rather supply-siders in disguise. Certainly, whereas Mr Denis Healey took a Napoleonic approach to the money religion, worshipping only when in the City, Sir Geoffrey persisted in a revivalist view, rejoicing at each instance of born-again entrepreneurship observable in Surrey. The trouble is, as Keynes might have warned them, that changing human nature is a long-term project and in the long term under their policies we would all be unemployed or bankrupt.

Guardian, 3 December 1981

CHAPTER FIVE

'From New Politics to Megalomania'

The Rise and Fall of the SDP

The new divisions of British politics provoked a renewed crisis in the two-party system. Those who felt that democracy should occupy the centreground of political discourse felt abandoned. Jenkins had argued in the mid-1970s that the answer for Britain was a coalition of the centre Left; he now argued that the Labour Party was being destroyed by extremism. As the dim outline of a new party emerged, and the realignment of British politics became a real possibility, Jenkins found a new political home, and a new political hero in the person of David Owen.

If Owen was to be the saviour of social democracy, then it was the appeal of Tony Benn to the old Labour Party which needed to be countered. The years 1980–81 witnessed the zenith of Bennism, and in this article Jenkins strove to portray Benn as a relic of history rather than as the harbinger of the future.

His greatest strength is that he is the champion of an aspiring élite against a discredited and dispirited ruling class

Mr Tony Benn is seen less often in the House of Commons these days but he is being heard all over the country. Three or four times a week he is down in the grassroots preaching his evangelical Socialist message, increasingly to trade union audiences. His chances of winning power for socialism or for himself at the hands of the Parliamentary Labour Party are minimal; that is why he spends so much of his time at Transport House or out in the sticks, fighting for the hearts and votes of the broader Labour movement.

His analysis is a startling one. He sees the country at the brink of an industrial abyss. Capitalism is ceasing to be compatible with parliamentary democracy; the ruling class no longer has effective means for containing either the strength of trade unionism or the spirit of equality as expressed through the ballot box.

Unable to govern, morally and intellectually bankrupted, the British ruling class has transferred its allegiance, almost treasonably, to the European Economic Community. At the same time capitalism in one country is ceasing to be possible and ruling classes everywhere are looking to supranational institutions, such as the IMF, for the authority they lack. What Mr Benn calls Democratic Socialism is the only means of resolving these contradictions and is therefore, in his opinion, inevitable.

There are two striking features of this analysis. The first is its similarity to a great deal of right-wing thinking, especially of the neo-conservative school in the United States. The second is that what Mr Benn is describing is a pre-revolutionary situation in an almost classical form.

Many who have departed the postwar political consensus to the Right have done so for the very reasons which have driven Mr Benn to the Left. They have concluded that the 'passion for equality' – Tocqueville's phrase is appropriate – is no longer compatible with liberal democracy; only two decades of rapid economic growth enabled it to remain so. The inability of the State to assuage the egalitarian appetites of the people is due to the power of the trade unions to impede production and the power of the ballot box to insist on ever higher levels of public expenditure.

Tocqueville attributed the demise of the *ancien regime* in France to the desire for equality. He gave two chief reasons for the coming of the Revolution – the persistence of obsolete privilege, which impaired the efficiency of the ruling class, and over-centralisation of government. Mr Benn's analysis is remarkably similar.

When Mr Edward Heath took Britain into the Common Market he 'lit the slow fuse to revolution.' Apparently Mr Benn later used this phrase in Cabinet, which must have irritated his colleagues. What he meant, it seems, is that if national governments no longer accepted responsibility for unemployment and slump they would find themselves without the basis for government by consent. The revolution would not necessarily mean all power to the shop stewards; indeed, more likely, there would first be a breakdown resulting in a, perhaps, Salazar-like near-dictatorship.

Mr Benn purports to see signs of this already and excites his audiences with claims that the Army, the security services and the Civil Service are already out of control while police repression is becoming an arm of industrial policy.

These latter points seem to me to be demagogic exaggerations but I would nevertheless not lightly dismiss Mr Benn's analysis. It was he who in 1975 coined the word 'de-industrialisation', and his warnings have come true with a vengeance.

They are underlined this week by the latest report from the Cambridge Economic Policy Group. Critics of Mr Benn's remedies (of which I am one) are inclined to ignore how closely his diagnosis resembles their own pessimistic prognostications. The strength of his political position is that it addresses the coming crisis head-on.

As to the shortcomings of his proposed cure, a critique of pure Bennery rests on two key points. One is that he sidesteps the trade union question and is unable to explain convincingly why his policies will produce a better industrial result in conditions of continuing liberty. The other is that his account of the democracy which he envisages has an ominous ring about it, again from the standpoint of liberty.

His economic position is often misunderstood. He is not interested in protection as a macro-economic device as advocated by Kaldor and Godley; for him it is no more than the necessary accompaniment to the regeneration of industry through a massive programme of State-funded investment. He is talking, as he always does, about socialism.

Questions about productivity tend to be brushed aside. He challenges the figures. The failure of the working class to work is a convenient alibi for a discredited ruling class. Capitalism has forced trade unions into a destructive role, obliged them to negotiate only for money wages. The implication is that things will be different under changed patterns of ownership and new power structures. That is the perennial hope of the Socialist millennialist.

The Bennite version of industrial democracy is, in effect, workers' control expressed through shop stewards' combines. He has no use for workers' representatives on boards. He seems to me to mistake the character of today's acquisitive collectivism, to ignore the problems of relating pay in the public services to the sectors where productivity can be measured and increased, and to underestimate the ability of the national trade union bureaucracies to impede progress in any direction.

Mr Benn has claimed often that he is a democrat first, a Socialist second. But what kind of democrat is he? Rejecting the authority both of the market and the ruling élite, he said in a recent lecture: 'We believe that the self-discipline of full democratic control offers our best hope for the future, and is the only real answer to inflation, because it confers real responsibility.' This sounds to me ominously like the doctrine that the will of the majority of the minority should prevail over the opinions of the greater majority. Mr Benn's proposals for 'democratising' the Labour Party point in the same direction, always towards more power for the activists.

And what if he is wrong about 'full democratic control' offering the 'only real answer to inflation'? And what if he is wrong in his belief that massive State investment programmes will halt Britain's industrial decline? And what again if he is wrong in his blithe claim that import controls could be negotiated with the rest of the world so as to avoid retaliation or isolation?

Nowhere in the world has socialism on the scale which Mr Benn envisages proved compatible with political freedom and socialism of his kind in one small island is a still more dubious prospect.

There are two great strengths to Mr Benn's position and one great weakness. His greatest strength is that he is the champion of an aspiring élite against a discredited and dispirited ruling class. On the rare occasions when the political map is changed it is often because some leader has arisen to articulate the aspirations of an emergent class or interest.

Mr Benn's appeal is to the meritocracy of the shop-floor level, to the burgeoning and growingly radicalised ranks of the public sector, to the lumpenintelligentsia of new university, polytechnic and comprehensive school; he is head boy of the class of '68.

His second strength is that there is a patriotic ring to his rhetoric. His prescription is for a kind of Socialist nationalism. Explaining his advocacy of trade protection he says things like 'it would mean waiting longer for a Toyota but less long for a hospital bed.'

The great weakness of Mr Benn's position is that there is no enthusiasm in the land for socialism. Class loyalty to the Labour Party remains strong but this seems to be more in spite of its residual socialism than because of it. All opinion surveys show that nationalisation is as massively unpopular as ever.

Mr Benn is preaching his version of Democratic Socialism at a time when nearly everywhere else in the Western industrialised world the Socialist era seems to be drawing to its close. Wherever it has been practised, although sadly not in Britain, Continental-style social democracy has been an immense success and has drawn the teeth of left-wing socialism.

The proletariat is a dwindling force in society and on its way to becoming not the vanguard but another minority group. The spirit of the times is acquisitive and once more individualistic, although these urges find their expression still through existing collectivities. The Socialist faith has been largely shattered by Stalin and the Gulag.

Mr Benn has taken a chance on history. He believes that events are working in his direction, that the coming collapse of British capitalism may bring with it his kind of socialism and his kind of workers' power. Maybe he will be right.

But the sight of Mr Benn speaking around the country with all of his passion and elegance, making news and drawing large audiences wherever he goes, reminds me of another politician who believed that destiny had beckoned to him. I mean Mr Enoch Powell, the man who finished up a prophet without a party.

Guardian, 19 March 1980

The crisis in the Labour Party came to a head at the Labour special conference held at Wembley on 24 January 1981. The Gang of Three – Shirley Williams, Bill Rodgers and David Owen – had been considering their position for months. The constitutional reforms carried in the name of party democracy were countered by the social democrats with demands for the system of direct election by the membership. The result was changes in the Labour Party which would elect the leader through an electoral college made up of 40 per cent trade union, 30 per cent constituency parties, and 30 per cent Parliamentary Labour Party, a formula shifting power decisively away from the more moderate PLP. Reselection of MPs within the lifetime of each parliament was also made mandatory. Finally, and perhaps more damagingly from a policy perspective, the manifesto of the Party would henceforth be written by the Bennite-dominated National Executive Committee of the Party. This change would ensure that at the next election the Party would be committed to the alternative economic strategy, withdrawal from the EEC, and unilateral nuclear disarmament. It was, as Austen Mitchell was to say, the longest political suicide note in history. It was this mixture of institutional and policy reform which taken together convinced the social democrats that the Labour Party was beyond redemption. Their response to the Wembley Conference was the Limehouse Declaration which, as Jenkins correctly identified, led inexorably to the formation of the SDP.

The muddle that ended in a leap in the dark

The special conference at Wembley on Saturday was a threefold disaster for the Labour Party. It provided a perfect moment for yesterday's launching of a new Social Democratic Party. It opted for a constitutional reform which for all the world looked like bringing the Labour Party under trade union control. It humiliated Mr Michael Foot before he had had a proper chance to show that he was something more than a lame-duck caretaker of a leader.

The 'Limehouse Declaration', as it may come to be known, does not exactly launch a new party, but it commences a countdown which will now be immensely difficult to stop. A new party has been launched in all but name and organisational form. At least 10 MPs are expected to support the call and they will most likely decide to form themselves into a Social Democratic Group in the House of Commons.

If so, they will ask the Speaker to recognise them as such and allow them to express their views on major questions. The Council for Social Democracy which is to be established in the country will be the embryo of a national party organisation. A manifesto is likely to be published within a few weeks. In due course Mr William Rodgers will resign from the Shadow Cabinet and Mrs Williams from the National Executive Committee.

One of the MPs who will be declaring himself today or tomorrow said that he regarded the step as a 'judicial separation': he expected divorce to follow in due course. The impression is that most of those taking part would be quite happy to be expelled from the Party but otherwise will continue to take the Whip until it suits them to resign it, and their Party membership, by July at the latest. Nothing short of a declaration of independence by the Parliamentary Labour Party is likely to persuade them to continue the fight from within.

Whatever the electoral fortunes of the breakaways over the next few years, it is probable that the events of this weekend will become a milestone in the realignment of British party politics which is now in progress. Wembley, coming after Blackpool, marked what seems to be a decisive stage in the disintegration of the Labour movement as we know it.

The defections to a new Social Democratic Party are by no means the sole measure of this. Those who are quitting are the tip of a despairing iceberg and many more MPs will either join the defectors later, run as independents if reselected in their seats, or start looking for new careers outside politics altogether. Moreover, the schism in the Party is now carrying over into the trade union movement, which in time could itself split along the same political line.

While the Bennite Left was celebrating its brilliant tactical victory at Wembley, many other MPs, including several members of the Tribune Group, were to be found ruing the day which had produced at least the public appearance of a trade union takeover of the Party. What exactly happened is more complicated than that, but the adverse electoral impact of an arrangement which gives the unions the largest say in the election of the parliamentary leader could well prove disastrous. The unions have long been unpopular with the voters and one of Labour's strongest claims to office, at least until the 1979 'winter of discontent', was its superior ability to cope with them.

What happened at Wembley was not the result of a deliberate takeover bid, rather it was the product of an unholy alliance between left-wing singlemindedness and trade union incompetence. If the unions have extended their empire as a result it was done in a fit of muddle-mindedness.

There was no majority for the constitutional amendment adopted at Wembley on Saturday, only a majority against all other alternatives.

The only reason the principle of an electoral college was agreed at Blackpool in October was as a stratagem for heading off a college based on an unacceptable formula.

Some trade unionists – and Mr Clive Jenkins was one of them – have had no qualms about extending direct trade union control over the Party, but other prime movers in the affair, notably Mr David Basnett, believed themselves to be engaged in saving the Labour Party and were tragically unable to see that they were being duped into a process which would destroy its independence.

The scales fell from Mr Basnett's eyes at around four o'clock on Saturday – too late. Mr Jenkins had taken him to the cleaners and made him look a fool. 'I think David has rumbled Clive at last,' said one of Mr Basnett's advisers, somewhat wearily. Not only was Mr Basnett duped, and duped from the very day he initiated the commission of inquiry and embarked along the fatal road which led via Bishop's Stortford to Blackpool and Wembley; so was Mr Callaghan and so was, most humiliatingly of all, Mr Michael Foot.

For it was Mr Jenkins, and Mr Moss Evans, with Mr Basnett as usual in tow, who so strenuously urged Mr Foot to reconsider his decision not to seek the leadership of the Labour Party and helped to persuade him that he uniquely could hold the Party together. Yet there he was on Saturday, less than three months later, ditched by his friends – a dejected figure, the Party splitting before his eyes.

What happened on Saturday made it perfectly plain that Mr Jenkins was hand in glove with Mr Benn. Members of the executive council of the Union of Shop, Distributive and Allied Workers had been facing re-election and, in a muddled fashion, had opted for the 40:30:30 formula. They intended, however, to shift their vote as soon as their own proposal was defeated and to back the formula proposed by Mr Basnett and supported by Mr Foot. This was the one which would have given MPs 50 per cent of the votes.

By moving their supporters in behind the USDAW motion, Mr Jenkins and Mr Benn ensured that the union could not escape the hook on which it had impaled itself. NUPE and the TGWU were made to realise that defeating the NEC's 33:33:33 formula was the only way of achieving the defeat of the Basnett 50 per cent. It was a brilliant piece of manoeuvring, the only clues to which were the open Bennite support for what was not most obviously the most left-wing solution (although it was the most anti-parliamentarian) and its endorsement in the Labour Party's Trotskyist paper, *The Militant*.

Not only was Mr Basnett left standing, so were left-wingers such as Mr Eric Heffer and Mr Neil Kinnock. Mr Heffer hadn't a clue what was going on and after the first ballot came down to the press table to complain that the Left had botched it and handed the victory to the Basnett camp.

What happened at Wembley was exactly the kind of floor manoeuvre I have seen at several American political conventions. There was nothing particularly reprehensible about it but it amply demonstrated how eminently unsuitable is a nominating convention for the election of a leader in a system of parliamentary and Cabinet government.

The style and the ruthlessness of this coup will have consequences other than the favourable launch it gives to the Williams–Owen–Rodgers–Jenkins enterprise. It means the ending of the alliance called Trade Unionists for a Labour Victory in which Mr Basnett and Mr Clive Jenkins sat side by side as colleagues. It could give a bit more impetus to an emerging group of politically right-wing unions within the Labour Party and the TUC.

After what happened at Wembley it will be interesting to see whether Mr Basnett can swallow his resentments over the Isle of Grain dispute and enter into a more natural political alliance with the AUEW and Mr Frank Chapple's EEPTU. Mr Chapple is talking about balloting his membership on continuing Labour Party affiliation. The others will not go that far, but it is within their combined power to purge the NEC and reverse most of the Blackpool conference decisions.

Inside the Party we are likely to see a more clearly defined split on the Left. Mr Heffer, Mr Kinnock and their friends (known these days as the 'inside left') are ready to consolidate the gains they have made and rally behind the leadership of Mr Foot. They fear that further gains by the Bennites (the 'outside left') will jeopardise the chances of electoral victory. However, the tide in the constituencies will not be easily stemmed. A good few Tribunites are coming under Militant pressure in their local parties as the reselection process gets under way. Mr Benn, for his part, has declared that his next objectives will be to bring the manifesto under the power of the conference, to elect the Cabinet, and to bring councillors under the same Party control as MPs.

Mr Foot was elected leader as the man to keep the Party together as opposed to Mr Healey who was seen as the man who might bring it to the point of split. Mr Foot has now presided over both the split and the rape of the PLP. At the same time his standing in the public eye (as recorded by the Gallup Poll) has sunk to a record low with the exception of Mr Edward Heath's in 1967.

After what happened at Wembley, confidence will be low in Mr Foot's ability to mobilise the unions behind a steadying operation. Nor are some of his policy circles easily squared. In a series of interviews in the last few days he has not succeeded either in explaining how unilateral and multilateral nuclear disarmament are compatible policies, or his plan for getting out of the Common Market without actually leaving. He might find it even more difficult to explain how he proposes to give an international lead in disarmament while breaking partnership with the European Allies.

The weakness of Mr Foot's position many mean that Mr Healey will feel able, if not obliged, to exert himself as deputy leader. If he does, that will mean the old game of trying to fix the block votes in time for the next conference. Perhaps he may succeed where both Mr Callaghan and Mr Foot failed. At best it is a chancy game although there is no other obvious way of recouping what has been lost to the Left.

The two longer-range questions are: what are the prospects for a Social Democratic–Liberal Alliance (which is what Mr David Steel would like it to be called), and could Labour win an election on a left-wing programme and under left-wing control?

Mrs Williams, Mr Rodgers and Dr Owen are making a brave leap in the dark. The odds have to be against their success and yet there is a feel in the political air which is favourable to their enterprise. As long as Mrs Williams is prominent among their number they will not be easily dubbed as traitors in the eyes of Labour voters, whatever may be said of them at Westminster. In putting as Dr Owen said 'country before party' they have also put it before their own careers and ambitions.

Labour leaders officially pooh-pooh the chances of their winning seats at the next election, but they take an entirely serious view of the damage they could do to Labour's chances. Moreover, these leaders know quite well the extent to which traditional Labour voters have become alienated from the existing party system.

As for the Left, its victories have not been brought about by accident. Something resembling a 'vanguard party' (which was the Leninist concept) has grown up within the Labour Party and is aspiring to power. The Left constitutes a minority, but it is a powerful minority and believes itself to be the true majority, the true vehicle of the working class.

In a period of economic decline and growing social dislocation, and in which old political patterns are breaking up, conditions may prove favourable to a realignment of party politics on the centre Left or equally to the capture of power by the Left. We have all of us moved into unknown territory and there is no clear vision of what the future will resemble.

Guardian, 26 January 1981

Peter Jenkins's enthusiasm for the new party shines through his early journalism about the prospects for the SDP and the chances of 'breaking the mould'. For a few months after the Limehouse Declaration it seemed that anything was possible; the new party was launched on a tidal wave of media interest and unprecedented public support – if the opinion polls were to be believed. Besides the Gang of Three, 12 Labour MPs declared themselves for the new party and speculation abounded as to who else was just about to join. Neither the media hype nor the public support lasted very long, and Jenkins spotted the hazards of founding a new party on little else but goodwill in this, his first piece on the new party.

It will need a lot of luck but it could just work

In the few weeks since the fateful Labour Party conference at Wembley the embryonic Social Democratic Party has become the focus of political attention. Everybody seems to be talking about it. The public response as measured by the opinion polls has been astonishing and without precedent. Its opponents in the established parties are no longer sneering or laughing; rather they are addressing themselves to the challenge in deadly earnest.

The breakaway from the Labour Party which became formal and

final on Monday is no sudden aberration. The Wembley conference in January was merely the trigger for a fission which had been building up for some time. The 12 who have gone (and others will be following or will be driven after them) had come to the conclusion that the way forward to a social democracy on the Continental model had been finally closed.

For years British politics have been striving towards the kind of realignment which may' now at last be taking place. The two-party system has been in decline since 1951 and through the sixties and seventies it became increasingly unable to produce strong, stable or effective governments. Demographic changes and changes in voting behaviour look as if they will make it still more difficult in the future to produce legitimate majority governments.

The decline of the Labour Party has been even more marked. At the last General Election its share of the votes cast was down to 37 per cent from 48.8 per cent in 1951. Ivor Crewe, of Essex University, has reckoned that by 1979 only one in 10 voters could be counted as staunch Labour loyalists compared with one in five in 1964. The manual working class is declining as a class but the erosion of support for Labour within that class is even more striking. The Labour Party has become increasingly alienated from the working class; by 1979 (according to Crewe's researches) only a third of the manual working class supported nationalisation or higher social spending.

Conventional wisdom is not to be relied upon in assessing the prospects for the new Social Democratic Party. That wisdom is rooted in the conventional party system and it is this which is being undermined by social and political change. For example, it is said that the two-party system effectively prevents the success of a third party. Yes, but only for as long as there is an effective two-party system. It is said that the new party will flounder in the proverbial loyalty and class solidarity of the Labour vote. Maybe, but that has been in the process of disintegration for a couple of decades.

It is said that the opinion polls are registering no more than a middle-of-the-term protest, a flash in the pan of the kind which has from time to time excited Liberal hopes. But this is unlikely to be so. In 1962, the year of Orpington, one opinion poll put the Liberal vote at more than 30 per cent; this year six polls have all put a Social Democratic–Liberal alliance in a lead over the two established parties. The three most recent ones give it more than 40 per cent of the vote.

That is quite without precedent; something is up.

The opinion polls also show that an electoral alliance with the Liberals is absolutely imperative if the two-party stranglehold is to be broken. The prospects for such an alliance have improved greatly in the last few weeks. The polls themselves may be largely responsible for this. Opinion in the Liberal Party has moved strongly in favour of an alliance with the new party. That policy now looks as if it will be carried overwhelmingly at the Liberal Party Assembly in September.

There is going to be some jockeying for position as the leading 'third party' in the system and, later on, some tough bargaining on the ground, but an effective electoral alliance now looks more probable than not.

Conventional wisdom dwells upon the importance of policy and organisation but what the new party needs above all is the capacity to win. It needs credibility of the kind which the Liberals have never quite managed to achieve. The Liberals always do better under the Tories and their revival is now in full swing. The latest Gallup poll puts them round about where they were in February 1974 when with more than 19 per cent of the votes they won only 14 seats.

The first-past-the-post electoral system starts to yield seats when a party wins more than a quarter of the votes. On their own the Liberals have never been able to make that breakthrough and the expectation that they will fail deters people from 'wasting' their votes. The polls are now showing clearly that a vote for a Social Democratic–Liberal alliance would not be a wasted vote. If the electorate gets that message the electoral barriers of the two-party system can be smashed.

The new party will call itself the Social Democratic Party and some of its leaders are still using the word 'Socialist'. They are hoping to be admitted to the Socialist International. They may be right to insist on a distinctive identity and it is natural that they should hanker after a continuity with their Labour past. What is likely to emerge, however, is a non-Socialist party of the Left which will incorporate some of the values of the Socialist era, just as that era incorporated some of the values of 19th-century Liberalism and radicalism.

They would probably be wise not to put themselves forward as another Labour Party or a Labour Party in exile. The public doesn't like the word 'socialism' and the people who are launching the new party are not in any meaningful sense Socialists. The party is likely to stand for broadly liberal economic policies (Keynesian liberal, that is) combined with more collectivist social goals. To say that this was the formula which was tried and failed is to forget the extent of which Labour governments have been institutional prisoners of the Labour movement as well as encumbered by old-fashioned ideological baggage.

The Social Democratic Party does not propose to accept institutional affiliations from the trade unions or anyone else. Unlike Labour governments, it will not be bound to do something silly as the price of doing something sensible. For the mixed economy to be managed by a party committed to its success (rather than to changing its mix) would be a novelty in British politics.

That is one reason why proportional representation is becoming an issue of importance. Surprisingly, this arcane subject is becoming a matter of interest, almost a cause, among younger people. The debates in the Labour Party about democracy, the cynical misuse of that word and the travesties of the block voting at Labour conferences may have played a part in exciting interest in electoral reform.

The Liberal Party was never able to make much progress on this because its case sounded too much like special pleading or an admission that it was impossible to win under the existing rules of the game. The Social Democratic Party, with its greater credibility in alliance with the Liberals, may succeed in making proportional representation into the keystone of its programme for democratic reform, the symbol of its break from the old corrupt and ossified patterns.

The most conventional wisdom of all says that the new party will get nowhere because it lacks grassroots organisation. This is the endless refrain from those who seek to exalt the indispensability of the party worker, that hero of the doorstep on a wet Saturday night, if only in order to lay his claim to a controlling power over the elected representative of the people. The argument is sentimental and bogus.

Party organisation is of less and less importance in winning elections; the national campaign in the media and the personality of the local candidate count for far more. In any case, the Labour Party has no armies of the doorsteps any more and when it comes to putting up candidates the new party is not likely to be short of enthusiastic volunteers. In the United States, the decline of party opened the way to new styles of electoral politics, of which George McGovern and Jimmy Carter were the exponents, and the same sort of thing could happen here.

Many hazards stand in the way of the new party. It may strike the electorate as too élitist and London-based. Voters may perceive the armies of capital and labour as too powerful and deeply entrenched to permit the development of a new politics. The new party may make the mistake of playing the old game when it should be playing the new one, overloading itself with trendy policies or replicating the bureaucratic organisations of the major parties.

Tribal allegiances to class-based parties combined with the first-past-the-post electoral system may yet prove too strong for it. There is the possibility too that by election time the centreground may be looking somewhat overcrowded although it is more probable that the Labour Party is too far gone to obey the centripetal forces of two-party politics.

At the moment, however, conditions are eminently favourable for the launching of the new Social Democratic Party. Only six weeks ago few were predicting that as many as a dozen MPs would dare to make the break, few imagined the scale and the enthusiasm of the public response, and the difficulties of making the indispensable pact with the Liberal Party seemed greater than they now do.

Public disillusion with the two parties and their leaders continues to grow. Labour is failing to benefit from the incompetence and unpopularity of the Government. The leaders of the new party stand high in the public's esteem. Mr David Steel and Mrs Shirley Williams are the two most popular political figures in the land. A sense of excitement and even of fun is developing around the new enterprise. It will need a lot of luck – such as the right kind of by-election at the right moment – but it could just work.

Guardian, 18 October 1980

The political fallout from the launch of the SDP infected not only Westminster but also Fleet Street. Political allegiance going back generations were shattered as much among journalists as politicians and voters. In an unusual and candid essay Jenkins surveyed the ideological wreckage in Fleet Street, and also came out publicly as a member of the new party. But as the article makes clear, he was embracing the SDP as much out of desperation as of hope.

Fleet Street's political map redrawn

These are exciting and bitter times. The political earth seems to be shaking and friends are falling out as at no time since Suez. The Social Democrats and the Socialists have quarrelled and the left-wing Socialists are all quarrelling among themselves. Meanwhile, there are three million unemployed in the land and some of them are getting angry. Other people are getting angry because they aren't getting angry enough. How is it that the news can be bad simultaneously for capitalism and socialism?

Tempers are warm because just as socialism at long last seemed to be laying hold of the Labour Party the Social Democrats defected and the Tribunites began to fall apart. Once again the jaws of victory were spitting out their prey. No wonder there is rancour and mutual recrimination in the air. Even at Mr Michael Foot's last birthday party, a happy occasion reserved to oldest and dearest friends, a flaming row broke out – the subject: Benn. It is the same wherever men and women of politics and letters gather together.

Newspaper offices are no exception. The mould of two-party journalism is breaking. Down at the House of Commons the party hacks prefer the newspaper hacks to be identifiable, each a Labour hack or a Tory hack. Mr Michael Jones of the *Sunday Times*, on joining the Lobby, was quizzed by a Conservative Party press officer. 'Come on,' the man said, 'of course you must be Labour – you used to be an industrial correspondent.' It was simpler that way: there were two sides and everyone played to the rules.

It was the same at the BBC. Central Casting (Current Affairs) had us all in its ideological card index. With dear Bill Hardcastle in the centre, on his left Peter Jenkins, on his right Peregrine Worsthorne; on his left Alan Watkins, on his right Andrew Alexander. Mr Ronald Butt tells the story of how, on such a programme, he was asked why Sir Alec Douglas Home had postponed the 1963 General Election. He replied: 'Because if he were to have it now, he would lose.' The producer was not pleased, his balance was upset – Butt had been cast as the Conservative.

Indeed, until recently, you could say that the BBC *was* the centre party, the impresario of the consensus with a national monopoly in moderation, and we were all shaded nicely into its spectrum. Now all that has changed too: the centre has become hotly contentious and highly political, moderates have had to be recast as extremists and the BBC, always a bit scared of its political paymasters, is having to take account of the fact that the old parties loathe the SDP and its Liberal allies more than they loathe each other. It is obliged, at the same time, to balance Tory 'wet' against Thatcherite and Labour Right against two brands of Left.

At the *Guardian* it is a bit like Waterloo Station with people coming and going carrying their own ideological baggage. As I was making my own exit from the Labour Party, our Features Editor, Mr Richard Gott, was coming in the other door from the revolutionary Left. Down at the House of Commons our Political Editor, Mr Ian Aitken, remains on the Foot-ite Left of the Labour Party but two out of five of our leader-writing staff have gone over to the SDP.

The Correspondence Editor is on the Left but not a member of a political party. The letters column is under the control of an editor, Mr Peter Preston, who has never taken out a party card. He is pursued down the editorial corridors by the spectre of Mr Benn and the ghost of C. P. Scott which is, perhaps, enough to keep any man straight.

Under the *ancien regime* the lines between party politics and political journalism were always somewhat blurred. Mr Hugh (now Lord) Cudlipp, as editor of the *Daily Mirror*, would translate the Labour Party manifesto into English prose. The old *Daily Herald* seconded a journalist to carry Sir Harold Wilson's bags. The Conservative Central Office has customarily provided indoor relief for superannuated Lobby Correspondents of the *Daily Telegraph*, employing them as press officers.

Now questions are being asked. The advent of the SDP has upset the old game and nobody quite knows what the rules are any more. A recent editorial in *The Times* warned editors to be on their guard against too great a commitment among their political journalists and urged them to remove the possibility of 'perceived bias'. But in political journalism one man's 'perceived bias' is another man's honesty of opinion.

Some Labour Party journalists now complain about the activities of SDP members – Mr Anthony Sampson, for example – when not a word was said when he was thought to be a Labour Party sympathiser. Mr Anthony Howard, back with the *Observer*, when I consulted him on the matter, made joining the Labour Party sound like something you should do in your youth and joining the SDP like leaving your wife for a young mistress. He wouldn't join the Labour Party, he assured me, if he wasn't already a member.

The Times thought that editors ought not to belong to political parties but many do. Sir William Rees-Mogg was a Conservative and, indeed, is said once to have said he would consider himself a failure if not a member of a Conservative Cabinet by the age of 40. Instead he became editor of *The Times*, which was the next best thing, perhaps.

Most political journalists do have political allegiances or affiliations. Mr Mike Molloy, editor of the *Daily Mirror*, is a Labour Party card-carrier himself and most of his senior staff are engaged in Labour Party politics or, in a few cases, now the SDP. He sees nothing at all wrong in this although his star columnist, Mr Keith Waterhouse, himself as Labour and pie and peas, likes to regard journalists as 'ragamuffins' who have no more business, he says, joining political parties than actors have joining national theatres.

Sir Robin Day belongs to no party but claims to have given invaluable advice to them all. Mr Alan Watkins of the *Observer* is not a Labour Party member but he attributes this chiefly to laziness. Mr Hugo Young, the political editor and columnist of the *Sunday Times*, says that he had never joined a political party because he would have too great a difficulty deciding which. I remember a conversation with a former political editor of the BBC in a restaurant at Brighton in which he said that it would be grossly improper for him to reveal to me his opinion on the subject of capital punishment.

There is not much connection that I can see between commitment and involvement. Party membership is a poor guide to voting behaviour among political commentators. Mr Henry Fairlie, the leading Conservative commentator of his day, supported Gaitskell against Macmillan in the 1959 General Election. Mr Ronald Butt, then writing in the *Financial Times*, left the readers of his column in little doubt that he believed the country needed a Labour government in 1964.

At the 1979 election I was unable to summon any enthusiasm for the re-election of Mr Callaghan's Government after its 'winter of discontent' although I had been generally sympathetic to his Prime Ministership. Sir William Rees-Mogg's valedictory editorial bequeathed the nation, and *The Times*, to social democracy.

Lady Falkender (née Marcia) once said – and not without some justice – that while Labour journalists seemed always to be leaning over backwards to be fair to the Conservative Party, Conservative journalists also seemed always to be leaning over backwards to be fair to the Conservative Party. What she might also have said was that there are a great many more Labour sympathisers working for the Tory press than there are Conservative sympathisers working for the fewer number of pro-Labour papers.

Political journalists are adept at scoring own goals, and seem to enjoy it as much as shooting at the other side. From what used to be regarded as the right wing of the Conservative Party, Mr Peregrine Worsthorne turns regularly on Mrs Thatcher; no one could ever accuse him of toeing anyone's party line. For a long while Mr Butt and Mr Edward Heath were scarcely on speaking terms.

Recently, two Conservative journalists, both of them on the Conservative Party's candidates list, Mr Godfrey Barber of the *Daily Telegraph* and Mr Keith Raffan of the *Daily Express*, led the pack in rubbishing the Conservative candidate in the Crosby by-election. It was put about that this was due to sour grapes, they having failed to be selected for the seat themselves; the reporters on the spot, however, were of the opinion that justice had been done by honest reporters.

It seems to me that there is no need to become pompous about all this or to prescribe elaborate rules. There is no such thing as objective journalism, only fair and honest journalism. Reporters usually prefer good stories to party lines and commentators like to get things right and not fall for propaganda. Nobody but a political animal would engage in political journalism and most who do it know how to live with honour in the no-man's land between the jungles of party politics and the media.

Where I stand is not exactly a secret. Mr Watkins in his *Observer* column has most kindly absolved me from explaining myself on the grounds that he can detect in me no signs of political ambition. He is correct about that. I can detect no signs of political ambition in him either, although in Fulham he may still be remembered as Councillor Watkins.

For the record, nevertheless, I allowed my subscription to the Labour Party to lapse at the beginning of last year and wrote out an admittedly somewhat larger cheque to the SDP. Occasionally I have given my friends there the dubious benefit of my advice but it is seldom asked; it is available to friends in all parties and, in any case, most of what I have to say, and sometimes rather more, is to be found in this column on Wednesdays.

It is not my practice to engage in local political activity on the grounds that I have quite enough of that sort of thing without doing it in the evenings or at weekends. My wife, Ms Polly Toynbee, who is a member of the SDP's National Steering Committee, intends to put up for the Lambeth Borough Council. That is her affair and I shall go canvassing on her behalf if weather permits. I expect, in the fullness of time, to become the Denis Thatcher of the SDP.

In changing my party card I don't believe I've changed my politics much. I had hoped to see the Labour Party become a non-Socialist party of the Left, more on the model of Continental social democracy. I don't believe the country will take to left-wing socialism, nor prosper from it, and I can't see how the Labour Party has much of a future as the political tool of the unions.

For a long while now I have been writing about decline and pointing out how the failure to arrest it encourages a polarisation which denies the country what it probably most wants, namely moderate government from the left of centre. In other countries this is usually what works best too. Thatcherism and Bennism are the twin disorders of decline.

Is the SDP the perfect cure? Of course it isn't. I see no new dawn, rather a prolonged period of political instability with no clear outcome. I remain pessimistic about the prospect of arresting and reversing our decline. However, because it seems to me that the Labour movement is no longer a desirable or viable instrument of government I shall hope, although without much confidence, to see its effective replacement on the left of centre. For the same reasons I would welcome the emergence of an overtly left-wing Socialist party, seeking power on its merits and finding constitutional expression through a proportionately elected parliament.

That, more or less, is what I think. Readers of this column know how I look at things and where I stand and if they don't like it they can shop elsewhere. Everybody else can shut up until the revolution comes.

Guardian, 8 March 1982

As it turned out, the hopes Jenkins had placed in the SDP were confounded by the resilience of the two-party system. After peaking at the 1983 election in terms of its share of the popular vote (coming within 2 per cent of Labour) in alliance with the Liberals, the SDP never made a real breakthrough in terms of seats. With its tiny number of MPs in Parliament the public face of the SDP increasingly became that of David Owen. Jenkins had considerable admiration for the political skills of David Owen and was personally close to him throughout the 1983 parliament. He broke with Owen after the SDP failed to break through again at the 1987 election and the Party was plunged into internecine warfare reminiscent of the old Labour Party over the issue of merger with the Liberals.

From one-man band to megalomaniac

This political season opens unusually with a funeral. The SDP is dead. A pity though that it could not have been given a decent burial. It deserved better than the unseemly scenes now being enacted in Portsmouth. For in its lifetime it drew support from large numbers of people who had recoiled in repugnance from party politics as conducted in the 1970s and early 1980s. Innocent and too fastidious perhaps they were, those apolitical 'virgins' who responded to the Limehouse Declaration: politics is a rough and dirty business. But they were entitled to expect that when their leaders regressed into mutual hatred and recrimination the brawl would be about something, about power if not principle. Fighting with knives about nothing is the lowest form of political life.

The SDP only ever had one real hope of succeeding. Roy Jenkins at the outset likened it to an 'experimental plane'. A better image might have been a one-stage booster rocket. The Liberal Party, that perennial vehicle of protest, had prospered moderately in the turmoil and disillusion of the 1970s but nobody could seriously suppose that the Liberals were going to form a government or, if they did, would know how to govern. Everyone knew that a Liberal vote was a 'wasted vote'. But maybe, just perhaps, a new party, formed by real politicians with Cabinet experience, could bring to third-party politics the credibility it had lacked hitherto.

That always depended primarily upon the Labour Party. For the Tories were never going to make room for a third party, but if Labour remained determined to lose it was conceivable that an alternative non-Socialist, progressive party could establish itself in the left centreground of party politics. That chance effectively came and went in 1983. With Michael Foot for leader, its policies miles from the people, Labour was unelectable. The new Liberal–SDP Alliance came within two whiskers of relegating it into third place. But the reward for 26 per cent of the votes was 3 per cent of the seats in the House of Commons.

Having fought one election as two parties with two leaders – a bewildering arrangement – and having failed in the most propitious circumstances to lift off, it was improbable the same arrangement would prove more successful on a second occasion unless the Labour Party could be relied upon to do still worse. It was obvious therefore, after 11 June, that neither the Alliance nor the SDP as an entity had an electoral future under the existing voting system.

That was the reality which had to be faced. For those who could not stomach merger with the Liberals, either for policy reasons or because they couldn't stomach Liberals, it was time to go home or move elsewhere. In David Owen's case an honourable and dignified course would have been to have gone on speaking his mind in Parliament as an independent social democrat. Once the members of the SDP had shown in a ballot their preference for merger over continuing separate identity there was no honourable, dignified or rational alternative to bowing to the inevitable.

The alternative which Dr Owen is pressing upon the party conference today is a fraudulent prospectus. There is no room for a fourth party in the British two-party system. There is not enough room for a third party. An Owen party consisting of himself and two MPs can have no electoral future whatsoever. The Owenite claim to be the exponents of a 'new politics' is nonsense. There is no possibility of practising 'multi-party politics' under the British system.

The claim to be the one true voice of social democracy is also bogus. Social democracy is not a sectarian creed. It is a broad approach to politics, one shared by some in the Labour Party and more in the Liberal Party. The Liberals may be unsound on defence, maverick in other respects, but the decision was to see what could be done in uniting the two parties. Those who do not like the result must shop elsewhere.

Dr Owen has no title to the SDP. The result of the ballot cannot reasonably be construed as a vote for 'amicable separation'. SDP members were asked whether they favoured the idea of merger or not and a majority said they did. They were not asked if they would support Dr Owen splitting the Party to set up one of his own.

He hasn't a leg to stand on in his bunker. But there he is, surrounded by a last-ditch entourage, inventing new schemes for the confounding of his enemies and moving imaginary armies on the map. The bitterness of defeat seems to have got the better of his judgement. The virtuoso one-man band performance which in the last parliament made him the most impressive politician in the country after Margaret Thatcher has degenerated into a display of megalomania.

It happens that I agree with Dr Owen about nuclear weapons and on other matters. I share his low opinion of the Liberal Party. But the politics of sectarian fantasy are even less attractive. There are – or, rather, were – 23 per cent of the people who wish to vote for a third party. They should be allowed the best possible opportunity to do so.

Independent, 31 August 1987

CHAPTER SIX

'Taking Leave of Our Senses'

The Heyday of Thatcherism

On the night of 2 April 1982 Argentine armed forces invaded the Falkland Islands. The British Government was caught by surprise and Mrs Thatcher, after recalling Parliament for a stormy Saturday debate, took the enormous political gamble of sending a task force 8,000 miles to reoccupy the Islands, by force if necessary. The political repercussions of the Argentine invasion included the resignation of the entire Foreign Office ministerial team and the transformation of Mrs Thatcher's standing in the polls. It also accelerated the slow recovery of the Government's fortunes which had begun in the last months of 1981.

Jenkins's principled opposition to Mrs Thatcher's Falklands adventure was rare in Fleet Street. In his Falklands pieces he combined a dispassionate analysis of the strategic shortcomings of the Falklands operation with a heartfelt rejection of the dominant mood of jingoism. He also put the events into an historical perspective by attacking both the Establishment's obsession with the supposed lesson of Munich and its long-running failure to face up to the reality of Britain's impoverished world role.

Taking leave of our senses

One has to keep pinching oneself. A week ago we were in Brussels listening to some bellicose talk about Britain's contribution to the EEC Budget. Mrs Thatcher wasn't going to stand for any degressivity from the perfidious French. She didn't want to fight but, by jingo, if she had to, she'd fight on the pastures, in the cornfields and cowsheds of

149

Europe. It was thought somewhat eccentric, although typically enough British, when Lord Carrington – on his way to Israel – flew home to make a statement in the Lords about the Falkland Islands. The Falkland Islands!

In underlining the total unimportance of these faraway dots on the map one does not wish to show unconcern for the fate of their unfortunate, but happily few, inhabitants nor to condone aggression or give comfort to dictators, 'tin pot' or otherwise. Yet I could hardly believe my ears listening to the Commons debate last Saturday. Nearly everyone seemed to have taken leave of his senses.

By what gigantic lack of proportion was the loss of the Falkland Islands to be seen as a major national humiliation? How could it be seriously said that this was the gravest international crisis since the war? By what weird calculus was it reckoned that the fate of all free peoples might hinge upon the fate of these 1,800 islanders and their 600,000 sheep?

The indignity – surely a better word than humiliation – of being outwitted by the Argentinians in the 20- or 30-year-old game of bluff which has been going on over these insignificant territories, left over not only from the British Empire but from its Spanish predecessor, brought to the surface every harboured grievance and suppressed fantasy. The Foreign Office was a nest of traitors; the Navy cuts, Trident, the Common Market – they were all to blame.

It had not, apparently, dawned on the House of Commons that it had long been beyond our national capability to defend the Falkland Islands from a major assault from a nearby irredentist power. Nor, it seemed, that the purpose of our national defences were to defend the British Isles, not the Falkland Islands, and that the Russians, not the Argentinians, were to be considered our chief adversary. Nor, in the emotional heat and mental confusion, was it reckoned that the Navy cuts had not yet scuppered the Navy nor yet a penny been spent on the Trident system.

Moreover, it was contended – by Mr Edward du Cann no less, he of the treacled dagger – that 'the defence of our people begins wherever British people are.' Nor was he alone in spouting such cant. Not only are we unable to defend our citizens around the world – how could we when the mighty United States is unable to recover diplomats held hostage in Iran? – but we are in the process of withdrawing from many of them their full citizenship rights. Under the Nationality Act it is improbable that Don Pacifico would have qualified as a British citizen.

Nevertheless, the fleet has been dispatched to the Falkland Islands with Palmerstonian flourish. A huge political crisis has been manufactured out of their loss. An able Foreign Secretary has seen fit to resign. The Prime Minister has staked her future and the future of her Government on a naval adventure. Lives are being risked, vast sums expended, everything else dropped and forgotten – all for 1,800 islanders and their 600,000 sheep. Why?

Chiefly, one suspects, because the ghosts of Munich still haunt the British Establishment. One does not appease dictators. A sound principle, no doubt, but one elevated out of all proportion when applied to a Latin American dictator seizing hold of a territory the size of Wales. Will a British show of naval force in the South Atlantic deter the Russians from direct intervention in Poland? Will it help to prevent another Afghanistan or Cambodia?

Another explanation, one fears, is wounded national pride. A 'tin pot' dictator provides the chance to avenge the loss of empire, the true 'humiliation' of Suez and the long slide in power and influence. A traditional naval expedition, a task force sailing out of Portsmouth, all hands lining ship – a wonderful, nostalgic sight, as good as a Royal Wedding or Trooping the Colour.

There is also the Prime Minister's pride to consider. Her Government's reputation, or what remained of it, rested heavily upon her gutsy style; she enjoyed her 'Iron Maiden' sobriquet; how could she talk tough to the Russians if she allowed a 'tin pot' dictator to get away with it? And never mind the Russians, what about her irate backbenchers? She is an impulsive politician. Her impulse, oh so British, was to send the fleet.

But what will it do when it gets there? Unlike a missile which may take 16 minutes to reach its target, a fleet takes 16 days. Its setting sail was the equivalent of an old-fashioned ultimatum. Each night for the next couple of weeks or so, we shall be seeing pictures of young sailors queuing up for their Mars Bars and Double Diamonds, playing fierce games of ludo and listening to 'Don't Cry for Me, Argentina' played endlessly over the tannoys. The Argentinians will probably be shown the same pictures. There will be plenty of time for everyone to wonder what happens at the end of the voyage.

Mrs Thatcher's war aims are far from clear. In the House of

Commons on Saturday she referred – with some care, one supposed – to the restoration of British 'administration' on the Falkland Islands. On television on Monday night, in the wake of the Carrington resignation, she was speaking loosely and – it seemed to me – wildly about the restoration of British 'sovereignty'. The Falkland Islands were to be 'regained', 'retaken', 'redeemed'.

One of the first casualties of war is conventional political journalism. From the moment hostilities become imminent nothing is said, on or off the record, for the purpose of public enlightenment: everything is for the purpose of creating some effect. So when Mr John Nott is asked if he would be ready to sink the Argentine Navy he must say 'yes' and roll his eyeballs in a warlike manner. He would have to do the same if asked if he was ready to nuke the Jockey Club in Buenos Aires.

Mrs Thatcher's own words and demeanour are consistent with her having embarked on a foolhardy attempt to reconquer the Falkland Islands or an attempt to regain some kind of negotiating position through the threat of force. There is no telling which, for in each case she would be bound to do and say the same things at this stage. One can only hope that it is true, as reported to me, that 'Jingoism is not rife at Number 10.'

The trouble is that warlike threats breed warlike deeds. You can't spread fear and confusion in the enemy camp without whooping up your own side. As the ships reach their destination matters will pass out of Mrs Thatcher's sole control. She may be prudence and caution themselves but she will have placed herself at the mercy of the folly of an Argentinian general.

If the General is still there. There is talk in London – wishful thinking perhaps – of the Galtieri regime being toppled before Mrs Thatcher's fleet arrives on station. The Government seems to be hoping that the combination of military threat and intensifying international pressure, political and economic, may yet lead Argentina to comply with the UN Security Council resolution.

The unpredictability of both Mrs Thatcher and General Galtieri may scare the United States into a top-priority effort to avert a naval confrontation between two important allies. Somewhere near the bottom line is the notion of some kind of 'two flag scenario' by which the Argentinians obtain sovereignty over the Islands while the British retain administrative rights on behalf of its people. The Labour Party is to float the idea of temporary UN supervision. How many Falkland Islanders will wish to remain after what has happened is another factor which could affect the eventual outcome.

What if none of these outcomes is in view by the time her fleet arrives on station? She can rely on international support and bi-partisan backing at home only for as long as force appears to be the servant of diplomacy. The minute she goes too far, or things go wrong for her, she will be out there on her own – nailed to the flag mast of the *Invincible*.

Her military options are not enticing. A blockade might take a year to work. Could the fleet sustain it for so long, more than 7,000 miles from home? Naval battles or bloody attempts to regain the Islands by force would soon forfeit her support at home and abroad.

The Labour Party's support has become more conditional ever since Mr Michael Foot contributed to Saturday's fervour with his patriotic oratory. The Opposition will back the Government's rational endeavours to alleviate the plight of the Falkland Islanders but it is not going to help Mrs Thatcher pull her chestnuts from the Tory Party fire.

The British people, too, are likely to arrive at a sensible view of the matter. It is doubtful whether they feel that some terrible national humiliation has occurred or that the Falkland Islands are worth a war. Doing what you can for fellow Britons in a far corner of the world is one thing but engaging the Navy to appease the Tory Party is another. There were cheers for the ships as they sailed away from Portsmouth on a sunny morning. There will be few cheers were Mrs Thatcher fool enough to turn her rash words into rash deeds.

Guardian, 7 April 1982

The islands will become a besieged Antarctic Berlin, without importance or meaning, doomed to wither on the vine of distance and unconcern

Now that it is all over bar the shooting, let us begin again at the beginning and consider what it is that we – or, rather, 'our boys' – must be prepared to die for. According to the Prime Minister, they will be fighting to make the world safe for democracy.

Firing on her usual moral two cylinders she said once more, when interviewed on the radio on Monday, that two principles were at stake: the principle of self-determination and the principle that aggression shall not pay.

She asserted the Falklanders' right to self-determination on the ground that that was what democracy was all about. She warned that if aggression was allowed to succeed in this case, other countries would soon be invaded with international anarchy resulting and many lives at risk.

It is too late for arguing yet again that these are fallacious or simplistic grounds for war on the disproportionate scale now planned. It remains relevant to point out that they provide flimsy foundations for international support as hostilities intensify.

Britain's insistence on the Falklanders' right to self-determination, which seems to have become the breaking point of the peace talks, is the part of our case which matters most of latter-day colonialism. The Government's repeated claim to be making the world a safer place would be more convincing if our friends and allies were cheering us up the beaches, but they are not; they await events with misgiving and foreboding.

They'll be happy enough when we have won the war, is Mrs Thatcher's reply to lily-livered objections of this kind. 'If we succeed, as we shall, we shall have the quiet acclaim and approval of all who believe in democracy.' This sense of unique mission, this Joan of Arc talk, rings dangerously in the ears. Does it seem probable that a small island in the North Atlantic is going to make the world a safer place by going to war over even tinier islands 8,000 miles away in the South Atlantic?

Let us make plain once again that the case for reason and proportion does not rest upon the proposition that aggression should be allowed to prosper or that, in this case, the aggressed are of small concern. It rests, first, upon the proposition that the world is not a simple game of dominoes and that in each case of conflict costs must be calculated and responses weighed. What happens to the Falkland Islands could have some consequences for, say, Belize but is likely to have not the slightest effect on future Soviet behaviour or Western responses to it.

As for the Falklanders, they are the victims not so much of

aggression as of geography and history. They are also the victim of British irresponsibility and self-delusion. They can no more expect to determine a British future for the Falklands than to determine that the map is coloured British pink again. The right of self-determination, made absolute and abstract, is absurd and worth not a drop of anyone's blood. The Falklanders have the right to the best deal which can be obtained in the circumstances, either under Argentinian rule or repatriated to Britain.

The negotiations to avoid a war broke down on principle. For Argentina her claim to sovereignty was a matter of high national principle. Britain's commitment to punishing aggression and upholding the rights of the Islanders required the denial of that claim. Because there was no procedural escape from the substance of the sovereignty issue the negotiations revolved around a – perhaps – insoluble dilemma.

The more willing appeared the Argentines to discuss without prejudice the question of sovereignty, the more concerned became the British with the modalities of disengagement and interim administration. The more insistent were the British on guarantees and safeguards, the more suspicious grew the Argentinians that the sovereignty issue would be prejudiced in Britain's favour.

In fact, both sides wanted to prejudge the issue of sovereignty. Arrangements which might allow the Islanders a veto would prejudice the Argentinian claim. Arrangements which rendered nugatory that veto would seem to allow their claim and give aggression its reward. Had it been the British Government's policy to negotiate a transfer of sovereignty, while protecting the interests of the Islanders, there need have been no war. But that was not the policy.

A re-invasion of the Falkland Islands in order to make the world safer for democracy might have seemed more plausible had not the great principles said to be at stake revolved around a sovereign claim to insignificant and underpopulated islands which, if sound at law, made no geopolitical sense. What is more, the breaking point of the negotiations will look to much of the world suspiciously like an attempt to restore a colonial-style administration. A war fought on these grounds is unlikely to command enthusiastic international support.

Moreover, there is too great a symbiosis for comfort in the affair. To be sure, Argentina is a South American dictatorship and Britain a venerable Western democracy; yet when it comes to intransigence there is not much to choose between a Thatcher and a Galtieri, as the headline writers around the world have been busy noting. Each has achieved political popularity through war; each has given more weight to domestic political pressures, whether from officers or backbenchers, than to international good opinion; and each has presided over a cacophony of conflicting and obfuscating statements of policy and principle. The world may be excused if it sees two nations in need of war, each struggling to escape from a spiral of decline and in need of heroic respite.

The recapture of the Falkland Islands, it seems, is to be an extension of the Prime Minister's 'conviction politics' by other means. Beyond that, Britain's war aims are far from clear. The Defence Secretary, Mr Nott, when interviewed again at the weekend, seemed to be envisaging some kind of fight-and-negotiate strategy; but if the Islands had to be retaken by force, which was what he was really talking about, then the policy – he said – would be to seek a long-term solution for them with the countries in the area.

But what makes him think that others are going to act in accordance with neat British plans? A task force of invading size was dispatched in the rash hope that it would bring the junta to its senses; now it is obliged to invade or come home. The sinking of the *Belgrano* had the effect of rallying the Argentinian people more solidly behind their disreputable and hitherto unpopular rulers. The most probable effect of military escalation will be to further heighten patriotic fervour. And if the Islands should fall to British forces, the obvious course for the junta is not to sue for peace but swear eternal war.

Mr Nott talks as if he imagines settling down on the verandah, Union Jack flying safely once more, to discuss fishing limits and communications facilities with friendly, neighbouring Argentina. More likely he, or someone, will be saying, 'One more such victory and we are lost.' The prewar problems of sustaining the Islands, and discharging our promises to the Islanders, will be writ large. They will become a besieged Antarctic Berlin without importance or meaning, doomed to wither on the vine of distance and unconcern.

And this is where we came in. For nearly two decades, successive governments and parliaments declined to face the facts or geography and history, politicians on all sides deluded themselves and others, entering into irresponsible commitments which they had neither the will nor means to discharge; they put party, political convenience, and the importunings of lobbyists above the national interest and, indeed, the longer-term interests of the Falklanders themselves.

Let us remember, therefore, as 'our boys' go in to die for principles, that none of this might have happened had Parliament not been summoned on that fateful Saturday, April 3, and had policy been made in reason and not hot blood. Nor need the mission have continued to its bloody end had our leader preached proportion in place of patriotism and passion. Blood will now be shed, not for true principle, but to expiate false and broken promises.

Our sailors and our soldiers, no doubt, will do what England expects. Our friends and allies will look on with bemused concern. Our people have closed ranks and the Tories are singing 'Rule Britannia'. The Establishment, meanwhile, goes into this war with an uneasy conscience. There is an awful feeling that it has been too serious a business to have been left to Margaret Thatcher.

Guardian, 19 May 1982

After the failure of half-hearted efforts to find a diplomatic solution to the crisis, British forces landed on the Falklands on 20 May and, after a short and successful campaign, the Islands were retaken. The total casualties were 254 killed and 744 wounded. Even before the end of hostilities it was evident that there was now a Falklands Factor working strongly in Mrs Thatcher's favour.

Seeing the Falklands as a footnote to a fatal chapter of strategic over-extension

Is there a correlation between the Falkland Islands and the money supply? Quite probably; after all, Lord Kaldor and his colleagues at Cambridge succeeded in correlating monetary growth with the incidence of cholera in West Central Scotland and the coming of Christmas. I see no reason, therefore, why the Falklands Factor (FF) should not be added to the Government's list of economic indicators.

It might even manage to devise a Medium Term Falklands Strategy (MTFS).

How shall we define FF? The Prime Minister attempted to do so at Cheltenham racecourse last Saturday and where better to rally the nation to a new sense of unity and purpose. FF, by the narrower measure (FF3), is the knowledge that 'we can do it', that 'we haven't lost the ability'. It is 'the spirit of the South Atlantic – the real spirit of Britain.'

This, she said, caused shipyards to adapt ships ahead of time and dockyards to perform refits faster than anyone had thought possible. If we could do it in war why couldn't we do it in peace? And, she went on, 'Just look at the Task Force as an object lesson. Every man had his own task to do and did it superbly . . . By working together each was able to do more than his best. As a team they raised the average to the level of the best and by each doing his utmost together they achieved the impossible.' Try that at British Leyland.

Later in this same astonishing speech, she proposed a broader measure for FF (FF1) which incorporated the 'new mood of realism in Britain.' In this she included the realisation that it was no good printing money to accommodate inflation. The Government had abjured such a disreputable way of proceeding and, increasingly, the nation wouldn't stand for it. People were now confident enough to face the facts of life. 'The battle of the South Atlantic was not won by ignoring the dangers of denying the risks.' (Ergo, the Falklands were recaptured as a result of the Government's control of the money supply.) And, with a final flourish of logic, she added: 'And that's why the railway strike won't do!'

While Mrs Thatcher was at Cheltenham the Chancellor was at Cambridge, and where better to deliver a long, dull lecture on his economic policy? Sir Geoffrey gave two explanations of FF. First, he said, it had increased confidence in our ability to see difficult decisions through. By this he presumably meant that the winning of the war would assist him in meeting his monetary targets. Secondly, he said, turning to the supply side, events in the South Atlantic had 'graphically demonstrated the supreme importance of individual heroism and personal endeavour, of people – not institutions – working together against enormous odds to turn humiliation into victory.

Note the careful parenthesis '*not institutions*'. It was the soldiers and sailors who won the war, not their nationalised industries – the Army and the Navy. Sir Geoffrey, presumably, would favour the privatisation of the armed forces. As it is, his vision is of enterprising mercenaries, driven forward by the incentive of their pay packets and prepared to lay down their lives for the PSBR. The Battle of the South Atlantic was won not on the playing fields of Eton but on the enterprising zone of the Isle of Dogs.

At Cheltenham the Prime Minister quoted Churchill. He usually springs to mind with the mention of war. Churchill said: 'We must find the means and the method of working together not only in times of war, and mortal anguish, but in times of peace, with all its bewilderments and clamour and clatter of tongues.'

She might just as well have quoted Harold Wilson who said (on 12 December 1964): 'I believe that our people will respond to this challenge because our history shows that they misjudge us who underrate our ability to move, and to move decisively, when the need arises. They misjudged our temper after Dunkirk, but we so mobilised our talent and untapped strength that apparent defeat was turned into a great victory. I believe that the spirit of Dunkirk will once again carry us through to success.'

There is probably no postwar Prime Minister who had not at some time or another invoked the Dunkirk spirit. Why improvisation *in extremis* should be regarded as the talent required for economic success is a mystery. I suppose the reason is that for most of the postwar period we have felt our back to be against the economic wall. That, perhaps, is why we go on thinking and talking about the war, watching films and reading books about it, more than any other nation in the world. The Falklands war brought back some of those folk memories, became part of the nostalgia cult which distracts us from the present and the future.

The war was a Golden Age in which everybody pulled together, and nobody went on strike, and everyone was cheerful and sang in the shelters and made cups of tea for each other. In fact, a lot of people went on strike and fiddled and showed Howe-like enterprise in the Black Market; and, contrary to the myth, morale became very low during the Blitz, about as low as on Thatcher-blitzed Merseyside today. Nevertheless, there was during the war a greater social discipline and a stronger sense of national cohesion because there was a sense of national purpose. The problem with peace is that it offers no equivalent of 'winning the war'.

Wars in this century have produced social progress through collective action. People's wars can only be fought if they are given some social as well as military purpose. In the last war the State intervened to insist on fair shares; war production was planned and price control was the essential pillar of the Home Front. When the attempt was made to extend the national unity of the war into the peace it was done by massive social reform – secondary education for all, universal welfare benefits, a National Health Service. There would have been no way the war could have been won, or the economy reconstructed afterwards, in the spirit of Thatcherism.

There might be some relevance to the 'Falklands Factor' if there were today some purpose beyond the subjection of the nation to market forces. It is not easy to take patriotic pride in three million unemployed, declining industries, rundown public services, and a deteriorating urban environment. The power of the State scored a brilliant feat of arms in the South Atlantic but what does the State do at home but malignly neglect the economy and condition of the people?

FF is not going to create jobs for three million unemployed and the Government has no policy for doing so. It has a policy of cuts but not a policy for economic growth, no policy for improving public services, investing in the public sector, or alleviating the condition of the poor and needy. To be sure, combatting inflation is a necessary task and breaking the hold of restrictive trade unionism is a necessary condition for industrial growth: but the patriotic spirit, which the war has supposedly aroused, cannot be harnessed to such nebulous and negativist goals as this Government puts forward.

As patriotism in time of war requires the State to exercise its power, so it does in time of peace. If Mrs Thatcher wishes to cash 'the spirit of the South Atlantic' she will need to set the nation a task worthy of uniting around. It is not difficult to imagine the broad outlines of a Plan for National Recovery which would be consistent with Tory principles. The power of the State would be used to promote new industries and to invest in public services; social policy would be approached in a spirit of generosity and fairness; indeed, rather than invoking the spirit of war it might invoke the spirit of Churchill's successful peacetime administration.

Mrs Thatcher's Government came in pledged to arrest and reverse the nation's decline. It was the first government to admit to the condition and to dare to use the word. Three years on, the Chancellor in his Cambridge lecture referred grandly to 'our programme to reverse Britain's decline'. But the Government has no such programme, only a belief in market forces now supplemented by the mystical FF.

In so far as decline is a moral condition a taste of victory may do something for the national morale. But the relative decline of the British economy, and the absolute decline of British power and influence, are due not to moral lassitude but to cumulative errors, neglects and shortcomings spread over a hundred years or more. Indeed, when the history books are written the war in the Falklands is unlikely to be seen as marking the moment of national regeneration but rather as a footnote to a fatal chapter of strategic over-extension, one of the chief causes of the long decline.

Moral revivalism is no substitute for policy. FF is not the elixir of growth. The 'real spirit of Britain' may be 'the spirit of the South Atlantic' but the real Britain is a stagnating economy, still-rising unemployment and a depleted and uncompetitive manufacturing industry. The Prime Minister's racecourse vapourisings show an earnest wish to enlist the patriotic spirit of the nation in the arrest of its decline but they show also that she has not the slightest notion of how to go about it.

Guardian, 7 July 1982

Mrs Thatcher won a landslide victory at the 1983 General Election with a split anti-Conservative vote and a surge of support for her post-Falklands persona. With a majority over all other parties of 144 seats the Thatcher Revolution really began. After their worst ever election defeat the Labour leader, Michael Foot, resigned and Roy Hattersley, the candidate of the Right, agreed to support Neil Kinnock's leadership bid on the 'dream ticket'. On the eve of their coronation at the Labour Party conference in Blackpool, Jenkins took stock of the daunting task facing the new and inexperienced leader.

No Leader of the Opposition since the war has started out looking less like the next Prime Minister

For more than three months, during the loveliest summer of modern times, the Labour Party's leadership election has dragged on. To describe it as a struggle would be to exaggerate, for Mr Neil Kinnock was a shoe-in from the word go. Nor would I have ever put a penny on Mr Michael Meacher's chances of denying the second prize to Mr Roy Hattersley, although the press, in search of silly-season headlines, fell for the Meacher camp's endeavours to promote a bandwagon.

No real contest though there was for the leadership itself, the process had to be gone through. The four candidates – Mr Peter Shore and Mr Eric Heffer make up the field – have debated together, answered questionnaires, issued manifestos and made speeches up and down the country. With no hope of succeeding, Mr Shore and Mr Heffer have been the most able to say what they think and between them have defined the range of options for Labour in the aftermath of what everybody, except Mr Tony Benn, accepts to have been a catastrophic defeat on June 9.

One consequence of this long-drawn-out affair is that Mr Kinnock succeeds to the leadership as if the obvious choice. By declaring his willingness to serve under the younger man, Mr Hattersley, in effect, settled for second place – the so-called 'dream ticket'. As he was drawn into a contest with the Bennite surrogate on his flank he ceased to offer an effective alternative choice for the leadership itself.

Some regard these as tactical errors on Mr Hattersley's part and think that he should have gone all out for the leadership and considered his position thereafter. That is perhaps to misread his intentions in the matter. Mr Hattersley may wear his ambition on his sleeve but in his heart the Labour Party comes first.

Be that as it may, the outcome is the coronation of Mr Kinnock at Brighton on Sunday. The heir apparent will have mounted the throne in smooth succession. Might it have been a different story without the machinations of that inveterate king-maker Mr Clive Jenkins? It was he, you may recall, who prematurely revealed Mr Foot's plans at the beginning of a week in which important union executives were to meet. Mr Foot was said to have been upset and angry but, if so, he soon got over it. Four nights later he and his wife and Mr Jenkins and his wife were to be seen on an evening out at the Gate Cinema in Notting Hill. They saw *The Ploughman's Lunch*.

The manner in which the big unions rushed to decision, before the blood of June 9 was even dry, was a part of the unseemliness of the process by which Labour leaders are these days elected. An important by-product is the further disrepute into which trade union democracy has been brought this summer. Nevertheless, I doubt whether it made much difference to the outcome. Mr Kinnock it was always going to be.

By now everybody is accustomed to the idea, but a foreign correspondent arriving in Brighton on Sunday might well be perplexed by the replacement of an old man who was never taken seriously as an alternative Prime Minister by a young man devoid of governmental experience of any kind. One would have to point out to him Mr Kinnock's engaging qualities – his energy, his wit and his charm – and his more evident political skills – as a platform orator and television performer; one would also need to draw attention to a record of political courage since the refusal to vote for Mr Benn in the previous deputy leadership contest and an ability, not always pronounced on the Left of the Labour Party, to look a fact in the face. One would have to mention also a tendency to flippancy (and to be carried away by Jilly Cooper) and to place question marks against parliamentary performance and intellectual depth. At the end of the briefing, Mr Kinnock might seem a plausible choice but still not an obvious one.

How is near-automatic succession to be explained then? A long list of contributory reasons can be offered. Since Attlee's day it has been said that the Labour Party is best led from the left of its centre. Mr Harold Wilson (as he then was) became leader with the support of the Left. Since his day the centre has shifted further leftward and Mr Kinnock occupies just about the appropriate place in the changed spectrum. The consolidated gains made by the Left mean that any attempt to lead the Party from further right – Mr Hattersley or Mr Shore – would involve it in further convulsions. In other words the case originally made for Mr Foot against Mr Healey is part of the case for Mr Kinnock.

Another reason is that under the new system, which has relinquished the leadership of the Labour Party to the pleasure of the trade union bureaucracies, the king-makers are themselves the authors of the policies which so disastrously lost the election. In continuity lies the hope of vindication. In any case, they themselves are the prisoners of internal Labour movement politics, their unions committed to policies repudiated by the electorate at large and still involved in settling old scores. Mr Kinnock was the only candidate untainted by incomes policy (or, indeed, by office) and that counted for something in trade union meta-politics.

Another reason for Mr Kinnock's clear run may be that the full seriousness of Labour's predicament, fighting for survival as the natural party of opposition, has yet to be appreciated in spite of the brutally frank speeches which Mr Shore and Mr Hattersley have been making up and down the country. Many on the Left continue to delude themselves that a divided leadership, a failure to put forward conference policies with true conviction, and a hostile media were the chief explanations for the June debacle. Others, including Mr Benn, take comfort in a crisis of capitalism which will result eventually in the triumph of socialism and the vindication of themselves. Others, dazzled by Mrs Thatcher, trust in conviction itself as the elixir of modern politics; Socialist grace is to be achieved by faith alone.

Mr Kinnock suffers from none of these delusions. Nevertheless, he has committed himself, in public at least, to a strategy of persuasion. Policy is to be modernised, to be sure, and must be modified to suit changed circumstances; Labour's appeal must be broadened, directed at the advantaged as well as the disadvantaged; efficiency socialism must be put back on the agenda and the white heat of information technology applied in the cause: he has said all these things but the message, the approach and the policies, are to remain essentially the same; Labour must listen, yes, but it is for the Labour Party to educate the Labour Party. Mr Kinnock is no preacher but he has the fervour of a Welsh educationalist.

Of course, what he says now and what he does later may be different matters. I do not intend to suggest duplicity, merely a manoeuvrability essential to any politician interested in achieving real goals. That was how Harold Wilson led Labour to victory in 1964, taking policy as read and putting his own glosses on it, refraining from opening sore questions, enlisting enthusiasm behind a modernising drive. And he did it, we should recall, within five years of Mr Harold Macmillan's spectacular electoral triumph and Labour's third successive defeat, and in the face of a sheaf of premature obituaries of the Labour Party and predictions of decades of Tory hegemony. We must beware today of the kind of power worship, deplored by Orwell, which leads it to be supposed that whoever is in power must always be in power and equally against concluding that all trends, in this case Labour's decline, must necessarily continue.

Nevertheless, the task which Mr Kinnock faces is vastly more Herculean than the task which faced Mr Wilson. To note that Labour survived those obituaries of 1959 and went on to win four elections out of the next five is to disguise the fact that the secular decline in its electoral support continued the meanwhile. Since then all of the sociological, demographic, and ideological changes, now familiar, which have eroded Labour's standing as a national party have continued and accelerated. It remains possible, under the electoral system, to win power while on such a declining trend but it has become much more difficult since the Wilsonian days. It would mean winning 117 seats at the next General Election and in two-thirds of Conservative-held seats Labour now starts from third place.

Moreover, when Wilson took over the bomb had been unbanned and Labour's anti-Europeanism was in part a reflection of a staunch Atlanticism. Mr Kinnock may yet trim somewhat on disarmament but he has said enough times that he intends to see Britain free of all nuclear weapons and the electorate persuaded of the Labour Party's non-nuclear strategy. While others retain nuclear weapons, it will take some persuading.

The Wilson of 1963 and 1964 was also able to allay doubts about his leftish record, and his political trustworthiness, by presenting himself as a model of modern professionalism and expertise. He achieved a parliamentary dominance over Sir Alec Douglas Home, appeared to know everything about economics, technology and many other things besides, and dwelt heavily upon his Cabinet experience. To hear him talk of his days as President of the Board of Trade you would have thought he had been President of the United States.

Mr Kinnock does not have these advantages. No Leader of the Opposition since the war has started out looking less like the next Prime Minister. That is due not merely to his own inexperience but also to the fact that the party he leads has never looked less like an alternative party of government. He is starting virtually from scratch in his attempt at the moral conversion of Thatcherite Britain to the values of democratic socialism he learnt at Aneurin Bevan's knee, and he will need every ounce of that zealous energy and Welsh charm to do it.

Guardian, 9 September 1983

Mrs Thatcher's second term of office from 1983 to 1987 was dominated on the domestic political front by the success of the Government's privatisation programme and by the miners' strike. The Labour Party struggled to find a response to the increasing self-confidence of Thatcherite capitalism, while all its old wounds were opened by the miners' strike. The strike distracted the Party from the need to modernise policy in response to the Thatcher Revolution. In this piece Jenkins captures the experience of ordinary miners trapped between the intransigence of Scargill's revolutionary socialism and the austerity of the Thatcherite policy for coal.

You're fighting for your pit, for your village, for your kids and, I hope to God, for a police force that don't get out of hand

My friend lives in what is hopefully called Sunny Avenue, South Elmsall. The mining villages in this part of Yorkshire are strung together in small conurbations, never quite town or country. South Elmsall, South Kirkby, Upton, Hemsworth all merge into one another, eventually becoming part of Doncaster which is the capital of what sees itself as the most militant district of the Yorkshire coalfield.

As the villages sprawl together on the surface, their pits, Frickley (which belongs to South Elmsall) and South Kirkby, meet underground. Yet they are separate worlds. The pit in Upton closed a few years ago. 'Upton is a ghost town now,' a miner's wife informed me. Her husband had transferred to Frickley from Upton. 'You either have to move or travel,' she said. Upton is all of two miles away.

Bill travels to work at Hickleton in Thurnscoe, which is four miles away. He is a colliery joiner. His wife Janet has a secretary's job in

Doncaster. They both come from local mining families. Bill's brother is a police inspector in Sheffield who has been in charge of policing Cottonwood. Hickleton, which has a reputation as a left-wing pit, was the first to vote to support the Cortonwood men when the strike was triggered there in March.

At Hickleton it takes some 1,400 men to produce a bit under a million tonnes a year. It is the deepest pit in the locality and very hot down below; the men take salt tablets and work in four-foot seams. At the new super-pit at Selby 2,200 men can get 10 million tonnes a year. If those are the economies of mining where are all the men to go? Bill asks.

The Coal Board calculates the cost of production at Hickleton at £123 a tonne which, if so, makes it a champion uneconomic pit. Bill disputes this. Like nearly all miners he is a great expert on his own pit. 'This dispute hasn't happened overnight,' he says. His economic history of Hickleton goes back over eight years, a story of investment starvation and manpower reduction. Management has made the pit uneconomic in order to close it.

There is not much point in trying to check the facts and figures. All the miners say much the same thing. They say it not because Arthur Scargill says it but because of what they think is happening at their own pits. They would agree with Rousseau who said, 'The nature of things does not madden us, only ill will does.' They believe the policy of the Board and the Government is to run down their pits and then sell off the good ones, such as Selby, to private enterprise.

What the Government calls economics offends against what these miners call morality. The moral assumptions of Thatcherism are utterly repugnant to them. Working underground makes it seem self-evident to them that life is about mutual dependence. They set no store by economic individualism. Their saying is 'good seams make good colliers'.

The productivity bonus scheme is offensive to them because – they quote Scargill – 'it sets men against men'. Bill thinks it is right that low-cost pits should help the others. He says, 'This isn't just an argument between Arthur Scargill and Maggie Thatcher. It goes deeper than that. It is about the Government being ready to help people because people are dependent.'

At the Miners' Welfare Club old couples are dancing the Anniversary Waltz. Bill introduces me to some friends including local

NUM branch officials. They are back from court in Pontefract giving evidence on behalf of pickets. If they were witnesses they had attended a mass picket, said the Stipendiary, and bound the lot of them over for 'besetting'.

They were full of complaints about the police and the media. Frank's children had seen the recent *World in Action* programme. 'They wanted to know "were you there, Dad?" They're going to think I'm some kind of law-breaker.'

'His father's either a thug or television's wrong,' said Roy.

Reg said, 'I'm thirty-six and I've never been in trouble with police all my life. Now I'm enemy within. Some kind of criminal. My kids know that's not me. So does my wife. They resent it.'

Nothing is more resented, I discovered, than the Prime Minister's remark. A typical comment from a much older miner was 'they didn't call us enemy within when we were digging for fucking victory.' Margaret Thatcher's insult to the miners of Great Britain will not be soon forgotten. She will be remembered like Churchill for Tonypandy.

The president of the branch, Tony, was as bald as Kojak and wore his dark glasses. He tried to sum up what it was they were fighting for. 'It's such a broad issue,' he said. 'It's like chucking a stone in a pond and the ripples spreading. You're fighting for your pit first of all. But you're fighting for your village and your kids' future. And you're fighting, I hope to God, for a police force that don't get out of hand, 'cos we've got to have a police force. And you're fighting for trade union movement because this union has only been loaned to us by my grandfather.'

Then, as an afterthought, he added: 'It's brought us closer as a community, this strike. It's done a Falklands on us.'

We move on. If miners don't like travelling far to work they'll drive miles for a pint. At another club, Jack, who's a management man but with a great deal more sympathy for the miners than for Ian MacGregor or Margaret Thatcher, says, 'It's only loyalty to the branches that's keeping them out now.'

That loyalty is immensely strong and is much more of a factor than the intimidation which has been going on. At the three local pits the number of men 'going in' is two, four and six. The strike is going to die hard in these parts.

The next morning the pickets are out as usual. At four o'clock, Bill and I walk up to Frickley through cold, wet, orange-lit streets. Nothing happens; there's a shove and a shout and the two men go in. I go back to a warm bed.

When men first went in to Frickley a few weeks ago there were riot shields and horses and broken windows and arrests, and the usual mutual accusations of violence. The pattern, at least in this part of West Yorkshire, seems to be a flare of violent anger when a pit reopens after which things settle down to a routine morning ritual, usually without incident. Low-profile policing is the general order round here, and it does seem to keep the level of violence down.

The wives who run the meal centre have been dubbed the 'Frickley Wonder Women'. They have escaped from their own kitchens to cook 200 dinners and breakfasts a day for the men on strike. Brenda was managing on £32 a week from the DHSS and £13 in family allowance but her mortgage was £20 a week and there was the water rates and the phone and a video which couldn't go back. Barbara, with one son, was also 'managing' on £13.65 plus £6.85.

Her boy was having free school dinners and her husband coming into the centre for his breakfast and dinner. 'At night we have toast and a few chips,' she says with a cheerful laugh. 'It's the kids you feel sorry for, isn't it?'

'It's the kids' clothes are the main problem,' says another Brenda. 'There's an allowance from council, which we appreciate, but it's not enough for coat and shoes.'

'We didn't miss our summer holidays at all,' says the first Brenda with a happy smile.

'We did,' says Merle, who is married to one of Bill's many cousins.

'I mean we knew no one else was having a holiday, didn't we?' says Brenda.

Two of their sons are 'considering army'. There hasn't been a pit job in the villages for some years, or so they claim. Bill says: 'We've got lads of twenty-two who've never worked and never will.'

'The cold's the real thing. We're freezing,' says Merle.

'Aye, you should see the rubbish we put on fires.' We leave them complaining about the police chasing their men off the tips and merrily discussing the uses of bricks in grates.

Outside a man stops Bill to enquire about a turkey dinner which is planned. There's a problem about money and turkeys. He listens to the latest and says, 'We'll be having corn beef dinner, then.' Off he goes, laughing.

In the shadow of the tip (which is a phrase I heard a miner use) men are digging muddy holes as deep as themselves, sieving dirt for scraps of coal to burn. Last week someone found an 1806 penny and today it's a George V Coronation mug but the handle is broken off.

Inside the Empire Club the old men remember Manny Shinwell in the cinema across the road dealing with the hecklers. That was in 1947 when the miners of Grimethorpe started a famous strike which raged through Yorkshire, the first big one after nationalisation. But these old men had 'nowt against nationalisation'; before that they were 'slaves', they insisted. They showed me how the old colliery managers had selected miners for work by pinching their biceps. A young face worker, with biceps as big as his belly, chipped in and said, 'We could have done with Arthur Scargill thirty years ago.'

Friday night in the Coronation Club opposite the gates of Hickleton Colliery and the strikers are keeping up as best they can the old tradition called pay night. George is 51 and has worked 35 years at the face. He is said to have broken a record earning £400 in a week but complains that recently his take-home had been down to £80 or so. He is wearing an expensive lambswool pullover hand-washed and his hair is blown dry. He looks terrific, chest puffed out and chin up high, and he is a brilliant conversationalist. He tells me what he thinks of Nottinghamshire miners: 'In war they took two days to capture one fucking hill.'

Keith tells tales of the picket lines. He's been all over Yorkshire and into Notts. He was there at Orgreave and advised Scargill 'Thee get down there, Arthur', but Arthur didn't and was nicked. Keith's stories are not of police brutality but of mindless, petty harassments: he was held eleven hours in cells for a trumped-up minor motoring offence and then not charged. But on another occasion, in a municipal car park where they had paid 35p for the van, there were 40 pickets and only seven police, who tried to move them on. 'I put one in bramble bush and asked others, "Does thou want seven shades of shit kicked out of thee?"'

How will the strike ever end?

'Once we're past Christmas and they see we're not beaten, they'll find a compromise.' 'We've survived this far. No good going back for nowt.'

'In the end they'll move coal by army. That's either her downfall or her victory. Could go either way.'

'It's not up to Arthur Scargill. When there's to be compromise, it'll come up from branches and areas, and Arthur Scargill will have to compromise.' 'People go on about Arthur Scargill, but only thing Arthur Scargill can do is what he's told. At end of day it's how many stick their hands up.' 'You can't get less than nowt, can you?'

The men and women of these mining families are of a proud species threatened with extinction. A great pestilence has been visited upon their communities and, in their innocence, they now await some more benign intervention from outside. London, Westminster, the TUC, the Labour Party are worlds away from their villages. The Prime Minister and her government inhabit a different moral universe.

My friend Bill sees it this way. 'People round here aren't prepared to lie down and have their bollocks kicked off like the rest of the four million unemployed. Personally, I'm prepared to stay out until the day the Government recognises that what I'm doing is beneficial to the country. I'm even prepared to see my pit close. If pits are going to close it's going to be our decision, not Thatcher's.'

Guardian, 21 December 1984

On 4 March 1985 the miners' strike came to an end with defeat for the NUM. The year-long strike had left trade union power broken and the NUM, once the most militant and politically powerful union in the land, emasculated.

Why Maggie will have to rejoice alone

The miners are beaten, although almost a hundred thousand of them are fighting bravely to the end. The power of the State has prevailed. But the gladiatorial fight to the finish at the heart of the war has still to be settled. Final victory eludes the Prime Minister. Arthur Scargill is not down yet.

The exciting clashes between police and pickets which filled the television screens last summer and autumn have given way to the circular scholasticism of Mr Scargill and the ubiquitous Mr Michael

Eaton. The public is bored stiff by the endless wrangles over procedures and words. Why don't they simply end the long dispute in some reasonable and honourable fashion?

Whatever the formal terms of settlement may say the reality at the end of the strike will be that the balance of power has shifted decisively from union to management. That is the true meaning for the NUM of defeat. The miners' will and capacity to fight closures will have been severely impaired for, perhaps, years to come. The hardships involved in paying off accumulated debts are going to be scarcely less than the hardships of the strike itself. Moreover, everyone knows that in the new circumstances the closure programme is likely to be more radical and more costly in jobs than the programme put forward at the beginning of the dispute last March.

Why then is formal surrender deemed necessary? Why is such importance attached to the NUM's conceding in writing the principle of closing uneconomic pits? Because Mr Scargill has said a thousand times if he has said it once that there is no such thing as an uneconomic pit and for Mrs Thatcher's victory to be complete and clear he must be made to eat those words.

Always build a golden bridge for your enemy's retreat was Scipio's wise advice. But if she builds a golden bridge for Arthur he'll use it as a platform from which to address the cameras.

Imagine the speech he might make. Nowhere in this document, he would say, waving it in his hand, is there any mention of an uneconomic pit. What is more, he would go on, the Coal Board has withdrawn the March 26 closure programme. And not only that but it has withdrawn its plans to close Cortonwood and the other four pits which were the trigger of the strike. Defeat would begin to sound remarkably like a victory.

The *Daily Mail*, the *Express*, the *Sun* would not like it at all. Nor would a substantial section of the Tory Party with its vivid folk memory of the humiliations of 1972 and 1974. It would be even more upset if, in the name of magnanimity, an amnesty had been granted to the some 600 miners dismissed by the Coal Board during the dispute for offences including arson and sabotage.

There would seem to be no way at the moment in which the Government could show a generosity of spirit towards the proud but beaten miners without the risk of Mr Scargill turning it to his political advantage. Why should the Prime Minister snatch defeat from the jaws of victory in order to enable Arthur Scargill to retain his revolutionary purity? It is his ruthless intransigence which prevents the dispute from being settled on reasonable terms. It is he who is determined to fight to the last miner.

Mr Scargill keeps saying that he is prepared to engage in unconditional negotiations but all the private diplomacy, conducted chiefly by the TUC, has failed to obtain his approval for any language which would admit closures on economic grounds on to the agenda of his 'unconditional' negotiations. No one is now asking the NUM to acquiesce in advance in such closures.

Under pressure the Prime Minister made that clear in the Commons on Thursday. When the colliery review procedure agreed with Nacods was exhausted it would remain managements' prerogative to close a pit if it so decided. But, she conceded, the union would have an equal right to oppose the decision and take strike action if it so decided.

It is pretty obvious that Mr Scargill has no intention of eating his words for Mrs Thatcher's sake. He has no need to do so. He remains in control of his executive. Even if a delegate conference were eventually to acquiesce in the principle of economic closures Mr Scargill's signature would not be on the piece of paper. As closures take place he will be able to claim that his was the voice of truth; behold, everything he prophesied has come to pass.

He will have more than that to say. His political defence will go something like this. He and only he has taken Mrs Thatcher on. For a whole year the miners fought and fought alone with amazing endurance and loyalty. In the end only starvation brought them to submission. The opportunity was there to put a stop to Thatcherism and monetarism. It was lost because the TUC and the Labour Party failed to join the miners' struggle. The lesson, he will say, is that only mass struggle can succeed. Even the miners cannot do it alone.

This will become the basis of a powerful myth within the Labour movement. Mr Scargill's critics, who are legion, will some of them try to point out that it was his disastrous generalship which brought defeat upon his men. Had a national ballot been called it might have been won. From the moment the Nottinghamshire miners were alienated from the strike the struggle was lost. Twice could the dispute have been settled on honourable terms. Victory could even have been claimed. Twice pig-headed Arthur marched on towards the last ditch.

These things may not be said very loud, however, and they will sound like the whinges of armchair critics. Disastrous though it has been his leadership of the strike has been a prodigious feat of endurance and resourcefulness. His professional adversaries within the Government were lost in admiration for the man last week when just as it seemed that all was nearly lost he conjured the Nacods once more out of the hat to keep the dispute going a little longer. The idea that Arthur Scargill will conveniently fade from the scene when the strike is lost is distinctly wishful.

All through the hope of the Labour leadership has been to somehow contrive the defeat of Arthur Scargill and of Scargillism while sparing the miners themselves from defeat. But that was to underestimate the man. We may now see the myth of betrayal take root in the narrowing sectarian ranks of the Labour Party.

In the broader trade union movement 'Scargillism' has come to mean trade unionism with a revolutionary tinge pursued with the tactics of the football terraces. The majority of trade union leaders will be pleased enough to see the suppression of that.

But the defeat of the miners themselves is liable to paralyse them with guilt and make it even more difficult than before to come to terms with the changed environment in which trade unions are obliged to operate.

For the country as well as the trade unions themselves the outstanding salient fact of an historic event has been the refusal of the mass of organised labour to lift a finger on the miners' behalf. The call for 'total support' which went out from the Brighton Congress was as totally unheeded as Mr Len Murray knew that it would be. It was a disastrous move which may take years to live down. Here is the stuff of another myth to supersede the events of 1974 and the 1978 winter of discontent; the plebeians decline to join the uprising.

However, the hopes of the SDP and the Liberals that the miners' dispute might prove a mould-breaking event are liable to be disappointed. Undoubtedly some unions will disaffiliate themselves from the Labour Party by voting down their political funds when the Tebbit-ordered ballots begin in April, but rather than proving a catalyst to the political dealignment of the trade union movement the defeat of the miners is more likely to prove a stunning and immobilising event.

For the Government the outcome is an undeniable plus. A victory is a victory. The ghosts of '72 and '74 have been exorcised at last. The authority of the State has been shown to prevail over the miners. If the outcome contributes to the continuing stasis of the Opposition so much the better. The best way to read the latest poll is to imagine what it might be saying were it not for the 'Scargill factor'.

Nevertheless, there is something wrong about the way this strike is ending. In my opinion it was necessary and right for the elected government to prevail over Arthur Scargill and the NUM but the ending of the strike does not leave me in a mood for celebration. It is all very well for Mrs Thatcher to laud the working miners as the heroes of the day, but we are being called upon to rejoice in a victory not over 'Argies' but our own people. At the end of civil wars noble and generous words are needed and there is an end for expiating ceremonies.

In all reason there should be a negotiated return to work and, perhaps, in a few more weeks, that is what will happen. But emotion might be better served and some measure of catharsis achieved if it were done the Welsh way, bands playing, choirs singing and banners proudly flying. What a show it would be to warm the national heart, a sight to compare with the return of the Task Force.

Guardian, 13 February 1985

One of the big issues of the Thatcher decade was her style of government, which became increasingly 'presidential'. The Westland crisis of January 1986 was the most profound constitutional crisis of Mrs Thatcher's premiership, as a minor dispute over the future of the Westland helicopter company quickly escalated into a full-blown political confrontation between leading Cabinet Ministers. The crisis was triggered by the dramatic resignation of the Minister of Defence, Michael Heseltine, who alleged that the normal practices of collective Cabinet responsibility had broken down. There was intense speculation as to the exact role of Mrs Thatcher and her closest officials in the series of leaks and counter-leaks between Heseltine and the Secretary of State for Trade and Industry, Leon Brittan. Brittan was forced to resign, Heseltine embarked on the longest leadership campaign in British political history, and Mrs Thatcher, although wounded, survived.

Lesson: tell all quickly

We veterans of Watergate learnt to ask the question 'What did he know and when did he know it?' By that time everyone had forgotten the original break-in to the Democratic Party headquarters which happened then to be housed in the architecturally monstrous Watergate complex. By then the crime had become the cover-up, a many-layered affair of cover-ups. President Nixon was ruined by the lies and evasions that were his response to that incessant question: 'What did he know and when did he know it?'

The Watergate story is a cautionary tale for all politicians, the moral of which is that it pays to come clean and come clean quickly. Leaking a government document in the heat of a war of dirty tricks may not seem a very heinous offence, but nor did tapping the phones of your political opponents seem particularly shocking to most Americans in 1972. It was the cover-up which brought them to see their President as a crook. It is the cover-up since the leaking of the Solicitor-General's letter to Mr Michael Heseltine on January 6 which has done the damage to Mrs Thatcher's reputation.

Who did know what and when? That question remains following the resignation of Mr Leon Brittan, hounded by the Tory pack. From the information available it is possible to construct three broad versions of what may have happened.

VERSION ONE:
She really didn't know, or at least not all of the facts, until Wednesday of last week. She didn't know because Mr Brittan hadn't told her. 'Why didn't you tell me, Leon?' it is said she asked him four times on Wednesday in bitter scenes between them.

The decision to leak was the decision of Mr Brittan's Department. Her private secretary, Mr Charles Powell, was informed of this decision and acquiesced in it although only in a 'neutral' fashion.

The leaks inquiry was not ordered as a cover for what she already knew. It was instituted at the request of the Attorney-General, Sir Michael Havers, who insisted that it must be discovered whether the law had been broken at any level. There was never any question of prosecuting Miss Colette Bowe, who had cleared her lines all round, but she insisted upon immunity before revealing to Sir Robert Armstrong the names of all those with whom she had checked her authorisation to leak.

176

Question: Why had Mr Brittan not told the Prime Minister the full extent of his role before January 22?

Answer: Because he thought that what had happened had been cleared with No. 10 or, say his enemies, because he was hoping to get away with his ineptitude.

Q: Why did Sir Robert Armstrong not tell her earlier?

A: Because he did not discover Mr Brittan's involvement until last Monday, January 20.

VERSION TWO:

Infuriated by Mr Heseltine's activities, the Prime Minister and Mr Brittan between them put the Solicitor-General up to writing a letter which it was their purpose to leak. The discussions between their private and press offices were merely about who should do it, how and when. The leaks inquiry was ordered by the Prime Minister as a cover, she knowing full well who was responsible for the leak. At their meeting on Wednesday she asked Mr Brittan to resign only on the understanding that subsequently he would implicate her. Therefore she felt obliged to defend him.

Q: Would Mrs Thatcher take such risks as these?

A: Possibly, in the heat of a fast-moving game and in her fury with Heseltine.

Q: Is it in character for her to first deceive and then lie directly to the House of Commons.

A: No.

VERSION THREE:

What really happened was something like this. Brittan thought it would be a good idea to make public the contents of the Mayhew letter. On the phone from Yorkshire he told his private secretary to put this to No. 10. The matter was arranged in a great hurry between the private offices. Mr Ingham insisted that the Department of Industry, not No. 10, should do the necessary. There was not time to further consult Mr Brittan, who had not intended, or authorised, a direct leak to the Press Association without the Solicitor-General's consent.

Q: Why, if this is what happened, was Mrs Thatcher not consulted?

A: Perhaps because she has conceded large discretion to Mr Ingham.

Q: Why wasn't she told subsequently?

A: Either she was or there are things which it is thought best not to tell her.

Q: Why was it thought necessary that Miss Bowe should have legal immunity?

A: Because it was not clear at that stage whether Mr Brittan would accept the responsibility for the excessive zeal or misjudgment of the officials who authorised her to leak.

Of these three versions, the first seeks to save Mrs Thatcher by blaming Mr Brittan for everything.

The second version is a neat conspiracy theory, probably too neat. It rests on systematic deceit by the Prime Minister. To order the Cabinet Office to conduct a leaks inquiry when she already knew exactly what had happened would be a monstrous imprudence. The Prime Minister may be more compromised than she has yet admitted, but version two does not ring quite true. Version three consists of a shabby cock-up. It rests on malice and ineptitude in about equal degree and reflects badly on officials as well as on their political masters. It would say something about the extent to which the Civil Service has been politicised under Mrs Thatcher's administrations. However, cock-up is the stuff that history is often made of. Version three, or something like it, could be the nearest to the truth.

Of my three versions, only version two provides an answer to the Watergate question: What did she know and when did she know it? If version two could be established she would have to follow Mr Brittan and resign. All other explanations point either to some degree of cover-up on her part or to astonishing failures of communication by her officials.

Mr Brittan has died the political death of the courtier. He owed his rise entirely to the Prime Minister and had no base of his own from which to defend his reputation. Inept he may have been, but his departure leaves behind it a nasty stench of scapegoat and important questions still to be answered by the Prime Minister. What did she know and when?

Sunday Times, 26 January 1986

CHAPTER SEVEN

'Waking Up From the Long Communist Nightmare'

The ideological distance that Jenkins travelled as a political columnist was illustrated in one of his most influential articles. Surveying Mrs Thatcher's first two terms of office just prior to the 1987 election, Jenkins, now writing for the Independent, *articulated his vision of post-Socialist politics. The themes that he touched on in this article were expounded at greater length in his book* Mrs Thatcher's Revolution.

The politics of the post-Socialist era

Sir Isaiah Berlin remarked the other day that this was the first time since the French Revolution that there is no project on the Left among the Parisian intelligentsia.

That is a striking way of drawing attention to the ending of the age of socialism. But at the same time it draws attention to the lacuna which exists as the twentieth century moves towards its close. For it is improbable that man, or woman, can live by incrementalism alone. The modern age is characterised by hope.

High expectations make societies difficult to govern but it is the expectation of something better, in heaven or on earth, which makes them governable at all.

Yesterday I wrote about what I called a crisis of opposition in Britain and described how slow and problematical the realignment of the Left was likely to prove. Today I want to say something about the politics of the post-Socialist era.

In one sense they have already dawned and their name is Thatcherism. For there is little doubt that in the eight years since 1979 the assumptions on which political argument is conducted have shifted a great deal. Democratic Socialists have felt obliged to try to wrest back the idea of liberty from the libertarian Right, although with no great success as shown by Mr Hattersley's recent ponderous tome.

We have all been obliged to concede a greater role to markets, the corporatist tendencies of the seventies have lost most of their force, and a new consensus has begun to form around the diminished power of the trade unions. We are, perhaps, all populists now.

Yet what we call Thatcherism is probably a transitional phenomenon which belongs still to the age of socialism. This is because a great deal of its thrust is anti-Socialist. Attitudes may to some extent have changed – productivity figures suggest so – but there are few signs of the cultural transformation required to bring about the American-style enterprise society of the Prime Minister's dreams. The clearest evidence of this is that, in so far as attitudes may have changed towards the role of the State in managing the economy, this has not been accompanied by any discernible change of attitude towards the duty of the State to provide welfare, medical care and education. We are not much nearer to a free-market society than we were to a Socialist society.

In trying to imagine the post-Socialist twenty-first century we can be sure of one thing. It will incorporate a good many Socialist values in the same way that the Socialist twentieth century incorporated a good many values from the preceding age of liberalism. Liberty and democracy are words much bandied in the vocabulary of socialism, although socialism has little to do with them; and because it was famously asserted that socialism was about equality it is often assumed, wrongly, that equality has to be about socialism. The distinctive idea of socialism is that economic organisation is the key to liberty, equality and human happiness. The pre-Socialist notion was that these were natural rights which could be advanced independently of economic conditions; indeed, Adam Smith regarded political liberty as the necessary condition for economic freedom not, as does the New Right, the other way round.

In the post-Socialist age liberty, equality and justice may come to be reinstated as intrinsic virtues. We can already see how rights have begun to cut across the ideological divides – the right to a job, a home, the right to educational choice or private medicine, the right to rights as laid down in the European Convention on Human Rights.

Post-Socialist politics are bound to be in large part about the State, the limits of its powers and the extent of its responsibilities, for that is what politics have always been most about. In much of postwar Western Europe there came to exist a broad consensus in favour of social democracy or liberal capitalism, which is to say market-oriented economic regimes combined with State-provided welfare. This compromise was made possible by fast growth, and may become possible again; but what we now know, or should know, is that socialistic policies of production tend to be hostile to the wealth creation which is the necessary condition of its more just distribution.

The politics of the post-Socialist era will be characterised by a majority of haves over have-nots. Central to the Socialist century was the notion, or the myth, of the proletariat as the real majority suppressed only by the wiles of the ruling class or its own false consciousness. Justice was harnessed to class, the poor advised to cling to the coat-tails of the Transport and General Workers' Union. In post-Socialist society not only the poor but the working class itself will be minorities. Once that is realised, and it is grasped that producer interests are no longer paramount, it may become more feasible to build new coalitions of interest or principle around other issues of liberty or justice.

Independent, 2 April 1987

Jenkins did not confine his analysis to the Right, for he was also very concerned with the reform process in the Labour Party. Although Labour lost the 1987 election, the substantial margin of defeat at least served to accelerate the reform process which had been begun by Neil Kinnock in 1985. The policy review that was initiated in the wake of the 1987 defeat was the most far-reaching revisionist project since the 1950s. In this article Jenkins compares that 1950s project with its 1980s equivalent.

A belated version of social democracy

Neil Kinnock was quick to deny that he is doing a Gaitskell in presenting the Labour Party with an out-and-out revisionist prospectus. But he would, wouldn't he? He also rejected comparisons with the German social democrats' Bad Godesberg programme of 1959, in which they came to terms with the social market economy set in place by the architects of the postwar economic miracle. It says something about Labour's predicament that we find ourselves discussing its attempts to come to terms with Mrs Thatcher's third successive electoral victory with reference to events which took place nearly 30 years ago and have no meaning to the vast majority of today's voters.

However, if we are to appeal to the history books we should be clear about what Hugh Gaitskell was attempting and about why, and in what sense, he failed. The process known as revisionism had been in progress since the publication of Anthony Crosland's *The Future of Socialism* in 1956. It had been especially concerned with diluting Labour's commitment to nationalisation as enshrined in Clause IV of the Party constitution. After Labour's third successive defeat in 1959, Gaitskell proposed not to repeal Clause IV but to 'bring it up to date' by placing new language beside it. Crosland regarded this as a tactical error which would draw attention to Labour's ideological albatross.

Gaitskell's 'amplification' was accepted by the NEC as 'a valuable expression of the aims of the Labour Party in the second half of the twentieth century'. But the unions opposed tampering with the Ark of the Covenant and he was denied the symbolic impact of a constitutional amendment.

In contrast, the SPD at Bad Godesberg in 1959 adopted a programme which represented a symbolic break with its Marxist past. It did not reject socialism but, in effect, signalled a coming-to-terms with the social market approach. The Bad Godesberg programme went far beyond Gaitskell's 'amplification' of Clause IV in abandoning traditional Socialist means to egalitarian ends.

To measure Neil Kinnock's revisionist tendencies against Hugh Gaitskell's, or the path to power taken by the SPD in 1959, is somewhat academic today. Ideologically, the new statement of *Aims and Values* falls somewhere between Gaitskell's turgid exegesis of the creed and the Bad Godesberg programme. The latter declared 'competition as far as possible, planning as far as necessary', a more positive and enthusiastic endorsement of the market than is to be found in the Kinnock manifesto.

Nevertheless, the new statement of aims amounts to the adoption by the leadership, if not by the Party, of a broadly social democratic approach. Some of the language is reminiscent of the SDP's Limehouse Declaration which said: 'We need the innovating strength of a competitive economy with a fair distribution of rewards. We favour competitive public enterprise, co-operative ventures and profit sharing.' The Kinnock document describes the operation of demand and supply, and the price mechanism, as 'a generally satisfactory means of determining provision and consumption' of most goods. Defence is not touched upon in the Kinnock–Hattersley document but, that apart, there is nothing in it that those who broke from the Labour Party in 1981 could reasonably take exception to.

But making the ideological adjustment in 1988 that ought to have been made in 1960 is not the solution to Labour's present difficulties. Things have moved on a good deal since those days. Moreover, too much can be made of the Party's repudiation of Gaitskell over Clause IV. True, it was a symbolic celebration of the past, a defiant donning of the cloth-cap image we used to talk about in those days; but Gaitskell's assault on Clause IV led to a power struggle with the Left over unilateral nuclear disarmament which he eventually won. When he died suddenly in 1963 nobody associated Hugh Gaitskell with heavy-handed socialism and, by 1964, Harold Wilson was able to project Labour as a modernising force.

The crisis in the Labour Party today derives only in small part from obsolete ideology. Clause IV is a bit of an embarrassment, a stick in the hands of enemies, but no more than that. The crisis which, by the end of the 1970s, had engulfed not only Labour but also the German SPD was not the crisis of Clause IV socialism but of social democracy.

Gaitskell's task was to make the Labour Party come to terms with the flourishing mixed economies and the 'Affluent Society' of the 1950s. Today the task for Labour is to live down its association with inflation in much the same way that the task for the Conservatives after 1945 was to live down their association with mass unemployment.

What Gaitskell was after in 1959, and what the German SPD achieved in that year, was a symbolic break with the past. The

Kinnock–Hattersley document may be seminal for students of ideology but unless it results in dramatic policy reverses at conference, or in an almighty row which Mr Kinnock is seen to win, it is unlikely to serve the same purpose. By producing an ideological manifesto at this time Mr Kinnock has shrewdly made sure that if Tony Benn and the Left challenge his leadership they will be forced to pitch their antique socialism against his belated version of social democracy.

Independent, 9 February 1988

The momentous events of 1989 saw the collapse of the Communist regimes of Eastern Europe in a series of popular revolutions. Jenkins wrote many pieces on the events as they occurred and the articles reproduced here reflect the mixture of reportage and analysis that characterised his writing on the fall of communism. The first marks the ending of the Communist Party of Great Britain, while the second records the events of the year. In the final piece in this section Jenkins interviews and profiles the hero of the Czechoslovakian revolution, Vaclav Havel. The themes that emerge from these pieces reflected his often repeated thesis that the Thatcher Revolution could not be understood as a domestic event but had to be placed in an international context. They also reflect his increasing focus on the European dimension of British politics.

After socialism, what's left?

With just a tinge of sadness one notes the passing of the Communist Party of Great Britain. At its 41st Congress in London at the weekend, the Party was told that historically the game was up, its remaining 7,500 comrades as good as redundant. A banal event compared with what has been happening across Eastern Europe, compared even with the Italian Communists' abandonment of Eurocommunism in favour of social democracy. The British Communist Party was always a poor thing but it was our own.

Politically insignificant in Britain from the time of the schism in the labour movement which followed the Bolshevik Revolution, the Communist Party – or 'the party' as it was invariably referred to –

played a part in perpetuating Britain's conflictual industrial relations; the class war was fought on the assembly lines, the docks and the pits. But the Party could always bask a little in the march of history: lost deposits in Britain, yes, but across half the postwar world the Red Flag was flying.

Their subversive industrial role and their ties with Moscow gave the Communists I used to know as a young labour correspondent a certain exotic appeal. The Jesuits of the labour movement, they tended to be better educated and more various than your average trade union general-secretary. The young, militant ones boiled over with class rage and hatred while others kept vodka and caviare in their fridges. The older ones, especially the miners, were often amiable and colourful characters. To be English and a Party member was a heavy business by the early sixties, but for a Welshman or a Scot, with memories of the coalfields in the thirties, it was simply to be part of another culture. Mick McGahey, of the Scottish miners, rates among the great conversationalists of our times and there were few nicer men around than Will Paynter, the Welsh miner who became general-secretary of the national union. RIP, CPGB.

Pronouncing the obsequies this weekend was Martin Jacques, editor of the trendy monthly *Marxism Today*, which remains, astonishingly, the official theoretical journal of the Party. The essence of his message was contained in these words: 'It is the end of the road for the Communist system. Stalinism is dead and Leninism has had its day. We are witnessing the defeat of socialism.'

Mr Jacques was presenting the congress with its new manifesto, an out-and-out revisionist document entitled 'New Times'. Times have not entirely changed, however, for the advance hand-out of Mr Jacques's speech reported that his remarks were greeted with 'enthusiastic and sustained applause', the sort of behaviour expected when the death sentence was passed at a Moscow show trial in the thirties, whereas Ian Aitken, who was there for the *Guardian*, reported, 'The audience appeared dumb-struck by the horror of it . . . No standing ovation for Martin. Instead, he got a brief round of applause . . .'

In another way these 'New Times' are not as new as they are made out to be, for all the great razzmatazz with which *Marxism Today* presents its production numbers; and let me say, before I go on, that Mr Jacques is an editor of considerable flair who produces a lively magazine. But his 'New Times' are old hat. They could only bring the shock of the new to ideologues who for years have lived at far remove from any real world.

The chief feature of 'New Times' is that 'the old world of mass production for mass markets has increasingly given way to something far more diverse'. This is called 'post-Fordism' – everything has to be post-something at *Marxism Today*. The reference is to Henry Ford (who died in 1947), not to the All-out-lads stewards down at Dagenham, more recently extinct. Yet the American sociologist Daniel Bell published his *The Coming of the Post-Industrial Society* in 1974, defining such a society as one in which knowledge played the central role in determining power and wealth. The decline of the working class had already become a platitude when the French Communist turned new-philosopher, André Gorz, said his 'farewell' to it in a vogue book published in 1982. The new patterns of consumption, of which 'New Times' makes much, date back to the 'affluent worker' who was first discovered at around the time Harold Macmillan told people that they had never had it so good and was much studied by Socialist thereafter. Ronald Inglehart's pioneering studies of 'post-materialism' date back to 1971.

Did all this really pass Marxist intellectuals by? *Marxism Today* seemed more up with the times in the days when the Labour Party was in ideological ferment, Ken Livingstone was in residence at County Hall, the Militants were on the rampage in Liverpool, the Bennites were ranting at party conference. Those were the days when duty required a weekly visit to Collet's in the Charing Cross Road for the latest from the sectarian presses. The Left may not have been important (except as a plague upon the Labour Party) but, at least, it was interesting. Today I don't bother to read the *New Statesman*.

If the Left is going to regain some intellectual verve it will have to do better than 'New Times' and what passes for new thinking in the Labour Party. Having entombed socialism in history, Mr Jacques, at the end of his speech, declares its triumphant resurrection. Even now he has to reject the notion that 'because the old forms of socialism are dead, then so is socialism'. But why? To be sure, some of the values which played a part in the Socialist era – egalitarianism, fraternity, solidarity – will last into the post-Socialist age in the same way that many of the values of the liberal era were expropriated by the Socialists. But clinging to socialism, even the word, I fear, will only serve to cloud the mind. Already we can see the ecological crisis coming over the brow of history like the US Cavalry to replace the crisis of capitalism. But what comes after socialism ought now to be the question for the Left. Marxism, even *Marxism Today*, has had its day.

Independent, 28 November 1989

Europe with a new face

Even in retrospect, it is difficult to keep pace with the events of 1989. Europe was transformed. The future of Mikhail Gorbachev and his *perestroika* remains in grave doubt, but even if an ill-willed regime replaces his in Moscow, it will remain unlikely that the Soviet Union can recover its Eastern European empire, even should it wish to do so.

It will also be much more difficult to threaten the West than in the past: Soviet military power will remain awesome, but the Warsaw Pact is virtually defunct as a military organisation. The Cold War is over and, in all probability, will stay over.

This makes certain that the changes occurring within the Atlantic community in response will also be permanent. The United States will not disengage from Europe emotionally or politically, as during the isolationist years between the wars, but a substantial military disengagement seems now inevitable. This, as I was suggesting yesterday, should not be regarded as due to budgetary constraints, although they are part of the story, but flows from a radical change in threat perception in the US. This leaves European members of NATO with the choice of reducing their own military forces accordingly or trying to make good the deficiencies resulting from the American retrenchment. With public opinion convinced that the Soviet threat is now minimal, there can be little doubt in which direction the democracies will be driven.

Nuclear weapons will continue to provide mutual deterrence from all-out war and, in the new circumstances, the national deterrent forces of France and Britain will be at additional premium. But peace and stability short of general warfare will have to depend increasingly on political and economic structures. It is these which have kept the peace within Western Europe, ending the historic animosity between

France and Germany, and the next task will be to extend those structures to the east. In modern circumstances of open communication and economic interdependence there is no reason why the collapse of the Soviet empire in Eastern Europe should produce the same results as the demise of the Austro-Hungarian and Ottoman empires. The break-up of the Russian Empire itself might be another story.

The European Community, regarded everywhere except Britain (or 10 Downing Street) as a great success story of the postwar period, is allotted an important role as the superpowers recede as the arbiters of Europe. In its early days the EC was an engine of prosperity and may be so again after 1992 when it becomes an economic superpower.

Not only has it provided a firm fabric of peace in the West, making war quite unthinkable, but a powerful magnet to the East. Military resolve played an indispensable part in the winning of the Cold War, but even more important was the political and economic triumph of liberal capitalism over communism.

It may well be, however, that at this moment of triumph the historic role of the EC in its present form is complete. What became the EC was first conceived at the moment of Stalin's finally dividing Europe. Jean Monnet and Konrad Adenauer were among the founding fathers of this Cold War institution. Their model has served well but may not be the model for post-Cold War Europe. It will be a long while yet before Poland, Hungary or, probably, any of the formerly Stalinist economies of Eastern Europe can realistically contemplate full membership of the EC. In order most effectively to help them, its own integration must proceed. But with the prospect of a pan-European order replacing the postwar division, Western European integration ceases to be an historical end in itself.

The German question lies at the heart of the matter just as Germany geographically is at the heart of Europe. Last May I attended a conference in Berlin at which wise men from all sides agreed that the German Question was not on anybody's agenda. Now that it is so prominent on the Germans' agenda, the statesmen of Europe are rallying behind the status quo in the hope of managing the transition which must be made. The concert of Europe became complete when Eduard Shevardnadze visited NATO headquarters and made plainer Soviet objections to (or, perhaps, terms for) the unification of Germany. But at the same moment Helmut Kohl was being feted by the people of Dresden. Watching these events juxtaposed on the TV news left little doubt as to who would decide the direction and pace of events.

It has been a joyous year for freedom, and bliss was it in this dawn to be a journalist. But, as the year ends, our early-year reading should not be forgotten. Revolutions consume their heroes and are betrayed, July days give way to *Thermidors* and *Brumaires*, and Bastilles have a habit of rising from their rubble.

Independent, 21 December 1989

The playwright, the drama and the real world

Some of the correspondents grumbled that metal detectors had been introduced, but the security was light by Western standards. The citizenry can wander through the precincts of Hradcany Castle – 'the castle', as in 'the White House'. A small notice indicates the offices of the President behind unguarded glass doors. We took our places and awaited the President.

Vaclav Havel was reporting on his return from the Kremlin. Havel in the Kremlin! The idea was still absurd – a word much employed among his literary and intellectual friends-turned-politicians.

Havel – it is hard to prefix an artist with the word president as if he were Bush or Mitterand – was asked whether the invitation to President Richard von Weizsacker of West Germany to visit Czechoslovakia on the exact anniversary of the 1939 Nazi invasion was a good idea. (It was a put-up question, evidence that the playwright is no slouch as a politician.) Yes, he said, it was an excellent idea, and his own. Then he said: 'I like symbols in politics. Professional politicians do not have much experience in this, less than in the theatre and the arts.'

He went on to explain, in wonderful words, why he had contrived this symbolism to advertise Czech freedom and independence – 'more sovereign than at any time since Munich' – and the contrast between the Germany which could elect so admirable a president and the Germany of Hitler.

The ceremonial guard of honour planned for the occasion, I learnt later, will be wearing uniforms styled by Theodor Pistek, the film designer who won an Oscar for *Amadeus*, and perform to an anthem by the composer-pop musician Michael Kocab, who played a pivotal role at one moment of the November Revolution and is today an MP.

Later, in a restaurant, it was related how Havel, in New York, had teased Jane Fonda with a shocking account of how he was organising a motor-cycle brigade dressed in black leather and blue helmets, mounted on 950cc Hondas. But don't worry, he told her, there would be a red heart painted on each petrol tank.

A certain ambivalence here, perhaps, as in a Havel play – a touch of the absurd – but beneath it, also as in a Havel play, a deep moral seriousness. Havel, his friends say, is committed to restoring the dignity and power of the presidency, with his inter-war predecessor Tomas Masaryk as the model; at the same time he entertains at court the Campaign for a Merrier Present, one of the most engaging of the revolutionary groups gathered under the umbrella of Civic Forum.

The two styles – the sobriety of the moral Masaryk and the bohemianism of Havel and his friends of the *boulevard* – reflect the dramatic tension between the celebration of freedom and the addressing of formidable problems which are the twin tasks of a nation newly liberated from communism. Within Civic Forum are those who, in 1968-speak, can utter such meaningless prescriptions as: 'Create space, fill it with information, and let the people decide', and the more numerous hard and serious persons who grasp the acute dilemma of a post-totalitarian society essaying political and economic liberalisation at a stroke.

Czechoslovakia is going headlong for democracy. Elections are in June, but no programme of economic reform is yet in place. Already the economic consequences of democracy are presenting themselves. Tomas Jezek, economic adviser at the Finance Ministry (also the translator of Hayek) said: 'We liberal economists know very well that prices should immediately reflect relative scarcities, but this means increases in real prices which scare the politicians, with elections near.'

In the opinion of the Finance Minister, Vaclav Klaus, Czechoslovakia has never had, nor probably will ever have, a stronger government. The view is shared by the co-ordinator of Civic Forum, Jan Urban, a brilliant and appealing man (a historian of Byzantium by trade but a bricklayer these last few years) who says: 'The moment for belt-tightening is now. After the elections people will ask what were we doing for eight months? Today we can blame the Communists for everything. After the elections we will be to blame.'

But another group, centred on the Deputy Prime Minister, Valtr Komarek, preaches gradualism and structural reform. The two schools battle for the President's ear but on economics the President's attention span is short. His attitude is that economics are for economists to decide, not playwrights. By instinct he is a gradualist. When it was explained to him that subsidies must be removed he enquired about the price of the theatre tickets and flinched. A speech made Churchillian allusion to sweat and tears but left out the blood. Blood, metaphorically, is what the liberal economists are baying for; it won't work if it doesn't hurt.

Among the strengths of the Czechs are their democratic instincts and experience; their folk memory of a pre-Communist work ethic; a higher base of prosperity than in other Soviet dependencies save East Germany; and no foreign debt on the scale of Poland or Hungary. Their weakness is to have been the most socialised of all, forced to be the heavy workshop of the Communist world. There is virtually no private sector and a pattern of trade locked into supplying large quantities of low-quality goods to the starved Soviet market.

This condition leads to the conclusion that structural reform – privatisation and some decentralisation – should precede liberalisation. Otherwise, it is argued, there could be massive unemployment and wage-driven inflation. The liberals see no alternative; without price decontrol and currency convertibility, the Western investment will go to Poland and Hungary; Czechoslovakia will exchange one subservient role for another as the reserve army of cheap labour for the West.

This debate is not yet articulated between parties, although it will be before long; at the moment it is a debate within a powerful consensus committed to democracy, human rights, social justice and a free market – the declared aims of Civic Forum. Under that umbrella march eight parties, Social and Christian Democrats arm in arm, and many tendencies beside. Said the leader of the Socialist Party (now Social Democrat), Jan Skoda, who lent his Wenceslas Square balcony to Havel at a crucial moment in November: 'We all know what we don't want but we have no very clear ideas for the future.'

That is the danger for the moment, that the elections will be a plebiscite about the past and result in no clear understanding of what lies ahead. Anti-communism is the prevailing electoral passion, the word Socialist no longer usable in polite society, all schemes for a 'third way' sunk before launch; Havel himself, engaged and stimulated by Gorbachev, is reputed to have rated him 'a perfect human being save in one regard – he is a Communist.'

And yet this anti-communism, combined with a passion for freedom and independence, may be the greatest asset of these newly free countries, the basis of a national consensus which transcends for now the quarrels of party. 'Who cares about goods in the shops when we can think and say what we wish?' asked our housewife-interpreter.

Civic Forum urges that this revolutionary moment be seized in both respects, to mobilise the country behind the imperative of economic reform and to install a multi-party parliamentary democracy. Civic Forum is a citizens' movement with many of the attributes of a party. It will be endorsing candidates from eight parties in the elections. Havel, with his immense moral authority, is ostensibly above party, but what if voters in their inexperience mistake the endorsement of Civic Forum for the endorsement of Havel? When I asked this of Urban he merely smiled. He hoped to see from the June elections a constituent assembly in the hands of a stable multi-party coalition, effectively selected by Civic Forum.

And who will then choose the Government? Effectively, the President will. From the attractive disorder of revolution real power is emerging armed with great moral authority, a democratic order in the making. Looking down from Havel's hilltop castle on to the baroque splendours of one of the most civilised cities in Europe, it is hard to believe otherwise, difficult already to credit the long Communist nightmare.

Independent, 6 March 1990

CHAPTER EIGHT

The Revolution Consumes Its Hero:

The End of Thatcher

Throughout the 1980s Jenkins charted the progress of the American New Right project headed by the old actor Ronald Reagan. In this article he reviews the last act of Reagan's presidency.

Last line of the Ronald Reagan story

New Orleans – Ronald Reagan's last words, at the very end of his long, sometimes rambling and nostalgic Farewell Address to the Republican Party, were these: 'We did all that could be done. Never less.' A valedictory commonplace, you might think: just the thing the old actor might say accepting a special Oscar to mark the end of a lifetime's career. But the words have special significance. They were an echo of his entrance lines 24 years ago. In a sensational television broadcast on the eve of the 1964 San Francisco convention at which Barry Goldwater won the Republican nomination, later to lose the election in a landslide to Lyndon Johnson, Ronald Reagan declared to the American people: 'You and I have a rendezvous with destiny. We can preserve for our children this, the last best hope of man on earth, or we can sentence them to take the first step into a thousand years of darkness. If we fail, at least let our children say of us, we justified our brief moment here. We did all that could be done.'

Those words were to become famous and today seem prophetic.

The phrase 'rendezvous with destiny' was a straight lift from Franklin D. Roosevelt. Until 1962 Ronald Reagan had been nominally a Democrat. Rewriting history around himself on Monday night, he presented Roosevelt not as someone who used the power of the federal Government to lift the US out of depression and attack its social injustices but, rather, as a campaigner against too much government and a champion of states' rights. 'They left me, I didn't leave them,' he said of the Democrats.

That became part of the Reagan mythology, that he was the true descendant of Roosevelt and the New Deal. That he believed it himself, and talked as if he did, played a part in winning the support of predominantly ethnic, blue-collar workers who in large numbers in 1980, and in 1984, deserted the old Roosevelt coalition for the new Reagan coalition. But the clarion to the conservative wing of the Republican Party were those words spoken on behalf of Goldwater in 1964. Thereafter Reagan was their champion. He propelled himself to national political fame as Governor of California in 1968, and made his first stab at the presidency in that year. He came within a whisker of seizing the nomination from Gerald Ford in 1976 and, of course, won it triumphantly in 1980. In that year what Goldwater had begun finally came to pass: the conservative capture of the Republican Party was complete.

The message he preached, then and now, was simplicity itself. A favourite line, always a winner with his audiences, was to tell Americans 'It ain't easy but it *is* simple.' His agenda was economic freedom at home, political freedom abroad, and America strong again militarily and strong again morally. Part of the Reagan trick was to go on saying the same things regardless of what he was actually doing. Of the conservatives' social agenda he delivered not at all. But he kept the moral majority at bay by going on talking about constitutional amendments to ensure the 'right to life' and prayers in the schools. The technique had served him in California, where as Governor he had actually signed an abortion law, and it would serve him to the end as President. It became known as the Teflon factor – nothing would stick to him.

He was at it again on Monday, preaching a balanced budget while bequeathing a gigantic fiscal deficit brought about by simultaneously slashing taxes and increasing military expenditures. 'What do you do,' asked his first budget director, David Stockman, 'when your President ignores all the palpable, relevant facts and wanders in circles?' Reagan, according to Stockman, failed to grasp the link between taxation and the budget. 'The President can't spend a dime,' he told the convention on Monday. 'Only the Congress can do that.' Simple.

The Reagan legacy includes a booming economy, much stimulated by fiscal improvidence. Its foundations may be flimsy, given the size of the federal debt and, more important, the trade deficit. But for the moment, its political foundations are secure. Having tried it twice and failed, the Democrats this year have forsworn all talk of tax increases. Without tax increases the scope for increased federal spending is small. In this way they are obliged to live in the shadow of Ronald Reagan in much the same way as the Republicans lived in the shadow of Franklin Roosevelt until Goldwater and Reagan came along.

If Reagan was lucky in that at home he presided over the worldwide recovery from the recession and the great inflation of the 1970s, he was luckier still abroad in his adversary, Mikhail Gorbachev. Once again history is rewritten in the service of the Reagan myth. The man who denounced the 'evil empire' suggests now that all along the purpose was to negotiate with the Soviets from strength, the end of rearmament was disarmament. Simple. But in this case also, with peace breaking out seemingly all around the world, the political lines have been redrawn by the Reagan myth. A Democrat, aspiring to the White House, must champion American military strength as the foundation of American influence for peace.

Time now for change? 'We are the change,' declared Reagan in his Farewell Address. True, in that he bequeaths a powerful myth around which the election will be fought. But while Roosevelt built a coalition which held together for two decades, the Reagan majority may prove more flimsy and personal. The old actor's exit line, echoing his entrance 24 years earlier, sounded not like the seal on an era so much as the last line of the Ronald Reagan Story. Titles. Music.

Independent, 17 August 1988

In May 1989, Mrs Thatcher declined to celebrate the tenth anniversary of her premiership, reflecting the mood of insecurity which began to overtake the Thatcherites. Despite the transient success of the new free-market economics and the Lawson boom, by the end of the decade much of the gloss had been wiped off the Thatcher Revolution. Like many former admirers of David Owen, Jenkins had, by the end of the decade, found much to praise in Mrs Thatcher's record.

Reflections on the Thatcher Revolution: 1

Her achievements are scarcely in doubt. She has held power for a decade and wielded it with prodigious industry and unabated zeal. It has been an increasingly personal kind of power, based upon mastery of her party and of the governmental machine, but rooted in her imperious temperament. The decade which preceded her had been one of instability and discontinuity.

During her decade the economy has grown faster than in the one before and, although many problems remain unsolved, its underlying efficiency has improved. Britain's decline relative to others, for the time being at least, has been arrested and reversed, although it will take decades to catch up with Germany, France and other more prosperous nations.

The *ancien regime* has been in large part swept away. Few today would say, as was widely believed in the 1970s, that Britain could be governed only with the consent of unelected trade unions. The power of the public sector, as wielded through the nexus of nationalised board, municipal employer and trade union, has been broken. Other centres of power have been reduced, notably local control of taxation and spending, while patronage – used with an eighteenth-century lack of scruple – has built a power base for the new regime in all areas of national life including the Church, the universities, broadcasting and the arts.

By governing with the grain of social and democratic change, encouraging ownership, capital accumulation, consumer choice, and attacking restrictionism and welfare dependency, she has made the Thatcher decade midwife to the birth of a new society. Put dramatically and over-simply, the them-and-us model of a class society, ruling and working, has given way to a society the shape of a fat diamond, characterised by material majoritarianism and an excluded underclass.

This Americanisation, particularly of urban society, with its attendant growth of social violence, physical dilapidation and ostentatious degradation of the poor, has not been matched by an Americanisation of political society; rather, the reverse. Economic liberalism has gone hand in hand with an authoritarianism which has impinged upon personal freedoms as well as local and professional autonomies. Material prosperity confers freedoms of its own, but the rights of citizenship have not been similarly enhanced; in some respects they have been diminished.

The achievements, for good or ill, of the past decade cannot be distinguished easily from the consequences of the decade which brought her to power. She came in as liquidator to a bankrupt order. It is not of her doing, although it may well be to her liking, that for 10 years the country has lacked a viable and effective opposition. The exigencies of her inheritance to a large extent dictated national priorities; her often repeated cry that 'there *is* no alternative' was a typical piece of dogmatism but, at the same time, an accurate description of an ideological vacuum. These dislocations of the two-party system have given her an air of permanence which would not otherwise have attached to her as a fallible politician.

It is hardly surprising that tomorrow's anniversary should be attended by intimations of mortality. Ten years is a long time in politics. It is a long while to stretch the patience of a democracy. As Machiavelli knew, 'Men are fond of novelty, so much so that those who are prosperous desire it as much as those who are poor. For, as has been said before, and rightly, in prosperity men get fed up and in adversity cast down.'

The opinion polls commissioned for the occasion, including the *Independent*'s own, indicate a high degree of ambivalence towards the Thatcher decade and a brooding sense of moral dissatisfaction. Whether or not these responses are indicative of changing political attitudes, they must count as valid comments on the Thatcher years. Many people, it would seem, while recognising that they are better off, do not feel that their lives are better qualitatively. Of Gallup's respondents, only 37 per cent agreed that 'overall this is a better country to live in than it was 10 years ago', while more than twice as many (49 per cent) thought that national pride had diminished as thought it had increased (22 per cent).

In her foreign policy she has played to patriotic sentiment. It is odd that she has so ignored it at home. Britain is a run-down, dirty and congested place in which planning is subordinated to speculation. She has shown no pride in great national institutions – the National Health Service, the universities, the BBC – and no concern for the nation's art treasures housed in their crumbling museums. She has built no monuments.

'Thatcherism', as I have long insisted, is more properly regarded as a style than as a coherent ideology. Styles wear thin with time. Asked what annoys them most about her, 24 per cent of Harris's respondents say 'her voice' and 19 per cent her 'uncaring nature'. Seldom in a democracy can such ascendancy have been achieved by a leader so unloved. When people turn finally against her, they may do so with a vengeance.

Independent, 3 May 1989

Reflections on the Thatcher Revolution: 2

Revolutions have their own logic or, at least, their own powerful mythologies – their Fructidors, Thermidors and Brumaires, their Februaries and their Octobers. Mrs Thatcher's 'revolution' is no exception: it began with a burst of enthusiasm in 1979, was almost betrayed in 1980, took on new life with the seminal Budget of 1981, went to war in 1982; then, after the great victory of 1983, the Government drifted until saved by a booming economy. But the 1987 election was fought on a radical programme and, now, in the third term, we have seen a new burst of radical zeal. That is roughly how the official history is written.

The Prime Minister is much influenced by her reading of her own past. Ten years in office have given her history. Her sole regret is that she did not push forward harder and faster earlier on; she remembers how, each time the going got rough, she was warned to hold back by fainthearts and 'consolidators', the 'wets' as were; yet her instincts or convictions, when she stuck to them, usually paid off – 'Thatcherism' worked. Thus she is unlikely to be moved by the whingeing on the doorsteps that, this time, she has 'gone too far'. She heard all that in 1985. 'Momentum' is the order of the day.

So momentum there is, but only down certain narrow roads. Take water privatisation: who seriously believes that the ownership and organisation of the water industry is among the most urgent problems facing the nation? But privatisation is privatisation, quintessentially Thatcherite. Meanwhile, far more urgent matters lie in the Government's pending tray, while her Ministers sit petrified in the face of prime ministerial dogma.

Take two examples. The first is the issue of community care for the aged, the physically handicapped and the mentally ill. The present system is a chaotic shambles: somebody has to be in charge. More than a year ago, Mrs Thatcher's own special health adviser, Sir Roy Griffiths of Sainsbury, analysed the problem with great care and concluded that the only agency capable of co-ordination in this field was the local authority. But that was like telling Mrs Thatcher that Jacques Delors in Brussels should be put in charge of British industrial relations. A solution which required giving more power or responsibility to local authorities was politically unacceptable. So the Thatcher think tanks went to work. What about a new agency altogether? How about district health authorities or the GP committees? All such possibilities were studied by a Cabinet committee chaired by the Prime Minister. A year later and the Government has done nothing. At the last meeting it was forced back to square one and the conclusion that the Griffiths proposals should be given 'more study'; that is, at least as far as the elderly are concerned.

What to do about the homeless is a similar parable of paralysis. The plight of these families and their children has become quite shocking. Ministers know perfectly well that the bed-and-breakfast system is a cruel disgrace as well as being expensive and inefficient. Something must certainly be done. The answer is to enable local authorities to make alternative provision. The Audit Commission has told the Government how best to do it. Local authorities! Over Mrs Thatcher's dead body. So nothing is done.

Thus, while the rhetoric is of revolution and radicalism, the conservative arteries of this Government are all the while hardening with the passing of time. 'Momentum' may be the slogan, but immobilism is increasingly the result of her imperial prime ministership. The row slowly brewing up over British participation in the Exchange Rate Mechanism of the European Monetary System is another example, with the combined weight of the Treasury and the Foreign Office seemingly incapable of prying open the Prime Minister's mind.

We should remember on this anniversary day just how long in the job is 10 whole years. Like Queen Elizabeth I, she has outlived a whole crop of courtiers, chopping off the heads of a good few; her intricate knowledge of the government machine enables her to interfere lovingly in the smallest detail of its business; nothing much can be done, or dare be done, without her royal approval; increasingly her government is conducted by whim and diktat. She has grown set in her ways, set in her cronies, set in her ideas. 'Thatcherism' is Mrs Thatcher. *La révolution, c'est moi.*

It has been an astonishing *tour de force*, a triumph of stamina and of the will. History will surely recognise her achievements as Britain's first woman Prime Minister, a leader with the courage of her convictions, who assailed the conventional wisdom of her day, challenged and overthrew the existing order, changed the political map, and put her country on its feet again. She did all this with ruthlessness and much injustice and at a high cost in human misery, but she did it. Yet note how, 10 years on, we begin to slip into the past tense.

Independent, 4 May 1989

The most obvious faultline which ran through the Thatcher Cabinet was called Europe. The Prime Minister set out her own personal vision of a non-federal Europe, a Gaullist Europe, in a celebrated speech at Bruges in September 1988, in which she warned against the threat to the Thatcherite Revolution from the bureaucrats of Brussels, sneaking in socialism 'through the back door'. A year later Jenkins, an ardent supporter of a united Europe, reflected on the impact of that speech.

The sort of Europe Britain wants

Few political speeches are remembered or are worth remembering. In recent times there have been Winston Churchill's 'iron curtain' speech at Fulton, Missouri, Harold Macmillan on 'the wind of change', Hugh Gaitskell's 'fight, fight and fight again', and Enoch Powell's notorious

'Tiber foaming with blood'. Margaret Thatcher's speech at Bruges, made a year ago today, belongs – tentatively, at least – in the same class.

But was it truly such a seminal occasion? Re-reading it, it is not obvious why. It contains one famous, stinging line: 'We have not successfully rolled back the frontiers of the State in Britain, only to see them reimposed at a European level, with a European superstate exercising a new dominance from Brussels.' But the rest of it, a year on, seems neither as outspokenly provocative or wise as its enemies and proponents contend.

Speeches, however, are more than their texts; they are theatrical events, and the one she made to the College of Europe in Bruges, for some reason, got everybody going. It was seen on the Continent as a renewed declaration of war by a British Prime Minister on what, in the parlance of the European Community, is called the 'construction of Europe'. It was welcomed by the free-market wing of the Conservative Party as a belated declaration of British nationalism, the dropping of the second Powellite boot, so to speak. By the Heathite (or, by then, Heseltine) tendency in the Party it was seen as a display of the sort of behaviour to be expected when the supporters of Grantham United were let loose on the Continent. In other words, it was a speech guaranteed to reinforce prejudices all round.

To see why, it must be placed against its background. In the February of last year the long-running row over the Common Agricultural Policy and the Community's budget had been settled for the time being. The question became what next, what after 1992? Momentum built behind the idea of economic and monetary union, an old dream whose totem was a central European Bank. Mrs Thatcher's answer to the question 'what after 1992' was 'Hang on a minute, let's finish that job first.' There remained a long way to go in the process of deregulation (or the 'Thatcherisation' of Europe) which she took to be the essence of the 1992 project. However, lurking behind this pragmatic front was the notion that 1992 should mark the end of the march of European history, at least as far as the Community was concerned. A free market between sovereign states was a sufficient end in itself, not a means to some other, such as the United States of Europe.

It was against this background that at Bruges she restated – for there was nothing very new in what she said – her consistent and gut antagonism to any form of supranationalism. But if the speech she delivered had a shrillness of tone which lifted it above its content it was because she had been particularly infuriated by the appearance of Jacques Delors at the annual Trades Union Congress in Bournemouth, where his prospectus for a 'Social Europe' had received a rapturous reception. At Cabinet a few days later the Prime Minister was at her most loquacious and vituperative on the subject of how, having expelled the pestilence of socialism from British shores, she was not prepared to see it brought in again from the Continent like rabies.

It is by no means clear that the Bruges speech changed anything very much. It expressed somewhat aggressively what the other European leaders knew perfectly well to be her position. When they all next met at Rhodes in December the matter was not mentioned. Moreover, a good deal of what she said was true and some of it timely, for example: 'We must never forget that east of the Iron Curtain, peoples who once enjoyed a full share of European culture, freedom and identity have been cut off from their roots.'

At home, as well, it was not the Bruges speech itself which led her into conflict with her Chancellor, Nigel Lawson, and the Foreign Secretary, Sir Geoffrey Howe. Their rows were already well in progress. Mr Lawson, for his part, had no complaint against her opposition to economic and monetary union and the loss of national sovereignty that this involved. His argument with her was about exchange rate policy, not Europe.

The impact of the speech on the Conservative Party was somewhat greater. It reopened the latent divide on Europe, raising the temperature once more of an issue which had long divided not only the country but both political parties. But at the time it must have seemed to Mrs Thatcher like a blow well struck. Her postbag brimmed over, overwhelmingly with approval. She had spoken for the nation, or so she thought. Nor, subsequently, was there to be the slightest indication that she in any way regretted what she had said, or the way in which she said it.

Why then is the Bruges speech so remembered? Why has it entered into the shorthand of political discourse? Partly, because it served as a text for a genuine debate, an old one but important – what sort of Europe did the British people want?

Partly also, perhaps, because it struck a chord at that moment. Her declaration in favour of 'the willing and active co-operation between independent sovereign states' coincided with a general revival of the spirit of nationalism in both Western and Eastern Europe. Moreover, this may even have been her purpose, for on her way to make the speech she was heard to reflect on the difficulty of stirring the British to the patriotic endeavour necessary for the achievement of her 'enterprise society'. Perhaps in Mr Delors she thought she glimpsed her new Galtieri.

The Bruges speech, if not exactly seminal, was a classic expression of the Prime Minister's convictions and instincts. What happened later did not flow directly from it but flowed from her. For it was not what was said in Bruges last September but her aberrant behaviour in May and June this year which alarmed her colleague and her party. There was the ridiculous fuss over health warnings on cigarette packets, the ill-judged and unnecessary opposition to the Lingua programme and the notorious 'diet of Brussels' poster, all of it culminating in the debacle of the European elections. If this should turn out to have been the beginning of the end, it will be the word Bruges not Calais written on her heart.

Independent, 20 September 1989

In October the divisions in the Government became apparent to all with the resignation of Mrs Thatcher's long-serving and pugnacious Chancellor, Nigel Lawson. Ostensibly a dispute between the Chancellor and Prime Minister over the role of Mrs Thatcher's personal economic adviser Sir Alan Walters, Lawson's resignation was in fact the bitter climax to a long-running dispute over British membership of the European Monetary System. As Jenkins correctly pointed out in the following article, Europe was at the heart of all the Government's problems.

A deep crisis of confidence in Thatcher

We have a crisis of confidence in the Prime Minister. By refusing to dispense with her personal economic adviser she provoked the resignation of her Chancellor and sparked a major run on the pound. It was her most disastrous day's work in 10 years.

It required a singular lack of proportion to prefer a part-time monetarist don domiciled in the United States to the man whose economic policies won her the last election and who, by general consent, was the most qualified of postwar Chancellors.

The state of her Government begins to resemble that of Harold Macmillan's after 1962. There is now a smell of decay in the air. Governments do not become accident-prone by accident. A series of spectacular misjudgements says a great deal about the lack of balanced advice available to her and the absence of collective ballast to her Government.

Europe has been the issue underlying most of Mrs Thatcher's biggest errors. Europe was at the root of the Westland affair, which in 1986 provoked the resignation from the Cabinet of Michael Heseltine and, by her own admission, could have brought her down.

It was Europe which drove her to excesses which helped to lose her the elections to the European Parliament last June. Europe was the issue on which she sacked Sir Geoffrey Howe from the Foreign Office last summer, badly upsetting her party in the process. Now Europe is the issue underlying the resignation of her Chancellor.

His departure throws the Government into double crisis, economic and political. Markets were quick to take his resignation as a sign of diminished commitment to a strong exchange rate. Now that she is seen to be in effect in charge of the Government's economic policy, Mrs Thatcher may have to demonstrate her will by a further sharp increase in interest rates. That could tip the economy into a recession from which it might not recover by the time of the next election.

The political crisis centres on Mrs Thatcher's style. It comes hard on the heels of her embarrassment of John Major at the Commonwealth leaders' conference in Kuala Lumpur. He takes over at the Treasury with the reputation of being her creature. Although her party will close ranks, as it always does in such moments, she no longer enjoys the confidence of a substantial and growing element within it and may be hard-put to regain it.

Her senior colleagues will have to think hard about what is to be done. Had Sir Geoffrey, Mr Lawson, and Douglas Hurd (who becomes Foreign Secretary) formed a solid front against her earlier on Europe, the rot could have been stopped. The damage she has inflicted on the Government is in large part also the result of supine colleagues. Mr Lawson has shown himself the only one with the guts to take a stand.

A year ago, when she was considering bringing Professor Walters back to No. 10, Mr Lawson argued vigorously against. He foresaw in precise terms the difficulties this might cause and warned her of them. She was undeterred. Sir Alan returned in May.

The root of the problem was that Sir Alan's very presence at her side inspired a lack of market confidence in her own Chancellor's policy. Sir Alan's views were so well known to be the opposite of Mr Lawson's on key points of policy that her choice of him as her personal adviser, and her decision to bring him back, was bound to be taken as a sign of continuing policy differences at the top of the Government.

Recently one of Mrs Thatcher's closest confidants said privately that her attitude was 'trust your accountant, never trust the bank manager'. Mr Lawson was the bank manager, Sir Alan her accountant.

Moreover, it was made abundantly plain by those close to her that she had no intention whatsoever of observing the spirit of the compromise she entered into at the Madrid summit of the European Community last June. There she committed Britain to join the Exchange Rate Mechanism of the European Monetary System during phase one of the Delors Plan for economic and monetary union, provided certain conditions were met. In reason, that should have meant some time next year, but it remained her firm intention to spin it out beyond the General Election.

Mr Hurd is a proponent of Europe and the EMS. Mr Major is seen to be less enthusiastic about the EMS than was Mr Lawson. Divisions on Europe will thus persist at the most senior levels of the Government. Europe remains at the heart of Mrs Thatcher's deepest crisis.

Independent, 27 October 1989

Nineteen ninety brought no respite for the beleaguered Thatcher Government. As well as the internal disputes over European policy, the new Community Charge – or 'Poll Tax' – proved instantly unpopular with not only the electorate as a whole, but Tory Party activists in particular. The Government's poll ratings continued to slide and what had passed for brave resolution in previous crises now came to look like little more than wilful stubbornness. As the Government's problems deepened, Mrs Thatcher's House of Commons performances became increasingly hysterical; in the following article, Jenkins describes the scene as Mrs Thatcher responded to what became known as the 'Rome ambush', when her European 'colleagues' had tried to bounce her into accepting further moves towards European integration. Mrs Thatcher's diatribes against the European Community were now delivered with a sombre and privately resentful Geoffrey Howe sitting beside her. Finally, on 1 November, Howe's patience ran out and he resigned, precipitating the final crisis of Mrs Thatcher's premiership.

Hyperbole laced with hysteria

The House was highly charged for the occasion, anticipating the climax to a tale of passion. Would she or would she not take the European train? Sir Geoffrey Howe, the station master, was at her side, whistle at the ready. Would she climb on board and wave tearful goodbyes to loved ones on the platform or stand there in a cloud of steam and watch the train draw slowly out to credits and music?

What she did was to hand her ticket to someone else. Several times she insisted that any decision to surrender the pound sterling to a single European currency must be reserved for 'future generations of parliaments and people'. Here was the clue to what may be her intention. She will seek agreement with Britain's European partners on a common way forward but she will never herself be party to a further subjugation of national sovereignty. *Après moi*, perhaps, but Margaret Thatcher – never!

It was as fascinating a display of Mrs Thatcher at bay as any I can remember. All was revealed, her mind an open book, her native political caution tugging her in one direction, her passions in another. The statement she began with was carefully crafted, a professional and diplomatic piece of work which ended with the pledge that Britain intended to remain a part of the future economic and political development of the European Community and would seek practical solutions to enable it to move forward with its partners. No two-speed or two-tier Europe, no relegation to the second division for her.

But once she was free of her text she began to say what she really thought. Goaded by the Leader of the Opposition, who accused her of having forfeited all claims to influence through her 'tantrum tactics', she launched the next minute into what sounded like a manifesto for a 'who rules Britain?' election campaign.

Her purpose was to retain the power and influence of the House of Commons. What was Mr Kinnock's? Would he agree to extend the Community's powers, into health policy for example? More power to the European Commission? More majority voting? The name Delors flashed into her mind. Had not he proposed the other day more powers for the European Parliament, the Commission to become the executive government, the Council of Ministers to be a senate? 'No, no, no!' she shrilled.

A Labour backbencher called upon her to 'save Britain and galvanise the people of this country'. If she had believed that Britain was, indeed, on the slippery slope to federal Europe, 'then I believe I would do just what the Honourable Member has said'.

Accused of wrapping herself in the Union Jack she shouted back: 'Better wrap yourself in the Union Jack than the Red Flag.' Dr Owen, who has nowhere else to wrap himself, urged her to go ahead and veto the knavish designs of the federalists who had jumped her in Rome. She 'totally agreed'. She went on to equate 'national identity' with monetary sovereignty. This was not the European Community we were promised when we joined, she said. 'The Commission is striving to extinguish democracy,' she alleged. To extinguish democracy?

The Foreign Secretary, beside her, tried not to look like a toad choking. Even her mutant teenage Chancellor paled when she came to the ecu. He has been doing a soft sell of his hard currency scheme, door-to-door in Europe, presenting it as an evolutionary means to a common and, perhaps, single currency. Well, actually, in her view the hard ecu was unlikely to catch on; she couldn't see it becoming widely used throughout the Community; certainly in Britain most people would prefer to stick to the pound. Mr Major looked as if he was about to experience the death of a salesman.

So it all came blurting out, hyperbole laced with hysteria, in a great stream of conviction consciousness. No thought was hidden, no prejudice restrained. And yet, there was the repeated refrain – the abrogation of monetary sovereignty would be for 'future parliaments and future generations'.

In yesterday's column I noted two possible devices that would provide that escape by enabling Mrs Thatcher to sign a Treaty amendment providing for economic and monetary union while reserving final parliamentary decision for a later date, well after her election. I pointed also to the hazards of opting out to fight an election on the question of who rules Britain, not least of which was that it would split her party.

From yesterday's display of split personality it appeared that her intention might be to do both, to compromise and not to compromise at all. Suppose she were to reach conditional accommodation with the 11 other members of the Community and then throw the question to the country? 'The people will not have it,' she keeps saying. So let them decide. Maggie Thatcher or Jacques Delors? Pound sterling or ecu? The more she let go yesterday, the more she seemed to warm to the idea. First make diplomatic peace, then declare political war.

Independent, 31 October 1990

Scorned veteran of Thatcher's long march

Europe has claimed another victim. Heseltine, Lawson, Ridley, now Howe. It is the Bermuda Triangle for those who sail with Margaret Thatcher. That message will not be lost on the Conservative Party in its present rattled state, nor on the public wondering whether this Government has entered its death throes.

The Prime Minister, apparently, was stunned when Sir Geoffrey told her at six o'clock last night that he could no longer accept her approach to Europe. He had gone through his motions at Cabinet that morning, setting out the programme for the new session of Parliament which the Queen will open next week. But she should not have been surprised. She had assiduously cold-shouldered her deputy Prime MInister since she had reluctantly allowed him that honorific when firing him from the Foreign Office in July of last year. At the time Downing Street had made no secret of regarding it as a 'non-job'. Mrs Thatcher brooks no deputies and Geoffrey was not to be 'another Willie'.

By then their relations were just too bad. He had come to irritate her beyond endurance with the blinking, stodgy style which had once been the hallmark of his dogged loyalty to her. He is the last of her original 1979 Cabinet, the only remaining veteran of the Long March of Thatcherism. It rankled with him that what he regarded as the Thatcher–Howe Revolution had become the 'Thatcher Revolution', as if he – the architect of the 1981 Budget – had become a non-person in its annals.

Europe is the running thread through this lengthening trail of casualty, even though deeper resentments may have boiled into Sir Geoffrey's uncharacteristic *démarche*. He is not one of nature's resigners although, he admitted to me in a radio interview last summer, he had considered his position when discharged from the Foreign Office. His attempt to force her hand on joining the Exchange Rate Mechanism of the EMS on the eve of the Madrid summit of the European Community in June 1989 had made their continuing partnership virtually impossible, at least for her. He had demanded that she set a deadline of July 1990 on when the time would be right. The story was that she locked her hotel door against him in Madrid.

Although he failed in that enterprise, Madrid – in retrospect – was the moment at which it became almost inevitable that another would succeed in persuading her, as did John Major, before 1990 was out. But by then she had quarrelled to the point of no return with another colleague, Nigel Lawson, whose resignation shook her Government last November.

At the Conservative Party conference last month, banished from the rostrum to the fringe, Sir Geoffrey warned: 'The next European train is about to leave, for a still undefined destination, but certainly in the direction of some form of EMU. Shall Britain be in the driver's cab this time or in the rear carriage?' In private conversations at that time his unhappiness was plain: he feared that in the case of Europe prejudice would be placed above country.

He was no 'Euro-fanatic', in the parlance of the Bruges Group; he never had been. But as Chancellor and Foreign Secretary he had come to see what was at stake. His real concern was that the election would be lost and that Britain would slide back into the decline which it had been his purpose in politics to help arrest and reverse. A Thatcherite scorned by Thatcher, he increasingly attached importance to the language of politics and hated the abrasive tone which became adopted. He supported the Government's policies but wished for a 'softer voice'. His resignation letter refers to the 'mood' she adopted in Rome last weekend and in the Commons on Tuesday when he sat, for the last time, unhappily at her side.

There is no Howe faction in the Party as such (it was made clear last night that he would not stand against her for the leadership, although he could possibly be prevailed upon to do so) but he commands affection and respect across a broad swathe of the Conservative Party. His immense industry enabled him to do many favours. He attended to his party business, replied always to his correspondence, took up MPs' cases, spoke in their constituencies. There will be a sense that he was sorely treated. The damage which his resignation will do will flow from its valedictory character – when Geoffrey says goodbye to all that, to many it may seem like time for farewells all round.

Independent, 2 November 1990

Having resigned, Howe waited a few days before delivering his famous resignation speech. Belying his reputation as the 'dead sheep' of British politics, Howe managed to combine an obituary of the Government with an invitation to Mr Heseltine to challenge Mrs Thatcher for the leadership in the forthcoming leadership election. Mrs Thatcher narrowly beat Heseltine on the first ballot in the ensuing contest, but not by enough votes to avoid submitting herself to the indignities of a second round of voting. She was dissuaded from putting her name forward for the second ballot by her Cabinet colleagues, and resigned. This allowed two other candidates to enter the ring, John Major and Douglas Hurd. Jenkins wrote the following article on the eve of the second ballot.

To retread or to renew, that is the question

As in the last act of *Lucia di Lammermoor*, with the heroine dead in her dressing room, the final rounds of the struggle for the leadership of the Conservative Party looked as if they might be a bit of an anti-climax. The ranks would close behind whichever of the three candidates found most favour with Conservative MPs, all of whom were promising unity and continuity.

But it has not been so: the contest has developed in a way that reveals a continuing split in the Party and beneath the superficial gentlemanliness of the three-cornered campaign lies much rancour and mutual recrimination.

What has happened is that the old guard has piled in behind John Major as the favourite son of the old regime, with the result that today's ballot has turned into a test of the legitimacy of the deposed regime. In today's ballot Mr Major is the proxy for Mrs Thatcher.

Lined up behind him are, with few exceptions, all of the gang – the Thatcher loyalists: the true believers in the old religion, the redundant courtiers, the sycophants and hangers-on; and the media cronies and stooges led by the *Sun* and the *Sunday Telegraph*. The Queen is dead but long live Mrs Thatcher's boy.

Mr Major resists this but not very vigorously; he needs all the supporters he can get, Norman Tebbit included. It is said of him that he is a man with no enemies, but with the friends he has acquired he might not need any. For their part, they may have mistaken their man. As one of his old Blue Chip friends puts it: 'John is really to the left of both Douglas and Michael.' But in his interview with me last week he studiously distanced himself from his old 'wet' friends and the cock was heard crowing in Smith Square. This is how he is obliged to play it and, for the moment, he is a prisoner of the company he keeps.

The battle has been further embittered by Mrs Thatcher's last will and testament. At the end of last Thursday's Cabinet, when the tears were over, officials withdrew and they sat round and talked politics for a few minutes. Mrs Thatcher pulled herself together and launched into an impassioned attack on Michael Heseltine who, she said, had to be stopped at all costs or he would undo everything that she had achieved. One Minister reported afterwards that fighting Neil Kinnock – or, even, Saddam Hussein – paled into insignificance beside this crusade. In this way Mr Major was anointed as champion of the True Faith.

It is hardly a recipe for reuniting the Conservative Party and, least of all, for achieving the renewal necessary for a ruling party in the post-Socialist era which has left the Labour Party without clear purpose or function. Yet today's ballot threatens to be as much a verdict on the Tory past as a decision about the Party's future.

The price of legitimacy, if that is what Mr Major represents to Conservatives agonising over their act of regicide, may be to appear to the public not as a new government but a retread of the old one.

As a painkiller Mr Major may serve his immediate purpose but is he the man, at this juncture, to register the social and electoral change that is required if the party in power is not to fall victim to the electorate under our obsolete two-party system?

The final ballot, on Thursday, may force the Party to a different kind of choice.

The relative strength of the three tonight will be a measure of the scale and shape of the Party's split; then the more serious question of who really can best unite it and lead it forward will become more pointed. Then it may be a matter of whether Mr Heseltine or Mr Hurd is the second choice of most, for unless he can steal a commanding lead in today's ballot, Mr Major is unlikely to be the second choice of many.

Between Mr Hurd and Mr Heseltine as the best man to lead the Party forward from Thatcherism, Conservatives face a difficult choice. Both have had to take account of Mr Major's early surge, however hyped up it may have been, because of the bruised passions that lie behind it. But both know also that by deposing Mrs Thatcher in the secrecy of last week's ballot the Party voted, essentially, for change and to save its electoral fortunes.

Mr Hurd offers a transitional leadership – although transitions have a habit of enduring – both in the sense that he is the older man and in the sense that he was a loyal member of the old regime while at the same time possessing political roots in an older, broader Tory tradition. His glamour ratings are the weakest of the three candidates but he looks the part of Prime Minister and would come to the job with the foreign experience relevant to handling Britain's difficult relations with Europe and, if it came to it, the diplomacy of a Gulf war.

A thoroughly civilised man, he would make a thoroughly civilised Prime Minister, too damned civilised by half for the rough trade of his party. But his style of government might rub the abrasive edges off the Thatcher legacy sufficiently to convince the electorate that a change had occurred. The best young talent of the Cabinet has formed up behind him.

Mr Heseltine represents a choice at once more exciting and more dangerous. Any Conservative backbencher looking across the House in last Thursday's no-confidence debate at Mr Kinnock and the Labour benches and wondering which potential leader could best see them off at a General Election would surely, on those grounds alone, go for Mr Heseltine. It is not for nothing that he is the candidate most feared by Labour. Mr Major is the one they now pray for.

To be sure, the latest polls show the Conservatives with a chance of winning under any of them, with not so much to choose between Mr Major and Mr Heseltine. But the 'post-Thatcher factor' in these instant polls is likely to be short-lived. Mr Heseltine has consistently demonstrated over time his appeal to the skilled working class, the younger generation, and voters in the Midlands and the North, and these are the essential ingredients for reassembling the Thatcher plurality. Moreover, Mrs Thatcher won all of her elections against a discredited or disunited opposition; Mr Heseltine may be the best able to contest the claims of Mr Kinnock's new-model Labour Party. His form suggests so.

His disadvantage with his party is that he is an outsider, nearly five years in the political wilderness, and the man who brought down Mrs Thatcher to boot. But with the electorate at large these are advantages. He has clean hands, particularly on the poll tax, and would most clearly signal the ability of the Government to take on new life and new energy after 11 years in power.

The Thatcherite anathema is to his advantage in this respect although would make it more difficult for him at first to reunite his party at Westminster. The idea that he is some kind of pinko or counter-revolutionary is a nonsense and only the mullahs ranked behind Mr Major believe it. He is a traditional Tory in his bones given to managerial enthusiasms and with a romantic One Nation view. He has a touch of Kennedy about him: a man capable of harnessing fresh talents to explore new frontiers and who could cut across party lines and instil enthusiasm.

One of the chief legacies of the Thatcher Revolution is the change she wrought in the political landscape. The achievements of her first two administrations were put at risk not by treachery within her Government but by the wrong-headed failures of her third administration.

If the Conservative Party now persuades itself that everything was going swimmingly until last Tuesday it will stand little chance of winning the next election. It could go down the path of the French Right after De Gaulle, shadow-boxing with a dead giant. If it is able, on the other hand, to respond to changed times, new aspirations, and fresh challenges, the achievements of Mrs Thatcher can be preserved and the post-Socialist majority remobilised.

Independent, 27 November 1990

One of John Major's early successes was his conduct during the Gulf War. The parallels with the Falklands were stark and critical to establishing his own political image. There was little of the flag-waving and jingoism of the earlier conflict and little of the long-term electoral benefit because it was so clearly an American-led war with only a walk-on part for the British. Jenkins's attitude towards this war was therefore very different from his attitude towards the Falklands. He saw it as the first conflict of the post-Cold War era and the first test of the new relationship between the superpowers.

Balance sheet of Gulf victory

As Iraqi resistance collapses all round we may begin to draw up a balance sheet for the war. It is turning out to be not only a famous military victory but a triumph also of skilful diplomacy. The liberation of Kuwait is virtually achieved and Saddam Hussein's army encircled and captive. With or without one final battle, this adds up to the humiliation of Iraqi arms which became the chief war goal of the United States and its allies. It is being achieved under the aegis of the United Nations and without the invasion, occupation or full destruction of Iraq.

Gamal Abder Nasser wept at the humiliating spectacle of his army fleeing bootless across the Sinai desert but became, nonetheless, a hero in Arab eyes. Saddam is suffering no less a rout but in what, even in most Arab eyes, must seem a far less noble cause. That part of the story is not complete but some doubt must be cast upon the conventional Arabist wisdom which said that any triumph of Western arms would incur the renewed and lasting hatred of the Arab world. As it has turned out, Arab fought enthusiastically against Arab and it may be that in the aftermath of the Cold War the criminal follies of Saddam have changed some of the old equations.

The outcome of the war so far adds up to a formidable scoresheet for President George Bush. The motley coalition which he assembled behind the massive force of American arms held together remarkably. Israel was kept out of the conflict. Saddam was given the diplomatic rope to hang himself. Mr Bush successfully deflected the last-minute Soviet initiative which might have enabled the Iraqi dictator to retreat in good order and live to fight another day.

President Bush persisted patiently with the air war – the key to the swiftness of victory on the ground. He rallied the Congress and the American people behind his enterprise. He achieved his victory with minimal American and allied casualties and made good his pledge that this would not be another Vietnam.

The war was preceded by a great debate in Washington between the 'air warriors' and the 'ground warriors', a controversy which continued through the 38 days of protracted aerial bombardment. The 'air warriors' have been largely vindicated by the prudent delay of the ground offensive. Air power did not quite win the war alone but it very nearly did, and was the key to the spectacular two-day collapse of the fourth largest army in the world.

The experience will reinforce the attractions of a mobile 'fortress America' in a way which may have profound implications for American relations with Europe and its future role in the world. It has shown how military might can be exercised from afar, rapidly projected as necessary without the need for permanently entangling alliances or expensive overseas deployments on the ground. It is bound to accelerate the American disengagement from Europe.

The United States entered this war in a mood of uncertainty at a time when its superpower status had been called into doubt by the ending of the Cold War and the bipolarity which had been its central feature. Yet the great economic superpowers – Germany and Japan – were idle spectators at this event, which will go a long way towards reinstating military capability as the measure of super-power in the post-Cold War era.

One casualty of the war is the strain now placed upon the Soviet–American relationship, but this was the product of Mr Gorbachev's perilous position at home. The notion that the Soviet Union and the United States would serve as the twin pillars of a 'new world order' looks a good deal less plausible today than it did when Mr Bush met Mr Gorbachev in Helsinki last September and agreed to cut him in on the future action in the Middle East in exchange for his support in the Security Council for the crusade against Saddam's aggression. It is a part of Mr Gorbachev's predicament that he no longer has as free a hand to pursue *perestroika* abroad in the face of its failure at home.

There is more to it than that, however: if the polarised politics of the Cold War blocs is to give way to the politics of balance of power, that is and always was a game of rivalry. The Soviet Union has traditional and geopolitical interests in the Middle East different from America's, the ending of its ideological confrontation notwithstanding.

The war went America's way but the peace will not be so easy. The 28-nation coalition was a brilliant *ad hoc* construction for the limited purpose of defeating Saddam. But the power structures involved were essentially those of the Cold War era, a multilateralism masking an American hegemony. This offers no lasting solution to the problems of the Middle East.

When the sand has settled once again the Gulf war may come to seem a less-than-defining event of the post-Cold War period. For a time it has relegated to the shadows the more pressing questions of the world. These are the rehabilitation of Eastern Europe within the fold of Western democracy, the management of the crisis in the Russian empire, and the recasting of Atlantic relations to take account of the Cold War's ending. If 'new order' there is to be, it must begin in Europe and eventually embrace the United States and whatever succeeds the Soviet Union in its present form.

With Kuwait liberated and Saddam Hussein cut down to size, the chronic instabilities of the Middle East will become once more a secondary concern, although a perennial nuisance.

Independent, 27 February 1991

CHAPTER NINE

'The Tories Have Made a Mess of It, But Don't Let Labour Ruin It'

The 1992 General Election

Nineteen ninety-two was a big political year – a General Election and the launching of the Single Market. It was the year in which many of the concerns that had become increasingly central to Jenkins's journalism became dominant, and in which a reformed Labour Party failed to defeat the more middle-of-the-road Conservative Government of Major.

It was Jenkins's last General Election campaign and we feature here his interviews with the three party leaders. The contrasts with his early pieces are profound – not only in terms of the political discourse that these interviews reveal but also in terms of the nature of Britain and the extent to which it had changed since his piece about the campaign trail of 1970. These three articles are also subject-lessons in political interviewing – Jenkins is present but the interview is about and dominated by the words of the subject, not those of the journalist. They should be required reading on journalists' training courses.

From kippers to Kinnock-bashing

With health still dominating the election campaign, and the row over the Labour Party's election broadcast reverberating unabated, I tried on the Prime Minister a question he is repeatedly asked – had been asked that very morning at his press conference in Smith Square before leaving London: why did the NHS remain such a powerful negative for his party? Let's take as read, I said, your personal commitment to the NHS, and take as read the amount of real resources the Government has put into the service these past 13 years, the question remained why the public believed that the NHS was not much safer in his hands than in Mrs Thatcher's.

He answered with a thin smile. He referred to a survey which had asked people if they were happy with the service as it was now: more than 90 per cent said they were, said that it was very good – and that was after 12 years of Conservative government. When questions were asked in a non-political way about the quality of service, he said, people conceded that it had improved.

On what may turn out to have been a forlorn foray into the country – for York, where we were going, is the most marginal Tory seat in the land – we talked for half an hour in his campaign plane, Norma Major kindly holding the microphone to catch his voice above the engine noise.

I began by asking was it not true that, for all the accusations and counter-accusations, claims and counter-claims flying in this election, at the end of it whoever governed Britain would be in much the same position, working with the same constraints. He might say that Labour would not be able to carry out its spending plans without raising taxes but wasn't it equally true that he would not be able to cut taxes as he had promised and would have to deal with a very large public-sector deficit?

He said: 'There are always constraints imposed by an economic cycle – that's an inevitability – and there will be constraints after the election. It was precisely for that reason that when we were costing our manifesto in terms of cash expenditure it was very modest expenditure. A few hundred million at most and, at the very outside, during one parliament, an extra level of committed expenditure of around a billion.

'The second question is whether we can make tax reductions. I believe we can. First, you could have put the same question to me before the '83 and '87 elections and yet we were able to make progress on reducing taxes. We have said we want to reduce the basic rate from 25p to 20p. I have not said that is within a parliament, just as Geoffrey Howe didn't say 33p to 25p within a parliament.

'A further point is that by introducing a 20p band we have opened up the possibility of reducing income tax by less than a penny at a time by widening the 20p band rather than by reducing the 25p to 24p. So there is now a new possibility of making gradual progress towards the 20p and I am pretty confident – indeed I am totally confident – that we will be able to make a fair amount of progress during the course of this parliament towards the 20p. I cannot promise we will get there and I don't.

'The reason we are drawing attention to Labour's £38bn of verifiable expenditure is because they have made quite explicit promises in clear-cut terms. I do believe that if they have £38bn of verifiable expenditure set out in their manifesto it is encumbent on the Labour Party to tell us how they propose to pay for it.'

Financial markets, I said, were obviously giving the pound a good deal of benefit of the doubt at the moment, presumably because they would prefer to see a Conservative government to a Labour government. But if and when he got back to power, markets were going to want to know what *he* was going to do about it.

Mr Major agreed that markets had been pretty stable, except when the opinion polls had put Labour ahead, which was an indication, perhaps, of their concern about Labour's policies. One reason why they were so stable was the Government's clear-cut and unwavering commitment to the Exchange Rate Mechanism. The ERM was in some sense a constraint on policy, but he saw it more as a bulwark of future counter-inflationary policy.

The £28bn borrowing requirement might turn out to be higher, but it could be lower. 'But I think the real point is to ask why has it gone to £28bn. And the answer isn't an acceleration of expenditure: it is predominantly due to a reduction in government income because of the recession. As we come out of the recession that revenue will come back and the gap will narrow. It's not the case that our expenditure will roar ahead.'

That might explain the present position, but what was he going to do about it? How were we to get out of this recession?

'What do we need to come out of recession? I think we need several things. One of them is low inflation. We've got lowish inflation of 4.1 per cent. In some ways, more relevant than that is to look at producer prices inflation, which is running at about 2 per cent now – the genuine input of undiluted inflation, as opposed to the distortions you sometimes get in the retail price index. I know of no respectable economic commentator who does not expect inflation to continue to fall under our policies. So that I think is extremely good news.

'The second thing I think is necessary is a stable exchange rate, and we've discussed that. The third is, of course, the level of interest rates. They have fallen from 15 to 10.5 per cent. They're now down to the European average and the possibility of further reductions is there as inflation comes down.

'The other reason I expect recovery is this. What is the impact of cutting interest rates? It is to put a lot of money back into the pockets of people who will spend it when they have liquidated their debt. They are liquidating their debt. I believe they are poised to spend it and bring consumer demand back. Then there is the corporate sector. Is it going to reinvest? Well, what the businessmen say is: yes. They will cut investment if there is a Labour government. So I think the prospect is for increased investment, increased expenditure, continuing low inflation, stable exchange rates and an average level of interest rates. So add it all together and I think you have the ingredients for recovery.'

Changing tack, I remarked on the sharper tone, the more aggressive line he had adopted in the past few days. Was this still the nice Mr Major we had seen buying kippers in Brixton? 'If you read the speeches I made in the House of Commons long before I became Prime Minister you will find that when it's necessary on policy issues I will take a sharp line.'

Yes, but you were saying yesterday and again today that Neil Kinnock is unfit to govern this country. He hasn't said that about you, has he?

'I think you have to see what he's said about me over the past 12 months – and not only him, but I'm not going to comment on that. If you look at the policies that he has changed on issues of key importance to this country – the European Community, defence, a whole range of foreign and domestic issues – there has been a complete sea change. Now I don't think that is an attractive posture in someone who wants to be Prime Minister.'

How did he reconcile the 'One Nation' conservatism he professed, his talk of a classless society, with some of the other things he and his party had been saying lately? For example, he had defended an inequality of income by attacking Labour's tax plans on the grounds that they are redistributional.

'Let me tell you what I mean by the classless society and by a society of opportunity. What I mean is that people from wherever they start can achieve by their own efforts whatever it is in them to achieve. That there is a ladder of opportunity they can climb and that there are incentives on that ladder, not penalties. And the artificial distinction between the value we put on the work of the blue-collar worker and that of the white-collar worker, I think they are old-fashioned, old hat, and socially and economically damaging . . . I want everybody to have the same chances and opportunities.

'But that doesn't mean that you don't attack policies that would go in the other direction. The point that we have been repeatedly making about the Labour Party's tax plans, since you raised that, is not just that they are redistributive but that the redistribution involves a huge – *huge* – reduction in net disposable income for about one-sixth of the population and the gains at the other end for nine million people – on Labour's own figures – are tuppence a week and for another two million 34p a week.

'If you want to know whether I think there should be more help for people at the lower end of the scale, look at Norman Lamont's Budget. For the first time it actually took a large number of people into a 20p tax band.'

I mentioned his line on the unions. Surely Labour doesn't want to go back to the 'winter of discontent' any more than he did?

'They may not want to go back to the winter of discontent. Who would? But they are repealing the legislation which makes it unlikely we could ever go back to it. They are still the subordinate partners of the trade union movement, it seems to us. They'd have no constituency organisation without the unions, no financial resources without them; and many of their policies are driven by the needs and requirements of the trade unions.'

I suggested that a lot of people may think as polling day approaches that it wouldn't make very much difference whether Labour or Conservative won, and that it might be time for a change.

'I think it would be sharply different if you had a Labour government rather than a Conservative government. We've seen the difference of policies on tax. They would certainly be different on defence. They have different policies on the European Community. I very much doubt whether their relationship to NATO would be the same as ours. In terms of domestic policy they would reverse the education reforms which we have put in hand, they would stop our health reforms, they would reintroduce the trade union immunities that we have removed over the past years. I could extend that list, but it is a clear-cut list of sharp and distinct policy differences. There would be a very wide gulf between the policies which a Conservative government would continue with and the policies a Labour government would introduce.'

Did he feel that since, so to speak, stepping out of No. 10 to campaign around the land, the country had seen the real Mr Major? Was he happy with himself, with his image, as the campaign had developed?

'I am the same person. Because you have an ambition to provide a country at ease with itself doesn't mean that you won't sharply attack those who produce policies that will not achieve that end.'

But how do you propose to turn the campaign around now? Because it didn't go your way in the first week, and it's not clear that it is going your way now.

'I'm not sure that I agree. The response that we have been getting in the streets – you have seen some of it on the television – has been very positive indeed. I believe it is going to continue to be positive. The central issues have been advanced. We started with the education reforms. I think they were well received. It's perfectly clear the public are very concerned about that and they favour the idea of the concentration on the basics of education set out in the core curriculum. On the tax issue I believe it is very much getting through . . .'

The polls don't suggest so.

'I'm not so sure that the polls are right about that. The evidence we are finding on the doorsteps and elsewhere is that the tax issue is getting through.'

Yes, but the polls consistently show that people think of more than tax cuts.

'If you actually believe people should have choices and opportunities, the amount of their own money that is left to them *is* an important issue. But what I am continually saying is that the national dividend in terms of economic growth has to be divided between improving public services and reducing taxation. That is not just a piece of off-the-cuff oratory. If you look at what happened in the public expenditure round and the Budget you will have seen that public expenditure was increased in priority areas – mostly for health but not exclusively so – by something over £5bn. The tax reductions Norman Lamont introduced in his Budget were £1.8bn.

'The mistake the Labour Party is making is to say that, however well the country does, however the economy grows, all the dividend of the growth and effort, the work of millions of individuals, should go in the way the Government decides into public services. Of course I want to improve public services but I also believe that part of that national dividend should go back to the people who do the work and pay tax.'

We were on the ground now; time for one more question. What made him think he would be back in No. 10 on 10 April?

'The response we are getting on the doorsteps and the proposals we have for the nineties. I don't believe people want to turn around the whole range of policies which we have been pursuing for some years and suddenly go off in a different direction. The collectivist approach the Labour Party is putting forward is being rejected in Western Europe, in Eastern Europe, in Latin America and almost everywhere. All over the world people are turning to liberal free-market policies and I cannot believe that in one of the cradles of democracy they will turn away from that now.'

Independent, 27 March 1992

'I don't think the phone will ring'

The way it looked, there were two most probable outcomes to the election: a hung parliament or a Labour victory. The first would give him his big chance, the second would mean the end of his dreams.

'Not necessarily so,' said Paddy Ashdown. We were talking on his campaign plane on the way to Inverness and a day of pouring rain, grounded planes and six hours cooped up in buses, at the end of which the good news was that the Liberal Democrats had gained support in the opinion polls and the bad news that a Labour government was looking even more probable than I had suggested at the beginning of the day.

A hung parliament, he said, would in many ways be the toughest of the three scenarios, and require some pretty tough leadership from him, but, yes, it would have the advantage of enabling the Liberals to play a part in government so long denied to them.

A Conservative victory would provide the opportunity to play a part in what I believed historically would be the next act in British politics, namely the realignment of the Left, or the progressive forces as Mr Ashdown preferred to call it. That has been the dream since Jo Grimond first articulated it in 1963.

As for the Labour win, he remarked, it was important not to underestimate the upheaval in the Conservative Party that would then occur, the ideological ructions . . .

Yes, yes, yes, but surely it had always been the case that the Liberals had flourished during periods of Tory power, fallen back under Labour. Grimond had dreamt of realignment on the Left, so had the Two Davids, but if Labour were to become the Government on 10 April, for the time being at least, that would be the end of that dream again, wouldn't it?

All right, it could be argued that either of the two other scenarios would be preferable, he wasn't going to disagree about that. 'But you shouldn't underestimate the fact that we are representing a wholly different agenda than has applied for the last 30 years. It is my judgement that, even in a period of holding office, Labour could not adjust itself to the new realities people are seeking.'

That was to take the longer view, but what about the shorter view? Suppose there *was* a hung parliament. He'd been asked many times how exactly he would play it, and had very wisely refused to say. So I would simply ask: a negotiating position is, by definition, negotiable, is it not?

'Correct.'

So statements about non-negotiable preconditions and the rest of it *were*, in truth, negotiable?

'Yes. As you know, the PR condition is not negotiable. That is the key that opens the door to the talks about coalition.'

Why not put it the other way round? Because if you enter into a coalition – and I mean a real coalition for the purpose of governing, not just for a few weeks until there is another election – would you not be in a much stronger position to bring about electoral reform than by pointing a pistol at someone's head saying 'We won't have a coalition unless you commit yourself absolutely now to give us exactly what we want'?

He understood the argument but wouldn't accept it. Why? Because PR was the essential precondition for a stable coalition. There was no achieving that while the Prime Minister had the power to pull the plug at any moment he liked. The only way to diminish that power was by PR, for then if he did call an election he would end up with the same result as he started with – a coalition.

How did he weigh the advantages of this all-or-nothing position, which he had explained with great cogency, against the obvious advantages for a party out of power for 70 years of getting his bum on the seat of a Daimler again? I reminded him of Adlai Stevenson's quip: 'Power corrupts, but lack of power corrupts absolutely.'

'Look,' he said, 'our working hypothesis is that neither of the other two parties is going to do this. We expect them to try to go it alone.

'So I have to get the case for reform and coalition brought out before the election, because there is no possibility that I'll win the argument afterwards. Their propaganda armoury is too great. I am assuming we are actually not going to get PR and a coalition government until after a second indecisive election.'

Yes, Neil Kinnock was reputed to have said that in the event of a hung parliament 'Paddy will be given a short, sharp poker lesson.'

He'd heard that. But there were three points. Say the Conservatives lost 40 seats, but remained the largest party in the Commons? What legitimacy would John Major have to govern on his own? Suppose Labour, at the fourth attempt, could not get to be the Government of Britain? What legitimacy would Kinnock have to govern on 37 or 38 per cent of the popular vote?

Second, the one thing that would hold the Tory Party together would be the prospect of a minority government they could remove in nine months' time. If Kinnock could say I am here for four years, head of a coalition that would stand, then the Tories would fall apart in ideological dissension.

Third, if Kinnock thought he could run another 1974 he was wrong. The ERM would stop him. He would not be able to falsely inflate the economy and dash for a quick election.

Kinnock, I suspected, reckoned that with half the Liberal Democrats in Parliament Scots who had been in bed with Labour in the Constitutional Convention, Ashdown would not succeed in voting down a Labour Queen's Speech which provided for a Scottish

Parliament elected by PR, whatever it said or didn't say about PR at Westminster.

'Peter, Peter, I'll have difficulty either way. It is going to require a very considerable effort to carry this through. I can only tell you this in respect of my Scottish colleagues: you can be absolutely certain, for the reasons you have described, that I have consulted them thoroughly over months and our decision is a collective decision.'

Polling day is only a week away. The results are declared. No majority in Parliament. Then what? Did he just sit there waiting for the phone to ring?

'That's right.'

And if it doesn't ring, it doesn't ring?

'Yes. And as I've told you, I don't think it will.'

What about the constitutional procedures? Had he been in touch with Sir Robin Butler (Secretary to the Cabinet) and the Palace?

'Yes. We have taken constitutional advice.'

What was it?

'I understand that if Major is the leader of the largest party, he would be called upon by the Queen.'

And if he asked for a dissolution?

'I think very heavy pressure would be put on him not to ask Her Majesty that question.'

If Kinnock then formed a government and was defeated in the Commons he would be granted a dissolution?

'That is my understanding.'

Why were we talking about these things? Why should we want PR and coalition government? What made him think the country would be better governed? And why should we allow Paddy Ashdown to appoint himself the Hans-Dietrich Genscher of British politics, a man for all governments, a permanent feature of the power structure?

Because most of Britain's problems of the past 40 years were connected with the ability of a party to inflict its dogma on the country on the strength of 40 per cent of the votes. Nationalisation. Education and health as political footballs. The poll tax. The British system led to alternating extremisms of Right and Left, and that was a less desirable system than recognising the importance of the moderate opinion in the middle, as Genscher did within Bonn coalitions.

This election had begun with the Tories hoping the Liberal

Democrats would siphon off enough anti-Government votes, particularly in the South, to keep Labour out. Now they were alarmed that, by taking Tory votes, the Liberal Democrats were going to put Labour into power. Which was correct?

In the past, the third party had pulled about three votes from the Tories for every two from Labour, but he believed the Liberal Democrats today were taking votes equally from both parties. People were beginning to vote differently to achieve their larger political aims, and the Tories, as in Scotland, were becoming subject to a double-flanked attack. That's what was happening. There was a mood in favour of change.

But in the South, support for Liberal Democrats would help Labour to gain power?

'Because they hold most seats in the South, it will hurt them. But in the Midlands we might help the Tories to hold their marginals.'

He had struck me, from what I had seen on television, as enjoying this campaign.

Enormously. (Little did he know the trouble in store that day.) He so loved being out and meeting real people.

And the way the other parties had campaigned had played into his hands?

Amazing, but he feared they'd learnt their lesson and might not give him such an easy time of it in the final few days.

They had enabled him to take a very superior attitude and drone on about 'the issues' while really, if one looked at it, he had been the most shameless – or to be fair, shamelessly effective – in capitalising on image politics, photo opportunities and the rest of it?

He didn't dissent from this, but said that the 'one-man band' had been the media's doing, not his. He thought Major had made an enormous tactical error right from the start. To lower himself to the business of attacking Kinnock devalued his greatest assets as a nice sensible man. He should have treated Kinnock with due disdain and prime ministerial superiority.

With this advice to his opponents we were approaching Inverness on a roller-coaster of air pockets. One last question. In a short space of time he had brought his party from the outer wilderness back into the centre wilderness which it had inhabited for many years. What now? If Labour won and nothing happened did he go on as the Right Hon. Paddy, catching the Speaker's eye to add his condolences on the death of some statesman, invited to the State Banquet for the President of Senegal, allowed to lay his wreath at the Cenotaph once a year? Was that how he wished to spend the rest of his life?

He rejected the premise, once more. Labour was increasingly irrelevant. He could not believe that Labour could be the force to govern Britain in the nineties.

'But look, this is what my life was meant for. The whole of the rest of it was a preparation for this. I love the job. I will go on doing it for as long as my party want me, as long as I can be useful, and as long as I have the energy.'

Independent, 2 April 1992

'We'll do what needs to be done'

Politicians conducting election campaigns do not like hypothetical questions, but Neil Kinnock raised no objection when I interviewed him as if on Friday he would become Prime Minister. 'We'll do what needs to be done,' he insisted in response to questions about how he might be obliged to reconsider Labour's plans on opening the Conservative Government's books or in face of pressures on the pound. That included a pre-emptive rise in interest rates, although he saw no reason at all why sterling should be withdrawn from London.

As for the possibility of devaluation – a word that in 1964 Harold Wilson had also banned from the political vocabulary although he later devaluated all the same – he said:

'The circumstances are very different. And one of the differences is that we have before us the experience of both devaluation against a fixed rate and against floating rates and have learnt that it's much better to work to sustain the value of the currency and raise the performance of the economy than to hope that there's a hidey-hole somewhere that can give you the relief which enables you somehow to sprout a more virile economy. It doesn't happen.'

I had begun by asking him whether on taking office he expected to inherit an economic crisis of the kind that has greeted previous incoming Labour governments or to become the beneficiary of a recovery which will have come too late to help the present administration?

'What we know is that the economy will be in difficulty, very serious difficulty. Whether crisis will be the proper word to describe it I'm not so sure. And whether there is any prospect of the beginnings of recovery nobody is in any real position to judge. All of which produces the best possible reason for proceeding with our policies, which *are* extremely prudent, will sustain stability and at the same time ensure we can ignite an investment-led recovery.'

But what was his diagnosis? Did he regard this as a cyclical economic downturn or was he talking of something more fundamental and serious, a situation capable of degenerating into slump?

'It's only cyclical in terms of Conservative economic policy. If we were to have a continuation of Conservative government I think it would turn into a slump. The basic underlying problem is one of underperformance due to the virtual absence of effective supply-side policies over the 13 years of this Government. They have relied entirely on deregulation, privatisation and tax cuts to produce a supply-side response and there's no record of any modern economy becoming more productive and competitive simply by relying on that approach.'

During the campaign he had made much of his so-called 'programme for action' to kick-start the economy out of recession. But the present Government had launched a pretty considerable reflation last autumn and its increased spending plans were now coming on stream. Did he seriously believe that a billion pounds' worth of measures – some of which, such as help for training, were by their nature longer-term – could be presented to the country as a 'plan for recovery'; something that was going to lift the economy off?

Yes, he said, making two points. One was that the £1.1bn package was precisely aimed at promoting recovery. The other was that in addition there would be £1bn for health and £600m for education, and these would also have substantial demand effects because they would lead to refurbishment, rebuilding, the purchase of equipment, and so on. The total commitment to an investment-led recovery would thus be rather more.

How much more?

About £2bn altogether.

As for the slow working of some of the proposed measures, the anniversary was approaching of the Government's claim that a consumer-led recovery was just around the corner. Labour's proposed measures would work both more quickly and be more sustainable.

He had said a moment previously that Labour's economic policies would all be 'prudent'. But would it be prudent, for example, to go ahead and impose the tax changes announced by John Smith – especially the removal of NIC ceiling – when, as some economic institutes and forecasters had warned, they could prolong the recession by their depressing effect on the southern economy, which, rightly or wrongly, was such a powerful engine of the British economy as a whole?

'But it won't, you see. First of all there will be many more gainers than losers in the southern economy. Second, the fact is that every pound which is taken from people on the higher incomes is going directly to people on lower incomes. So at least as much money will be put into the economy. Indeed, because of the probably higher propensity to consume among people on middle and lower incomes, it might even be more reflationary.'

Nor would it hit the housing market, as some had suggested. This was because the housing market was driven primarily by first-time buyers whose average income was £18,000. They would have greater confidence to buy as a result of Labour's tax changes.

Did he suppose that they would be helpful to business confidence either at home or abroad?

There was no reason why they should upset confidence. At the height of the Tory boom people were paying higher marginal rates of taxation than Labour now proposed.

Yes, but not at such low levels of income.

What Labour proposed would compare favourably with comparable economies in the EC, he insisted.

'We can't keep putting off trying to operate in the same circumstances as the Germans. If they are the benchmark of success – and they are, certainly in the EC – then we've got to do anything we can to make the same inputs. That's the only way we are going to build our strength.

'I am not willing either in terms of the value of the currency, or in terms of other economic policies – and I know that this is John's [Smith] attitude as well – to keep on putting off the day when we really confront the need to achieve the best standards of production. It may take some time to get our training standards up and so on, but if we don't start we can only fall further behind.'

We had talked about Harold Wilson and devaluation; however, Wilson also, he might care to remember, had won a tiny majority in 1964 but had gone rushing ahead with his programme for a 'hundred days' until he was 'blown off course' in July 1966. It could be said he never fully got back on course. So wouldn't it be better, in view of that kind of experience, to say here and now: 'When I sit there in the Cabinet Room I intend to pause and think again before rushing into doing any of the things I said I would do during the election campaign'?

'Don't forget, we've never rushed. We have very deliberate policies which have been through a process of review that is unprecedented in British politics. Therefore, we do not enter office with our ties caught in the traces of the team, as it were, and get pulled along willy-nilly.

'So in office we'll do what needs to be done, but included in that is the need to get an investment-led recovery. And I am not using that as a mantra. It is a statement of the truth about the British economy and how we bring it to a higher standard of performance.'

So we turned to some other matters, although pursuing the same line of inquiry. The National Health Service: did he really intend to turn the whole thing upside down all over again, cancel all of the present Government's reforms, go back to square one?

'There isn't much to turn round – not yet. If the Tories were in any longer there'd be turmoil, no doubt about that. But as it is, 52 hospitals have been opted out for a year, a few more for a week or so. They've run up an enormous bureaucratic obligation, but there are other ways to use that labour. As far as GP fund-holding is concerned, it's 1,400 out of 25,000 so the movement back into the mainstream – the re-establishment of the *National* Health Service – is not a big disruptive act. The breaking up of the NHS so far is, happily, in its infancy.'

But surely there must be great numbers of doctors, managers and others in the NHS who, whatever they may have thought of the Conservative reforms at first, were now praying 'God spare us from Labour turning the whole thing upside down again'?

'I think the sentiment that comes across – for example, from the BMA conference last week – is not that one. They say the turmoil comes from a system that breaches the greatest qualities of the NHS. Conservative doctors say that, too, it's not simply a partisan point. I think their appraisal is correct.'

On constitutional reform, including proportional representation, you have argued cogently that this is something which should not be settled by backstairs deals, that it needs proper consideration, an open national debate. Yet in the case of a Scottish parliament, and of Welsh and English devolution, you are prepared to rush into a solution which was hatched up in exactly that expedient way in response to a party problem you had in Scotland. Why the difference?

He rejected this account. The Scottish Convention had deliberated for two and a half years . . .

Yes, but the English weren't asked. It involved them, too.

'Of course it did. And what was happening in England was various representations from the regions – from local government and MPs – about the need to establish regional institutions . . .'

But there wasn't much popular support for that, was there?

He thought so. But there had to be the necessary consultations to achieve consensus.

Did he mean he wouldn't do it unless there was consensus?

It would not be 'enforceable' unless there was. But there was evident a great deal more regional identification – a product of the times and what was happening in the EC. There was also a greater understanding of the need for greater economic co-ordination and promotion of the regions.

But he had said only that morning that consensus meant governments didn't always know best. What he was saying now sounded as if, on this subject, Labour did think it knew best. Here was something he was going to go ahead and do without giving it the same thorough considerations he was giving to other aspects of constitutional reform.

'No, it isn't being done over the heads of the people in any sense. It reflects widespread popular opinion, manifested in a number of ways.'

On PR he had explained why he was not prepared to show his hand at this stage. I suspected, as I had written in the *Independent*, that he was disposed to favour PR. This he neither confirmed nor denied. I asked him if he was prepared to say that on this matter he would be guided by belief and principle and not pull up the drawbridge once in office with a majority?

All he would clearly say was that the committee of study under Professor Raymond Plant would 'most definitely' go ahead in all circumstances.

'The first thing I want is a thoroughness and breadth of analysis so that everybody – and I include the last citizen as well as the politicians – can know why they are doing it, what the options are and what the implications are, not for the next 10 minutes of history but for far into the future. And that applies whatever the decision may be.'

On this point at least he was a conviction politician?

'Absolutely.'

Independent, 7 April 1992

Major's victory surprised many because of the opinion polls – although Kinnock has later said that he felt the election slipping away in the final days. The Conservatives played the national question hard and the longer-term effects of a powerful advertising campaign attacking Labour's tax plans also paid off when John Smith, the Shadow Chancellor, spelt out his plans for raising revenue in a widely criticised Shadow Budget. But, as Jenkins points out, the polls were wrong because people lied to the pollsters about their voting intentions. In reviewing the election in this piece, Jenkins also spelled out his conclusions on the Left in the 1980s and looked forward to the new agenda of the 1990s – his conclusion, that Major's brand of liberal 'and – we hope – progressive conservatism' was in tune with the times, seems to have been largely vindicated. Peter Jenkins would have embraced the politics of Tony Blair with gusto.

Finally, there really was no alternative

Politicians are not the only ones who tell lies at election time. The opinion polls were wrong because people lied to them. This has to be so, for it stretches credulity that there could have been a last-minute swing back to the Government large enough to explain the discrepancy between the final snapshots of opinion and the actual results.

Had there been such a swing, the polls would have picked it up, for at least they are pretty reliable detectors of movement. They sniffed enough to send the City running to the bookies on Thursday, but nothing that explains why the Conservatives held their 1987 share of the vote while Labour's increased by less than 5 per cent.

The most plausible explanation is that what voters told the pollsters was not an accurate indication of what they would actually do. The questions the pollsters asked, most of which could be answered only within the narrow framework of party choice, allowed no way of registering a protest against the Government except by threatening to vote Labour or Liberal Democrat. The whole dynamic was of an electorate torn between its disillusion with the Conservatives' record and its reluctance to bring back a Labour government. The second proved even stronger than the first.

It is important to begin with the proposition that the opinion polls were wrong in order to avoid bewilderment at what has happened. For the re-election of a Conservative government to a fourth term unprecedented in this century makes perfectly good sense when placed in the context of Labour's secular decline as an electoral force. Its 35 per cent share of the popular vote is very close to estimates of its core support as what was the working class diminishes, as people vacate the old class strongholds of inner city and northern industrial town, cease to be organised in trade unions and exchange their council tenure for home ownership.

Since 1987 this declinist thesis has been reinforced by similar trends elsewhere in the world. Marxist socialism has declared its bankruptcy and the social democratic era is drawing more gently to a close. Liberal capitalism is in the ascendant. In countries with proportional electoral systems this can take the form of fragmentation, giving scope for post-Socialist parties of both Right and Left; in Britain it can take only the form of an unequal contest between two parties and a third party of protest.

From the moment the Labour movement, still in the throes of the Bennite cultural revolution, threw up Neil Kinnock as its leader it seemed improbable that he would ever set foot in No. 10. This was not a reflection so much on his qualifications, although they were less than impressive, but due rather to the fact that he was a creature of his party who could not conceivably have come to the fore as parliamentary leader except through the newly established electoral college that transferred the choice of leader from elected MPs to unelected union leaders and party activists.

He turned out to be a party reformer. He came to accept a large part of the declinist thesis and saw increasingly that with its outmoded structures and obsolete ideological prejudices Labour could not command a winning coalition of voters. He did the best he could, purging the hard Left, abandoning the policies that did most to alienate the new working classes, paying lip-service at least to the economics of the market, but making little progress towards removing the dead hand of the trade unions. The illusion that this would be enough took hold as Mrs Thatcher entered into terminal unpopularity and her triumphantly proclaimed 'economic miracle' degenerated into another recession. It looked as if Labour had come far enough for the restricted pendulum of our two-party system to swing again.

Not so. The results of the election turn that judgement on its head. The most obvious first question is that if Labour could not win an election in such uniquely favourable circumstances, against a government self-condemned to fight at the bottom of a business cycle, then when in heaven's name could Labour ever hope to win? For it could scarcely be claimed that the Government had won the election on its brilliant record or on the strength of an inspiring campaign. No, Labour had lost again, seen still by too many as effectively disqualified from providing a better alternative. The verdict of the people essentially was: 'OK, the Tories have made a mess of it, but don't let Labour ruin it.'

Moreover, the centrist constituency that burgeoned in the eighties around the SDP in alliance with the Liberals proved impervious to inroads by the reformed, new-look and rose-scented Labour Party. To aggregate the Labour and Liberal Democrat vote into an anti-Tory coalition is to miss the point that an equally powerful anti-Labour coalition remains at large in the land. There may not be much ideological light between some of the parliamentary protagonists, but there was nothing to stop the voters turning the Tories out for Labour if they wanted. They did not want; for the most part they preferred to waste their votes in their own ways and to continue their peripheral games on the Celtic and West Country fringes.

The modest inroads that Labour did manage to make into the Conservative hegemony built around Thatcherite prosperity, a declining Labour movement and the divided forces of opposition do not represent a stage in the reassembly of a winning coalition of Labour voters. Rather, the gains in Lancashire, the Midlands and the South-East are seats temporarily on loan due to the contingency of the recession. When cyclically corrected, the geography of British politics remains unchanged, a conclusion reinforced by the target marginals Labour failed to win in which the forces of demographic and cultural change prevailed over present economic discontent.

The Labour Party must now try to read afresh the runes of its latest debacle. For this was no near-miss, no Everest half climbed, no pip at the post by a last-minute swing or the scare tactics of its opponents and their tabloid press lackeys. It was a reversal no less fundamental than in 1983 and 1987, indeed a confirmation of the watershed that flowed from 1979.

Blaming Mr Kinnock will not do, although he will likely now go with grace and honour, perhaps announcing this on Monday. That will open the way for John Smith to lead the Labour Party through the next stage of its wilderness, if he wants that hapless task, or perhaps one of the more zealous young reforming Turks around Mr Kinnock.

Two weeks ago Mr Smith was widely hailed as the architect of Labour's coming victory for having deftly deflected the Tories' tax assault with his 'shadow' Budget. Today he appears more clearly as one of the architects of defeat. For it was he who hoisted Labour with the tax increases which, when it came to it, helped to convince the electorate, especially in the South, that recovery from the recession would be safer in Tory hands.

The lesson of the election for Labour is not that it might have won with a leader other than Mr Kinnock. Indeed, Mr Kinnock – who had a good campaign – may well have been less of a liability to his party than his party was to him. Labour lost because it was Labour. Whoever takes over from Mr Kinnock will need to start from that fundamental diagnosis and treat his achievements as only the first instalment of a transformation process that has as far to go as the distance it has come in the eight years of his leadership.

No doubt there will be much chatter, excited by the mirage of a hung parliament that – thanks to the polls, again – wrapped so much of the campaign in a misleading haze, of a realignment of the centre Left around the issue of constitutional reform. But the moment for electoral reform may have passed with the chance of a Labour government acting imaginatively to secure its post-Socialist future.

Cooking up deals with the Liberals for an unforeseeable future may now only distract from the more important task of addressing present realities. With or without proportional representation, Labour can survive only by finding ways of reoccupying the centreground that it has progressively allowed to become the no-man's land of third-party politics.

Talk of consensus may also underestimate the extent to which the Conservatives will be in that business, too, now that John Major is his own man. Again the recession and the legacies of Mrs Thatcher's third term may prove a distorting prism through which to grasp the meaning of this election. For with economic recovery, more emphasis on social reform and the changes in train in Europe and the rest of the world, the re-election of a Conservative government in Britain is not some kind of aberration resulting from the distortions of our political system, defective though that may be. A more realistic assumption for those who will rightly now begin the search for a practical and relevant agenda for the Left in what will soon become the 21st century is that Mr Major's brand of liberal and – we hope – progressive conservatism approximates to the spirit of the times more closely than anything else on offer. That, also, is why he won.

Independent, 14 April 1992

Jenkins was also looking ahead in one of his final pieces for the Independent. *The fact that he was reporting on a British presidency of the European Community which would be responsible for promoting an agenda designed to expand the number of members and the scope of European unity was a vindication of much of his political journalism since the 1970s. His tone is expectant and his vision of a wider and deeper union representative of his matured political beliefs.*

On the brink of a plunge into a larger pool

A first priority of the British six-month presidency of the European Community, which begins on 1 July, will be to set in motion the process of its further enlargement, as was agreed in principle at Maastricht. The four candidates from the European Free Trade Association – Austria, Finland, Sweden and Norway – have now been joined by a fifth, Switzerland, although the Swiss people may not agree.

Enlargement will have many consequences, but the dilution of the

EC into a loose confederation of free-trading nation states on the model touted by Margaret Thatcher and her friends will not be among them. Parliament had better get that straight for a start when the debate opens today on the ratification of the Maastricht Treaty of Union.

All of the new candidates are hard currency countries who will have little difficulty in meeting the criteria for stage three of the monetary union agreed at Maastricht, and their accession would increase the probability of the project going ahead in 1999 if not 1997. By championing their admission in the cause of a wider Europe, the Government will be helping to ensure that the EC is also deepened.

On this, by the way, it is intriguing to note the logistics of the timetable. No doubt the Prime Minister today will emphasise once again that the opt-out clause he negotiated at Maastricht commits his government to nothing and reserves to Parliament the decision to participate or not when the time comes. But in order to participate, two preliminary steps would have to be taken. First, eligible countries must have been within the narrow band of the Exchange Rate Mechanism for two years prior to a decision to move to stage three in 1996. Britain would have to make up its mind on this by the end of 1994. Second, to be eligible countries must have in place a free-standing, independent central bank. Legislation to denationalise the Bank of England would have to be included in the Queen's Speech of 1994 unless John Major wants it caught up with the General Election he may wish to call in the summer of 1996.

In other words, the Government cannot indefinitely conceal its intentions behind the opt-out clause and certainly not if it hopes to stand a chance of locating the European Central Bank in London. Indeed, if he wants a successful British presidency, Mr Major may have to declare his hand this autumn. The decision would still be Parliament's (at least in theory) but he would make plain his intention to recommend to Parliament that Britain should join if enough other countries determined to go ahead on the basis of the criteria fixed at Maastricht. Being 'at the heart of European affairs' can have no meaning other than being at the heart of its monetary arrangements.

The British like to think of the Eftas as natural allies within an enlarged Community, but this sentimental affection may be misplaced. For example, they all have politically powerful and pampered farmers and are liable to strengthen the forces of agricultural protectionism within the EC. The Scandinavian countries and Austria are advanced social democracies and can be expected to support the Social Chapter of the Maastricht Treaty from which Britain, in isolation, also opted out. Four out of five were Cold War neutralists. They would be more inclined to become members of the Western European Union than of NATO. Britain is engaged in a running battle with France over the status of WEU. The French want it brought into the European Union, we insist that it complement, but not duplicate, NATO. Maastricht was at best a stand-off, with France, more probably, a winner on points.

Then there is the problem of Community institutions and the arrangements for majority voting. The British view of the Eftas as nice, house-trained countries that can be fitted smoothly into existing arrangements is not shared by other countries. The Swedes, for example, can be very difficult – ask anybody with experience at the United Nations. The arrangements agreed at Maastricht for conducting foreign and security policy have become a mockery already as a result of the Greeks' intolerable behaviour over Yugoslavia. Bring in the neutral Eftas, lacking all experience of the use of power in the pursuit of interest, and the whole business could become a total shambles.

The British might be inclined to say 'we told you so', but that will not be the reaction of others who will press hard to combine enlargement with extensions of majority voting. This was made plain to me by senior officials in Bonn last week.

What should be obvious is that a Community of, say, 25 – and probably a Community of 16 or 17 – could not function effectively with the present decision-making apparatus. Yet to allow enlargement to become simply an agent of dilution would defeat its purpose. The goal should be to make war in Central or Eastern Europe as unthinkable and impossible as it became in Western Europe when the traditional enemies, France and Germany, locked themselves into first the Coal and Steel and, subsequently, the Economic Community. Czechoslovakia, Hungary and Poland aspire to join the Community they see and admire, not some watered-down confederation of states open to all and sundry. The Maastricht Treaty of Union provides a multi-tier model on which the European Community can be both widened and deepened, but a country that aspires to be 'at the heart of European affairs' must be ready to swim in the deepest of its pools.

Independent, 20 May 1992

Index

TICKLE THE PUBLIC
One Hundred Years of the Popular Press
Matthew Engel

'A splendidly witty and readable history of the harlots of Fleet Street'
J. D. F. Jones, *Financial Times*

'For some years Mr Engel has been one of the most consistently read-able performers in journalism. He is an ornament to the profession'
Alan Watkins, *Spectator*

Taking his title from a rhyme that went around Fleet Street in the 19th century, award-winning *Guardian* journalist Matthew Engel presents his highly individual history of the popular press in Britain.

'One of the famous old adages of journalism is that there is no such thing as an old story. This book is a telling testimony to that theory . . . they were all there 100 years ago, and thank heavens they were. Matthew Engel's highly entertaining book . . . is a wonderful chronicle of the birth and growth of the tabloids'
Stuart Higgins, *Sunday Times*

'Elegant and amusing'   Francis Wheen, *Observer*

'Engel's analysis is brilliant . . . he has convincingly proved that papers do have an effect, whatever they say'   Roy Greenslade, *Guardian*

hardback   £20.00   0 575 06143 X

Gollancz

GROWING UP POOR IN LONDON

Louis Heren

The late Louis Heren was born the youngest of three children in Shadwell, a slum parish in the East End of London, in 1919. His father, who had been a printer on *The Times*, died when he was four, leaving his mother to run the City of Dublin Dining Rooms opposite the West Garden Gate of London Docks.

GROWING UP POOR IN LONDON is a delightful and often moving account of childhood in a vanished London, and a wonderfully faithful picture of Cockney life in the East End of seventy years ago, with its gaslit streets, its regular 'London particulars', the joys of jumping lifts on the tailboards of carts, and the extraordinary courage of 'our mother', as the author always calls her. It was always the ambition of 'our mother' that Louis should follow his father to Printing House Square. And so he did, starting as a messenger boy and finally retiring as Deputy Editor and Foreign Editor in 1981, having along the way served as the paper's correspondent in India, Israel and the Middle East, South-east Asia and Washington.

'Louis Heren fills these pages in the way that he once filled a room – with presence, depth, humanity and, above all, warmth . . . I knew Growing Up Poor was a classic when I first read it. I know it remains a classic today'   Peter Hennessy, from his Introduction

£6.99   0 575 40041 2

INDIGO

SOUNDBITES AND SPIN DOCTORS

Nicholas Jones

'Everyone at Westminster should read this book'
Boris Johnson, Daily Telegraph

In SOUNDBITES AND SPIN DOCTORS – fully updated for the paperback edition to include media coverage of the 1995 Conservative leadership election and publication of the Scott Report – BBC political correspondent Nicholas Jones draws on his extensive personal experience to analyse how politicians use the media, and vice versa. What motivates each side and which has more to gain and more to lose?

'Nicholas Jones will have made himself unpopular . . . because this bold, truth-telling book discusses practices that not only politicians but also news organizations would prefer to keep discreetly veiled . . . He hopes that the readers of his "investigation of the often private interplay between journalists, politicians and their advisers will obtain an insight into the hidden world of media manipulation". This hope is amply justified'   Michael Davie, Times Literary Supplement

'A report from the battle-front, a highly readable account of life at the Westminster sharp end'
Ivor Gaber, Times Higher Education Supplement

£8.99   0 575 40052 8

INDIGO

LONG SUNSET

Anthony Montague Browne

'Intensely revealing though these memoirs are, they slip down as easily as a piece of ripe Stilton, leaving a rich and lasting aftertaste'
Peter Hennessy

Anthony Montague Browne was Winston Churchill's Private Secretary from 1952 until his death in 1965. These memoirs shed much light on Churchill's activities and attitudes during his final decade and as the last member of what Churchill called 'my circle' to have written an autobiography, Montague Browne represents a last link with the greatest Englishman of the century.

'It is full of wit, mischief, affection – and, at the end, great sadness'
Alistair Horne, *The Times*

'This is one of the most perceptive and entertaining of the many books which "Boswellise" the great man and is on a par with those of Lord Moran and Sir Jock Colville'   Robert Blake, *Country Life*

'It is a memoir that achieves the ideal balance between author and subject, itself the reflection of the sympathy, integrity and humour of deep friendship'   Alan Judd, *Spectator*

£10.99   0 575 40040 4

*IN*DIGO

HONEST OPPORTUNISM

Peter Riddell

What is it that attracts people to politics? And of the 651 men and women who represent us in Parliament, why will some become ministers and a few climb to the heights of the Cabinet, whilst the majority remain on the back benches?

HONEST OPPORTUNISM – first published in 1993 and now updated to take account of the findings of the Nolan Committee's inquiry into standards in public life – describes the rise of the career politician, charting meteoric successes, spectacular failures and committed nonentities with equal relish for detail.

'Essentially a guided tour of the way Westminster politics works by one who's been buried deep in them over the years and appears to have spotted everything. This book is the best available substitute, on every level from gossip to academic inquiry, for spending countless hours in the place talking to politicians for yourself'

David McKie, *Guardian*

'Peter Riddell is an exceptional political commentator . . . His book should be read with care, if only to warn us that we can expect much more of the same kind of politician in the future'

Robert Rhodes James, *The Times*

£8.99   0 575 40039 0

INDIGO

SECRET SOCIETY
Emma Nicholson

'The Conservative Party has changed so much whilst my principles have not changed at all. I would argue that is not so much a case of my leaving the party but the party leaving me.'

Emma Nicholson's defection from the Conservative Party to the Liberal Democrats in December 1995 came as a bombshell to John Major's already tottering government. Long admired as an articulate and concerned politician, she represented the human side of Conservatism which was rapidly being drowned in a cascade of scandal, sleaze and a growing conviction that the Tories had been in power too long.

Now Emma Nicholson gives her own account of what led to that momentous decision – how lack of leadership, arrogance, tiredness, corruption and a pervasive lack of principle had corroded the soul of the party and reduced it to no more than a secret society.

Emma Nicholson's defection drove another nail into the coffin of a discredited government. SECRET SOCIETY tells how and why.

£7.99   0 575 40072 2

INDIGO

THE HIDDEN WIRING

Peter Hennessy

'Hennessy's discussion of his separate themes is . . . brimming with scholarship and erudition. He writes, as he speaks on both radio and television, with pace and verve' Anthony Howard, *Spectator*

Peter Hennessy is a demystifier who for twenty years has been searching for the concealed codes of state power, and in THE HIDDEN WIRING he unravels the mysteries of the British constitution to expose the true nature of the relationships between the five institutions at the core of public life: Monarchy, Premiership, Cabinet, Whitehall and Parliament. This paperback edition is fully updated and includes a new chapter on the constitutional implications of the Scott Report.

With the conduct of public affairs under scrutiny as never before, Peter Hennessy's characteristic wit, zest and incisiveness have never been deployed to better effect.

'The vibrant tones of the author's infectious enthusiasm ring from every page' Julia Langdon, *Glasgow Herald*

'Characteristically timely, lively and provocative'
David Cannadine, *Observer*

£7.99   0 575 40058 7

INDIGO

BALKAN ODYSSEY

David Owen

In 1992 David Owen, former Foreign Secretary and co-founder of the SDP, was appointed European negotiator charged with bringing the conflicting parties in the former Yugoslavia around the conference table to hammer out compromises that could then be implemented on the battlefield. For three years he and his counterparts – first Cyrus Vance, then Thorvald Stoltenburg – strove both to contain the various wars in the region and to impose a peace plan on a political impasse which consistently defied solution. BALKAN ODYSSEY is his personal account of these turbulent years and of the most traumatic event of recent European history.

'BALKAN ODYSSEY is the detailed diary of a man who was at the centre of international debate, negotiation and hesitation in perhaps the most crucial episode in the early life of post-Cold War Europe. His energy is unflagging, not only in the sheer hours devoted to shuttle diplomacy but also in the formidable detail with which his thoughts, words and deeds are recorded . . . As a source for future historians this book will be invaluable'   Robert Fox, *Daily Telegraph*

'Important and revealing . . . will be a tremendous resource'
William Shawcross, *Sunday Times*

£8.99   0 575 40029 3

*IN*DIGO

Out of the blue...
INDIGO
the best in modern writing

*IN*DIGO books are available from all good bookshops or from:

Cassell C.S.
Book Service By Post
PO Box 29, Douglas I-O-M
IM99 1BQ
telephone: 01624 675137, fax: 01624 670923